THE TRAEGER GRILL BIBLE • MORE THAN A SMOKER COOKBOOK

THE ULTIMATE GUIDE TO MASTER YOUR WOOD PELLET GRILL WITH 200 FLAVORFUL RECIPES PLUS TIPS AND TECHNIQUES FOR BEGINNERS AND ADVANCED PITMASTERS

BBQ ACADEMY

TABLE OF CONTENTS

INTRODUCTION	- 14 -
SHOPPING GUIDE FOR A TRAEGER GRILL	- 15 -
TRAEGER PRO SERIES	- 15 -
TRAEGER IRONWOOD SERIES	- 16 -
TRAEGER TIMBERLINE SERIES	- 18 -
MASTERING YOUR TRAEGER GRILL	- 20 -
THE FUNDAMENTALS OF WOOD PELLET GRILLING AND SMOKING	- 20 -
FIRST TIME	- 21 -
SEASONING YOUR GRILL	- 21 -
START-UP PROCESS	- 22 -
WHAT IS THE P-SETTING?	- 22 -
SHUT DOWN CYCLE	- 24 -
MAINTENANCE	- 24 -
HOW TO CLEAN YOUR TRAEGER GRILL	- 25 -
TROUBLESHOOTING FOR THE MOST COMMON PROBLEMS	- 26 -
THE GRILL IS NOT STARTING UP	- 26 -
HOW TO CLEAR AN AUGER JAM	- 27 -
MAINTAINING TEMPERATURE	- 29 -

CHOOSING THE RIGHT PELLET	- 30 -
WOOD PELLET REFERENCE CHART	- 30 -
MOST POPULAR PELLET BLENDS	- 31 -
HOW TO STORE YOUR PELLETS	- 31 -
ACCESSORIES	- 32 -
SMOKING, AND GRILLING, AND COOKING, AND BAKING ON YOUR TRAEGER	- 33 -
THE MOST IMPORTANT INGREDIENT: TEMPERATURE	- 34 -
SOMEONE LIKES IT SMOKED	- 34 -
FINAL STEPS	- 37 -
KNOW YOUR MEATS	- 38 -
PORK	- 38 -
BEEF	- 40 -
POULTRY	- 42 -
LAMB	- 44 -
FISH	- 45 -
PANTRY ESSENTIALS	- 46 -
COOKOUT TIPS	- 48 -
A FEW FINAL TIPS	- 48 -
MEAT RECIPES	- 49 -
BEEF	- 49 -
TEXAS SMOKED BRISKET	- 50 -
MESQUITE SMOKED BRISKET	- 51 -
SWEET HEAT BURNT ENDS	- 51 -

REVERSE-SEARED TRI-TIP	- 52 -
SMOKED TRI-TIP	- 53 -
SANTA MARIA TRI-TIP	- 53 -
PULLED BEEF	- 54 -
SMOKED ROAST BEEF	- 55 -
SMOKED BEEF RIBS	- 55 -
BRAISED SHORT RIBS	- 56 -
PERFECT ROAST PRIME RIB	- 57 -
PASTRAMI	- 57 -
SMOKED NEW YORK STEAKS	- 58 -
THE PERFECT T-BONES	- 59 -
REVERSE-SEARED STEAKS	- 59 -
ASIAN STEAK SKEWERS	- 60 -
TRADITIONAL TOMAHAWK STEAK	- 61 -
PEPPERED BEEF TENDERLOIN	- 61 -
KOREAN STYLE BBQ PRIME RIBS	- 62 -
BACON-SWISS CHEESESTEAK MEATLOAF	- 63 -
LONDON BROIL	- 64 -
TEXAS SHOULDER CLOD	- 65 -
CHEESEBURGER HAND PIES	- 65 -
PORK	**- 66 -**
BABY BACK RIBS	- 68 -
MAPLE BABY BACKS	- 69 -

SIMPLE SMOKED BABY BACKS	- 69 -
SMOKED SPARE RIBS	- 70 -
SWEET SMOKED COUNTRY RIBS	- 71 -
CLASSIC PULLED PORK	- 71 -
RUB-INJECTED PORK SHOULDER	- 72 -
MAPLE-SMOKED PORK CHOPS	- 73 -
APPLE-SMOKED PORK TENDERLOIN	- 73 -
TERIYAKI PORK TENDERLOIN	- 74 -
BARBECUED TENDERLOIN	- 75 -
PORK BELLY BURNT ENDS	- 75 -
APPLE-SMOKED BACON	- 76 -
CAJUN DOUBLE-SMOKED HAM	- 76 -
SMOKED HAM	- 78 -
BBQ BREAKFAST GRITS	- 78 -
LIP-SMACKIN' PORK LOIN	- 79 -
PINEAPPLE-PEPPER PORK KEBABS	- 80 -
JALAPEÑO-BACON PORK TENDERLOIN	- 81 -
COUNTRY PORK ROAST	- 82 -
PICKLED-PEPPER PORK CHOPS	- 82 -
SOUTHERN SUGAR-GLAZED HAM	- 83 -
STUFFED PORK CROWN ROAST	- 84 -
BACON STUFFED SMOKED PORK LOIN	- 84 -
SMOKED PORCHETTA WITH ITALIAN SALSA VERDE	- 85 -

CHICKEN AND POULTRY — 87 —

- BEER CAN—SMOKED CHICKEN — 89 —
- BUFFALO CHICKEN WRAPS — 90 —
- ROASTED WHOLE CHICKEN — 91 —
- SMOKED WHOLE CHICKEN — 92 —
- SKINNY SMOKED CHICKEN BREASTS — 92 —
- WOOD-FIRED CHICKEN BREASTS — 93 —
- CHICKEN TENDERS — 93 —
- BUFFALO WINGS — 94 —
- SWEET AND SPICY SMOKED WINGS — 94 —
- SMOKED DRUMSTICKS — 95 —
- SMOKED QUARTERS — 95 —
- SMOKING DUCK WITH MANDARIN GLAZE — 96 —
- EASY RAPID-FIRE ROAST CHICKEN — 97 —
- CINCO DE MAYO CHICKEN ENCHILADAS — 98 —
- MINI TURDUCKEN ROULADE — 98 —
- SMOKE-ROASTED CHICKEN THIGHS — 99 —
- SAVORY-SWEET TURKEY LEGS — 100 —
- JAMAICAN JERK CHICKEN QUARTERS — 101 —
- SMO-FRIED CHICKEN — 101 —
- APPLEWOOD-SMOKED WHOLE TURKEY — 103 —
- SMOKED AIRLINE CHICKEN — 104 —
- TRADITIONAL BBQ CHICKEN — 105 —

WILD WEST WINGS	- 105 -
BUTTERED THANKSGIVING TURKEY	- 106 -
SPATCHCOCKED TURKEY	- 107 -
SMOKED TURKEY BREAST	- 107 -
CORNISH GAME HEN	- 108 -
SMOKED TURKEY WINGS	- 108 -
LAMB AND GAME	**- 109 -**
SMOKED PHEASANT	- 109 -
SUCCULENT LAMB CHOPS	- 110 -
SMOKED CHRISTMAS CROWN ROAST OF LAMB	- 111 -
SPATCHCOCKED QUAIL WITH SMOKED FRUIT	- 112 -
YUMMY GYRO	- 112 -
VENISON STEAKS	- 113 -
GREEK LEG OF LAMB	- 114 -
ROSEMARY-SMOKED LAMB CHOPS	- 116 -
SMOKED RACK OF LAMB	- 116 -
BURGERS	**- 117 -**
SMOKED BURGERS	- 117 -
RANCH BURGERS	- 117 -
CHILE CHEESEBURGERS	- 118 -
BISON BURGERS	- 119 -
FRENCH ONION BURGERS	- 120 -
PORK FENNEL BURGER	- 121 -

PORK AND PORTOBELLO BURGERS	122
SAUSAGES	**123**
SMOKED BRATS	123
TRAEGER SMOKED SAUSAGE	124
SMOKED SAUSAGE & POTATOES	124
GRILLED BACON DOG	125
SAUSAGE PEPPER SKEWERS	125
POLISH KIELBASA	126
RUBS, SEASONINGS, INJECTABLES, AND SAUCES	**128**
PORK RUB	128
CHICKEN RUB	128
DILL SEAFOOD RUB	129
CAJUN RUB	129
ESPRESSO BRISKET RUB	130
SWEET BROWN SUGAR RUB	130
ALL-PURPOSE DRY RUB	131
ALL-PURPOSE CALIFORNIA BEEF RUB	132
SWEET AND SPICY CINNAMON RUB	132
COFFEE-CHILE RUB	133
CUMIN SALT	133
WOOD-FIRED BURGER SEASONING	134
JERK SEASONING	134
ROSEMARY-GARLIC LAMB SEASONING	135

TEA INJECTABLE	135
GARLIC BUTTER INJECTABLE	136
COMPOUND BUTTER	136
LOBSTER BUTTER	137
QUICK AND EASY TERIYAKI MARINADE	137
ITALIAN MARINADE	138
SPICY TOFU MARINADE	138
THANKSGIVING TURKEY BRINE	139
LEMON BUTTER MOP FOR SEAFOOD	139
WORCESTERSHIRE MOP AND SPRITZ	140
THE ULTIMATE BBQ SAUCE	140
EASTERN NORTH-CAROLINA BBQ SAUCE	141
WHITE BBQ SAUCE	141
HOT SAUCE WITH CILANTRO	142
BASIL PESTO SAUCE	143
VEGAN PESTO	143
FENNEL AND ALMONDS SAUCE	144
HONEY DIPPING SAUCE	144
GINGER DIPPING SAUCE	144
THAI DIPPING SAUCE	145
COCONUT DIPPING SAUCE	145
BLACK BEAN DIPPING SAUCE	145
MAPLE SYRUP DIPPING SAUCE	146

- SOY DIPPING SAUCE 146
- AVOCADO SALSA 146
- ALDER-SMOKED SALT 147

FISH AND SEAFOOD 148

- PACIFIC NORTHWEST SALMON 149
- GRILLED SALMON 150
- HOT-SMOKED SALMON 151
- WOOD-FIRED HALIBUT 151
- SEARED TUNA STEAKS 152
- BARBECUED SHRIMP 152
- CAJUN-BLACKENED SHRIMP 153
- OYSTERS IN THE SHELL 153
- CAJUN CATFISH 154
- GRILLED KING CRAB LEGS 154
- LOBSTER TAIL 155
- BARBECUED SCALLOPS 155
- CHARLESTON CRAB CAKES WITH REMOULADE 156
- CITRUS-SMOKED TROUT 157
- DIJON-SMOKED HALIBUT 159
- CURED COLD-SMOKED LOX 160
- SUMMER PAELLA 161

VEGETABLES 162

- TWICE-SMOKED POTATOES 162

BROCCOLI-CAULIFLOWER SALAD	163
CAROLINA BAKED BEANS	164
BLT PASTA SALAD	164
POTLUCK SALAD WITH SMOKED CORNBREAD	165

VEGETARIAN RECIPES 166

SMOKED EGGS	166
MEXICAN STREET CORN WITH CHIPOTLE BUTTER	167
ROASTED OKRA	167
SWEET POTATO CHIPS	168
BUNNY DOGS WITH SWEET AND SPICY JALAPEÑO RELISH	169
MEXICAN STREET CORN WITH CHIPOTLE BUTTER	170
SOUTHERN SLAW	170
GEORGIA SWEET ONION BAKE	171
SCAMPI SPAGHETTI SQUASH	171

VEGAN RECIPES 172

GRILLED RATATOUILLE SALAD	172
GRILLED BABY CARROTS AND FENNEL WITH ROMESCO	173

APPETIZERS AND SNACKS 175

SMOKED CASHEWS	175
SMOKED CHEESE	175
BACON-WRAPPED JALAPEÑO POPPERS	176
PULLED PORK LOADED NACHOS	177
PIG POPS (SWEET-HOT BACON ON A STICK)	178

CHORIZO QUESO FUNDIDO	179
SIMPLE CREAM CHEESE SAUSAGE BALLS	180
PIGS IN A BLANKET	180
BACON PORK PINWHEELS (KANSAS LOLLIPOPS)	181
DELICIOUS DEVILED CRAB APPETIZER	181
SMOKED TURKEY SANDWICH	182

BAKED GOODS 183

PRETZEL ROLLS	183
FOCACCIA	185
TRAEGER WHEAT BREAD	186
PIZZA BITES	187
IRISH SODA BREAD	188
BAKED WOOD-FIRED PIZZA	189
PUMPKIN BREAD	190
BEER BREAD	191
ZUCCHINI BREAD	191
SWEET CHEESE MUFFINS	192

DESSERTS 193

BACON CHOCOLATE CHIP COOKIES	193
S'MORES DIP SKILLET	194
SMOKED BLACKBERRY PIE	194
CARROT CAKE	195
SMOKIN' LEMON BARS	196

| DOUBLE CHOCOLATE CHIP BROWNIE PIE | 197 |
| BAKED BOURBON MAPLE PUMPKIN PIE | 198 |

CONCLUSION 199

© COPYRIGHT 2020 BY BBQ ACADEMY
ALL RIGHTS RESERVED

INTRODUCTION

We all love to make people happy with food. Sharing a meal is the one thing that everybody cherishes all around the planet. And you don't need to go out to enjoy a great barbecue, you can just have it in your backyard.

Traeger is the premium wood pellet grill. A grill that will allow you to transfer your kitchen to the backyard for the summer. In fact, the Traeger doesn't just allow you to smoke and grill, but also bake and cook. And you can use it anytime of the year to give an extra smoky kick to any dish you want.

Why don't surprise your family with a perfectly smoked Thanksgiving Turkey? Why don't delight your children with Sunday morning breakfast with apple-smoked bacon? And how about a long day of enjoying beers with your friend waiting for that perfectly juicy Texas-style brisket? You can craft an entire wood-fired meal from start to finish with the flip of a switch, thanks to the Traeger technology. This book will guide your through all the methods and techniques to fully utilize your Traeger. From maintenance to smoking techniques, from pulled pork to brownies: this is the complete guide to the best wood pellet grill money can buy.

The wood pellet grill was born from something all of us have experienced at one time or another: failure. A failed meal on an inferior grill was all it took for Joe Traeger to turn the outdoor cooking world on its head. He became the inventor of the pellet grill and founder of Traeger Pellet Grills. The wood pellet grill gave everyday consumers masterful results by removing the guesswork from barbecue and eliminating unwanted flare-ups and flames.

Since the introduction of the wood pellet grill in the mid-1980s, its use has spread across North America, giving customers enhanced temperature control and wood-fired flavor in each meal.

By using an indirect heat method of cooking, the wood pellet grill and smoker ensure you never experience those flare-ups that often occur on a traditional grill. On top of the moist results it delivers every time, wood-fired flavor has made the pellet grill a coveted item for everyone—from world-champion pitmasters to the weekend backyard warrior.

Over the years, the methods of achieving these moist, delicious meals have changed as more advanced controllers and drain systems, as well as adjustments in the augers and burn area, have been introduced.

New designs, including Wi-Fi control boards and direct flame searing, are all the rage today. Though the design has evolved, each pellet grill aims for the same result: amazing wood-fired flavor without the hassle of a direct flame.

Whether you have a Traeger grill or are considering buying one, we will guide you through an amazing journey to smoking meats, grilling fish, and beyond... If you try cooking with real wood, you will never want to go back!

SHOPPING GUIDE FOR A TRAEGER GRILL

Depending on your budget, space, and needs you can choose among 6 grills from the three series of Traeger grills. They all come with D2 technology, a brushless motor that adds pellets to the fire automatically in order to maintain temperature and Wifire technology to control your grill with your phone, even if you are not home. It can be hard to choose, so we decided to give you an overview of the best Traeger grills on the market. We would personally recommend the Timberline series for the most seasoned cooks and the Trager Pro for the smaller budget. But the Ironwood series is also a great compromise. You can't go wrong with any of the grills, they are all amazing grills that will change your way to cook and enjoy a BBQ. The only thing you should really think about is which size suits best your needs.

TRAGER PRO SERIES

Traeger Pro 575 Pellet Grill:

Capacity: 575 sq. in. 24 burgers, 5 rib racks, 4 chickens
Weight: 124 lbs
Black or bronze

Traeger Pro 780 Pellet Grill:
Capacity: 780 sq. in. 34 burgers, 6 rib racks, 6 chickens
Weight: 150 lbs
Black or bronze

The Traeger Pro Generation 2 series is fueled by an 18Lb pellet hopper on the right side of the grill. The hardwood pellets are available in a range of popular wood flavors to pair with whatever you choose to cook. The beauty of pellet grilling is, all you have to do is set your target temperature anywhere between 165F and 450F degrees and let the grill handle the rest. Once set, the auger will transport the amount of pellets needed to reach and maintain your temp.

This Gen 2 Pro series features Traeger's D2 technology, powered by an industry first brushless motor to power their variable speed fan and auger. Once the pellets reach the fire pot, the hot rod ignites them, and the variable speed fan stokes the fire, helping you reach your desired temperature quickly and efficiently maintain it.
Traeger's D2 system makes it easy to smoke, grill, and even bake with woodfired flavor. In addition to maintaining the fire, the variable speed fan of the D2 system also circulates smoke throughout the whole grill, making sure everything on the cooking surface gets surrounded by smoke.

The Generation 2 Pro series even adds the convenience of WIFIRE technology. Using the Traeger app, you can monitor and control your Pro grill from anywhere you are. This is particularly useful for slow cooking and grilling; you won't ever need to frantically check on it. And for times when you may want a little inspiration, Traeger's app even has plenty of great recipes to keep you busy. Simply press "cook now" and the app will send the settings needed to the grill for perfect results on whatever you choose.

The Pro Series comes with a temperature probe that can be run through a port on the right side of the grill. This makes it easy to monitor the progress of your cook through the app, and even set target probe temps to be sure you don't overshoot doneness.

The Pro 780 gets its name from the seven hundred and eighty square inches of cooking space it provides. To show you some scale, this is what it looks like fully loaded.

When needed, the top rack can be removed.

Underneath the cooking grids, you will find Traeger's grease drip tray. This provides a full coverage layer of diffusion from the firepot in the belly of the grill, and a surface for drippings to vaporize off of, adding smoking flavor.
This indirect heat setup also goes hand in hand with low and slow smoking, no need to worry about runaway flare ups burning your food.
The grease tray slants to the left, directing drippings to this grease bucket on the left side of the grill, for easy cleaning.

Underneath the grease tray, you will find Treager's heat baffle. This provides an additional layer of heat diffusion above the firepot. The baffle can be removed when cleaning is needed.

The fire pot sits in the belly of the grill and of course this is where your pellet's ignite and burn, maintaining your set temp.

For extra insulation, the bottom portion of the grill is double walled.

For times when you may want to change out the flavor of your pellets, there is a pellet chute on the back of the hopper.

It's worth noting, the Traeger Generation 2 Pro Series is available in two sizes. You can also choose from a bronze or black lid color.

TRAEGER IRONWOOD SERIES

Traeger Ironwood 650 Pellet Grill:
Capacity: 650 sq. in. 6 pork butts, 5 rib racks, 8 chickens
Weight: 149 lbs.
Black

Traeger Ironwood 885 Pellet Grill:
Capacity: 885 sq. in. 9 pork butts, 7 rib racks, 10 chickens
Weight: 175 lbs.
Black

With the Traeger's Ironwood series you can smoke, grill, bake... and it's packed with some pretty cool features. Let's check it out!

Traeger's Ironwood series is fueled by wood pellets that are held in this 20 Lb. pellet hopper. These hardwood pellets are available in a range of popular wood flavors to pair with whatever you choose to cook.

When it's time to grill, just power up the D2 controller and dial in your temperature anywhere between 165F and 500F. Once set, the auger will transport the amount of pellets needed to reach and maintain your target temp.
For more reliability, the Ironwood series uses an industry first brushless motor to power their variable speed fan and auger. Once the pellets reach the fire pot, the hot rod ignites them, and the variable speed fan stokes the fire, helping you reach your desired temperature quickly and precisely maintain it.
Traeger's D2 system makes it easy to grill, bake, or smoke with woodfired flavor.

The Ironwood series even adds the convenience of WIFIRE technology. The Traeger app allows you to use your phone to monitor and control your Ironwood grill.
When I was getting ready to smoke a brisket, I was able to monitor the preheat from my phone while getting it prepped. This was a 17Lb. Brisket, so I opted to let it smoke overnight at the office.
I used the included temp probe so I could keep an eye on the progress and headed home to let it cruise. The next morning it was still going strong with some good color. After letting it rest, the results were impressive. It turned out really tender and juicy. It was a huge relief to not have to worry about maintaining the temperature I wanted throughout the night, the Ironwood is not a grill you will have to babysit.

For times when you want guidance throughout the whole cooking process, the Traeger app even has a collection of recipes to choose from. These recipes are fully compatible with the Ironwood, simply press "cook now" and the app will send the target temps and timer settings for great results on whatever you choose.

When it comes to extra smoke flavor, Traeger's Ironwood series has a super smoke mode, which utilizes its variable speed fan to get the maximum amount of smoke between 165- and 225-degree settings.

For maximum smoke circulation, the Ironwood series features Traeger's innovative downdraft exhaust system. This forces the smoke to exit through these ports at the back of the grill, right near cooking surface level.
This design causes the fan forced smoke and heat to create a vortex around your food before exiting the grill.

The Ironwood series even has a "keep warm" setting, so your food can be ready whenever you are. For cooking surface versatility, the inside of the Ironwood Series has a two tier grate design. To give you an idea of what you can fit on the Ironwood 885, here is what it looks like loaded with a little bit of everything.

The top rack works well for low and slow smokes like a brisket, because you have plenty of room to put a water pan on the lower rack to add moisture during the cook.
For times when you don't need it, the top rack can be removed.

The larger bottom grate can either be used in the lower position for grilling, or set it a step higher for more delicate items.

Underneath the cooking grids, you will find Traeger's grease drip tray. This provides plenty of surface for drippings to vaporize off of, adding to the smokey flavor you get when grilling. The grease drip tray also provides a layer of heat diffusion from the fire pot in the belly of the grill, the burgers I made cooked really evenly across the grates and there is never a need to worry about runaway flames burning your food.
The grease tray slants to the left side, causing excess drippings to drain into this bucket on the left side of the grill for easy cleaning.

Underneath the grease tray on the Ironwood, you will find Traeger's heat baffle. This adds another layer of heat diffusion above the fire pot. This baffle can be removed for cleaning when is needed.

The fire pot sits in the belly of the grill, and this is where your pellet fuel ignites and burns. For added heat retention, the belly and side walls of the Ironwood are double walled. This allowed me to smoke the brisket overnight and still have pellets left in the morning.
The lid also has a gasket to add further insulation, and the included temperature probe can be run through this port on the side of the grill so that the wire doesn't keep the lid from closing all the way.
For times when you want to change out the pellet flavor you are cooking with, the back of the hopper has a pellet cleanout door.

The left side of the Traeger Ironwood has a stainless-steel side shelf with tool hooks, for keeping everything close at hand.

TRAEGER TIMBERLINE SERIES

Traeger Timberline 850 Pellet Grill:
Capacity: 850 sq. in. 6 pork butts, 8 rib racks, 9 chickens
Weight: 213 lbs.
Black

Traeger Timberline 1300 Pellet Grill:
Capacity: 1300 sq. in. 12 pork butts, 15 rib racks, 12 chickens
Weight: 226 lbs.
Black

The Traeger Timberline is fueled by a large capacity, 24Lb.

Pellet hopper on the right side of the grill. At the bottom of the hopper, the auger that transports the exact amount of pellets to the fire pot when needed to reach and maintain your ideal temperature.

The Timberline's large capacity hopper means you can comfortably fit a whole 20Lb. bag of pellets at a time, with room to spare. This large capacity hopper is especially nice when smoking something for a long time, because a full hopper can power your grill for up to 20 hours. Moreover, the Timberline series is the only one that features a pellet sensor to warn you when the pellets level is too low.

The control panel on the hopper has an easy to read digital display. Simply turn on the grill, and use the dial to set your temperature anywhere from a low of 165°F to a maximum temperature of 500°F.
Once your target temperature is set, just ignite the grill with the push of a button & the auger will transport the right amount of pellets to the fire pot.

The Traeger Timberline features an induction fan that rolls the smoke and heat over your food before exiting the grill's rear vent, forming their True convection system.

The body of the Traeger timberline features a double wall stainless steel interior, for heat retention & durability. The lid of the grill also has an airtight gasket, to make sure your heat & smoke stays in the grill where it's meant to be. This insulated design, paired with the True convection system makes cooking on the Timberline just as easy as using an oven.
I used cinnamon rolls to test the heat distribution, and they turned out great!

The Timberline series even comes with Wifire technology, which allows you to remotely control your grill through Traeger's app. Easily set your grill temperature and monitor the progress of your cook from the app.
For longer cooks like a turkey, you can set a target internal temperature, so you know exactly when your food is cooked to perfection.
Traeger's app even comes loaded with a wide range of recipes that have target temperatures pre-programmed. Your grill will then reach and maintain the ideal temperature for the recipe.
It's nice to take the guesswork out of managing temperature, especially when it comes to low and slow smoking.

When it comes to cooking large batches of food, the Traeger Timberline 1300 has you covered with a 3-tiered cooking rack design, which combine to provide 1300 square inches of cooking space.
Each rack can be removed when needed & the cooking grids are made out of stainless steel rods, for maximum durability.
The bottom rack can either be used in this top position, or moved lower for higher temperature cooking. I like to set it in the lower position when cooking something like burgers.

Under the cooking grids of the Traeger Timberline, you'll find a grease drip tray, this catches the drippings from what you grill & works to vaporize the moisture back toward your food.

In the back left and right corners of the grill, you can see the inlets that allow smoke to roll up the rear wall of the grill before exiting, a key component of Traeger's True convection design.
Beneath the grease drip tray, you can see Traeger's heat shield, this sits above the fire pot where the pellets burn, helping to even out the rising heat.

Under the heat shield, you will find the fire pot where the auger deposits pellets to burn and maintain the grills temperature. When you want to quickly change the type of wood pellet you are using, the rear of the hopper has a door that allows pellets to be emptied.

Other nice features of the Traeger Timberline include a magnetic cutting board, that secures to the top of the hopper, a side shelf with hooks to keep grill tools close at hand, and a grease management system that drains into a slide out drip pan on the left lower portion of the grill for easy cleaning.

MASTERING YOUR TRAEGER GRILL

Congratulation! You have just bought the best grill you will ever own. But what are the steps you have to take to make it also the only grill you will ever need. The Traeger grills are sturdy machines but nevertheless, a correct use, maintenance, and cleaning procedure will allow it to run smoothly for years to come and provide hours of enjoyable family dinners, without having to worry about unpleasant smells and annoying malfunctions.

THE FUNDAMENTALS OF WOOD PELLET GRILLING AND SMOKING

Real barbecue can be hard; you've got hot embers, dirty coals, dangerous fire, plus a lot of TLC and time to invest. But the results are the reward for the hard work. Succulent and savory smoke-infused dishes just can't be achieved without low temperatures, a bit of time, and quality hardwood smoke. Charcoal briquettes are okay, but they're messy. Hardwood logs are great for barbecue purists, but massive log-burning grills are overkill for most patios. Wood pellet fuel has made barbecue a lot easier. The tiny pellets burn just like logs, but leave very little ash and are easy to manage.

Today's wood pellet grills offer all the convenience of electric smokers with a few added benefits, including higher temperature options; real wood-generated cooking heat; and no soot or wasted fuel, because the pellets are devoid of any of the moisture you would get from green or wet wood.

The 6 variables of wood pellet grilling and smoking:

As the pit master, your job is to control the cook. Your life will be made a bit easier with a good pellet smoker, but there are still a few variables to which you'll want to pay close attention.

1. **Time:** From preheating to resting the meat after a cook, you'll want to put some extra thought and planning into the amount of time you will need. Most wood pellet grills have an important preheat time frame to observe. When working low and slow with larger cuts of meat, your cook times can be quite long. Start early and give yourself plenty of wiggle room to hit your desired serving time. Even after you pull the meat off the grill, there's an extra 10-minute "rest" recommended for large cuts of meat before carving.

2. **The meat:** Your "cooking" experience starts at the butcher shop or grocery with your selection of the best-looking cuts. Quality meats with more fat provide the best flavor. Remember: the bigger the cuts, the more cook time and seasoning you'll need.

3. **Spices:** We have great seasoning blends mapped out in the recipes in this book. Freshness makes a difference; use the freshest spices you can get your hands on. You can also "bloom" some spices in a dry frying pan over low heat to activate the oils and enhance flavors.

4. **Smoke type:** Choose your wood pellet flavor to match your meat. We'll cover this more later in the chapter, but the wood you choose affects the consistency of these recipes.

5. **Placement:** Your wood pellet grill has a very even cooking temperature devoid of typical hot spots, thanks to the convection-like heat circulation caused by the fan and the heat deflector. Still, try to position your food in the pathway of the smoke inside the chamber.

6. **Temperature:** Lower cook temperatures for smoking provide the most effective way to break down collagen and fat in the meat and absorb maximum smoke flavor. Outside temperature can also affect cook temperature and time. Try to position your wood pellet grill out of the way of direct harsh winds.

Just a few more tips on temperature...

On typical grills, I always suggest setting up hot and cold "zones" where you can move meats to control cooking speeds. That tactic is not an option on wood pellet grills. Instead, you'll be working with set levels of heat, such as hot-smoking, cold-smoking, and smoke-roasting.

Traditional smoking happens at lower temperatures—most low-and-slow meat smoking takes place between 225°F and 275°F. It's at these lower temperatures that the real magic happens. With this set-it-and-forget-it style of wood pellet cooking, low-temperature meats are gently coaxed into fall-off-the-bone succulence.

Cooking at lower temperatures, however, won't necessarily keep you from going too far and overcooking your food. Different foods have different internal-temperature targets. For example, leaner cuts of meat dry out easily. If you're not careful, you'll end up with jerky!

When you use your wood pellet grill at higher temperatures, it is best described as smoke-roasting. Like on a gas grill, you'll attain high-heat char and browning; unlike on a gas grill, you'll get smoke flavor. Most of the baking and cooking you can do in your home oven can also be done on a Trager.
The popular wood pellet grill smokers by Trager can all reach highs well over 400°F.
Electric smokers are also easy to operate but have a more limited temperature high end of 275°F. They are not nearly as versatile.

The pellet grill's ability to achieve higher temperatures than a typical smoker is a definite plus, so, when we get to the recipes, we'll sneak in a few specialties that take advantage of high heat, like reverse searing.

FIRST TIME

Before using your brand-new Traeger grill for the first time, be sure to read the instruction and familiarize yourself with the setting. We are not going to go through all the functions and instructions here, since you will find that in your owner's manual (if you have lost it, you can easily find it online in pdf). We would just like to point out some often overlooked but very important steps that you have to take for the proper use of your Traeger grill. Let's start with seasoning your grill, and no, you won't need salt and pepper!

SEASONING YOUR GRILL

Before using your Traeger grill for the first time you have to "season" it. That might seem weird but a one-time firing (without cooking anything in it!) will ensure that you will get the most out of your wood pellet grill. Seasoning a grill burns off the residual factory oils, so that they don't end up in your food.

Step 1 Plug in grill and turn on

Step 2 Prime your auger tube with pellets. You will see that it's going to start turning and feeding pellets into your hopper. You don't need to use the Traeger pellets for this, even if you decide to cook with them. Any sort of cheap, store-bought natural wood pellets will do the trick. More on pellets later.

Step 3 Add hardwood pellets to hopper

Step 4 Turn the main power switch to "on".

Step 5 Turn dial to "Select Auger" then choose "Prime Auger"

Step 6 Once pellets begin to fall into firepot, select "Done" to turn off auger

Step 7 Turn the selection dial clockwise to 350 °F and press it

Step 8 Make sure that all the components are inside the grill, then close the lid.

Step 9 Press ignite, and after the temperature reaches 350 °F, run for 20 minutes
Step 10 Increase temperature to 450 °F
Step 11 When the temperature reaches 450 °F, run for 30 more minutes
Step 12 Increase temperature to 500 °F
Step 13 When the temperature reaches 500 °F, run for another 30 minutes
Step 14 Turn off grill by pressing the selection dial for three seconds on a Pro Series Grill.
If you have an Ironwood or Timberline, press the Standby button for three seconds to initiate the shutdown cycle.

Step 15 Once the shutdown cycle finishes, seasoning of your grill is complete

That was easy, wasn't it? You are now ready to use your Traeger grill.
Please, think ahead that you need to season your grill before using it for the first time and don't skip it.

START-UP PROCESS

Unlike seasoning this is a step you have to follow every time you grill. Following the correct process is of the utmost importance, because it may affect your cooking even hours in. In our experience, if you cook without starting up your grill correctly you may experience temperature swings, flame outs, and other issues.

Most of the models produced after 2016 follow a simpler **closed lid start-up process**. Check out your serial number on the hopper lid and check it against the list of closed lid grills on the Traeger grill website.

Closed lid start-up process:
Set your Traeger grill directly to the desired temperature and preheat with the lid closed for approximately 15 minutes.

If you have an older model, chances are you will have to follow an **open lid start-up process**.
It involves a few steps, but it is just as easy.

Open lid start-up process:

Step 1 When ready to cook, set your grill to the smoke setting with the lid open
Step 2 Wait for the fire to start (approximately 4-5 minutes)
Step 3 Close Lid
Step 4 Increase the temperature to the desired temperature and preheat for approximately 10-15 minutes

WHAT IS THE P-SETTING?

If you own a trigger grill with a digital thermostat, you should learn how to adjust your Traeger's P setting.

You will be able to get more smoke at lower temperatures for your recipe, or more heat to compensate for cold or windy conditions.

On any of the labeled temperature settings, the Traeger's digital thermostat does a great job of staying within a fairly tight temperature range.
That's because when the temperature falls below a threshold, the auger delivers more fuel, that is pellets, to the fire pot. If the temperature is above the threshold, the auger doesn't run.

On the smoke setting the controller runs differently, cycling the auger on for 15 seconds and off for a set period of time.
If the interval between auger cycles is shorter, pellets will load the fire pot and the grill will get hotter with less smoke.
If the auger's off cycle is longer, the pellets will smolder giving off way more smoke at a lower temperature.

From the factory it's not obvious how to adjust the augers off cycle or P setting (pause setting): buried in the thermostat standalone installation instructions are directions on how to make the adjustment.
You can change the settings pretty easily.

Step 1 First, you have to access the switch. The thermostat ships with a small sticker over the switch.
To access the P hole, remove the sticker to the right of the LCD, labeled call service. The P hole is behind that sticker.

Step 2 Next, with the grill started and set to the smoke setting, take a piece of stiff thin wire, like a straightened paper clip, and poke it into the P hole until you hit the button.

Step 3 When you click the button, you'll see the readout change, showing the current P setting: the factory standard is P-3.
Each click of the button, increases the P setting by one. Once you reach P-9, the settings start over with zero.
The lower the P setting, the shorter the off cycle. Each increase in the P setting number, adds 10 seconds to the off cycle.

Traeger Smoke P-Setting		
P-0	15 seconds auger on	Pause 45 seconds (auger off)
P-1	15 seconds auger on	Pause 55 seconds
P-2 (factory default)	15 seconds auger on	Pause 65 seconds
P-3	15 seconds auger on	Pause 75 seconds
P-4	15 seconds auger on	Pause 85 seconds
P-5	15 seconds auger on	Pause 95 seconds
P-6	15 seconds auger on	Pause 105 seconds
P-7	15 seconds auger on	Pause 115 seconds
P-8	15 seconds auger on	Pause 125 seconds
P-9	15 seconds auger on	Pause 135 seconds

It is important to note that if you have the P setting set higher and the wind picks up, your fire will go out: the auger will keep feeding it pellets and you'll have to shut the grill down and follow the manuals instructions for clearing out the fire pot and restarting the grill. If you don't follow those directions, you'll light a giant pile of pellets that could burn too hot and damage your grill.

In 70-degree ambient temperatures with no wind, the factory P setting of 3 produces a temperature around 150 to 160 degrees.
We like to smoke fish at a lower temperature than that, so we use a higher P setting.

If you are smoking a brisket during a windy snowstorm, you will want to maintain a temperature around 160. So, you will have to lower the P setting to get more heat to compensate for the cold and windy conditions.

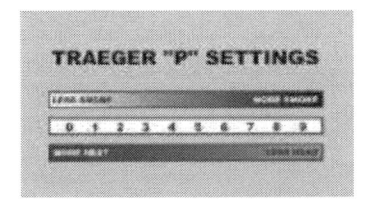

You can usually get good results from the factory setting but sometimes you might want to adjust the heat or smoke for your recipe or weather conditions.

- 23 -

In that case, if you want more control, poke it in the P- hole!

SHUT DOWN CYCLE

Here's the proper shut down method for a Traeger Grill; please follow it, if you want your Traeger to last years.
When finished smoking an epic meal or grilling a delicious dinner on your Traeger, make sure to turn the grill off.
Once you've taken your food off the grill, turn the temperature gauge to Shut Down Cycle.
Close the grill lid and let the internal fan run for about 10 minutes to cool down the grill.
When the fan has automatically shut off you are done.
You can flip the power switch to Off, unplug the grill, close any power outlets, and store extension cords and any remaining pellets.
If your grill is stored outside, put the cover on it, or a plastic sheet to protect it from rain and humidity.

MAINTENANCE

It is very important to know how to correctly maintain and clean your Traeger grill.
You made the great choice of buying a grill that will last a lifetime, so why don't ensure that it runs smoothly for years?
To care for your Traeger grills, you have to know its main components. Even if you are not a DIY expert, and you are most likely to call a repair service, if you have a problem, you still need to know how your grill is built, even just for cleaning it properly.
There are eight main components of the machine which work together to provide you with results that you won't have with any other grill.

The main components are listed below:

Hardwood pallets
These are the most important part of the grill. They function as the main fuel for the grill to work. All-natural hardwood flavorings can seep into your food while cooking through them. You can put any type of wood you want to bring a distinct taste to your dish.

Hopper
This is where you will put your wood pellets in. The flavoring happens here as the wood ignites and cooks the food. 100% wood with no charcoal or gas connection required.

Controller
The knob enables you to set the temperature of your choice and regulate it during the cooking process.

Induction Fan
The fan turns on as you turn on the grill and heat up the food evenly by using the convection process for cooking. The Fan transfers hot air to the entirety of the grill, making it evenly distributed.

Auger
It is a screw-like device that picks and places the wood pellets into the firepot to start the ignition process.
Hot rod
This is where the pellets meet the fire and fire catches on. It is at the end of the auger.
Firepot
Automatically fire is turned on, which ignites the hotrod and causes pellets to catch fire.
Drip Tray
This piece of metal just above the fire prevents it from directly reaching the grill and reduces charring on food. It allows heat and smoke to pass through.

How does it work?
The wood pellets are placed in the auger from the hopper. For higher temperatures, more wood pellets are added to the auger. The auger then transfers the wood pallets to the firepot where a fire is burning. The firepot makes the hotrod ignite the piece of wood, and smoke and fire from the wood are released. A drip tray stands just right on top of the hotrod and the burning wood to stops the naked flame. A fan inside the device is turned on, and it evenly distributes the smoke and heat to the food on top of the grill. For precise temperature controls, some grills are now equipped with an app that helps the cook control the temperature per his or her needs.
The Traeger wood pallets grill not only grills but also can be used for baking, smoking, roasting, and braising.

HOW TO CLEAN YOUR TRAEGER GRILL

Making sure your grill is clean and free of built up grease and debris is critical for keeping the pure, wood-fired flavor of your grill intact. The best way to ensure this is through regular cleanings and maintenance of your grill.

NOTE: Make sure that your grill is switched off and not connected to the electrical outlet!

You'll want the following items on hand:
- Wooden Grill Grate Scrape
- Grease Cleaner. Trager markets a Traeger All-Natural Grease Cleaner, but your normal kitchen grease cleaner will work just as well. Even better, if you clean it frequently, you might want to consider using vinegar or lemon juice diluted with water (at 60%) in a spray bottle.
- Drip Tray Liners
- Bucket Liners
- Shop Vac
- Paper Towels
- Bottle Brush
- Disposable Gloves

- Step 1 Spray grates with the grease cleaner
- Step 2 Spray inside of chimney
- Step 3 Remove and clean grates with the Wooden Grill Grate Scrape. Don't use wire brushes and wipe the grates down with a cleaning cloth or heavy-duty paper towels for this.
- Step 4 Remove drip tray liner
- Step 5 Remove drip tray
- Step 6 Remove heat baffle
- Step 7 Vacuum inside of grill.
- Step 8 Scrub inside of chimney with a bottle brush. Again, don't use wire brushes and wipe the grates down with a cleaning cloth or heavy-duty paper towels for this.
- Step 9 Spray walls with your grease cleaner

- Step 10 Let soak, and wipe down with paper towels
- Step 11 Reinsert heat baffle
- Step 12 Reinsert drip tray
- Step 13 Insert new drip tray liner
- Step 14 Insert new bucket liner
- Step 15 Reinsert grates

You don't have to go through the whole process every time you grill; after all the meat takes its flavor also from the charred and impregnated grates from all the previous barbecues. But you should do it twice, or three times per grilling season, if you use it frequently. If you are cooking something particularly greasing, we would recommend, that you clean it right after. It will make the job a lot easier, if you don't let the fat congeal.

To avoid problems and making the cleaning process a bit easier, here are some helpful tips for routine maintenance:

1. **Invest in a cover.** The Traeger covers are a bit expensive, but aesthetically pleasing. If you don't want to buy a Trager cover, then make sure to cover it carefully with a plastic sheet. If your Traeger grill is stored outside during wet weather, you risk that water gets into the hopper. When the pellets get wet, they expand and may clog your auger. Also, you cannot cook with wet wood.
2. **Change the foil on your grease pan often**, and clean underneath the foil as well. Grease is easier to clean when it is still a bit warm; so after you have finished barbecuing, even if you are tempted to sleep off the party, take the time to scrape the extra grease and debris from the grease pan and grease drain tube and replace the grease pan foil, to avoid grease build-up. If the drain tube gets clogged, you may risk a grease fire.
3. **Empty the grease bucket.** Yuck, I know! But it is a simple enough job: empty the grease in something you can discard, such as a plastic bottle; don't pour it down the drain or in the gutter! Clean the bucket with hot water and soap or, to make your job easier, line the bucket with aluminum foil that you can simply discard.
4. **Wipe down the exterior surfaces.** The Trager grills are beautiful objects, so keep the powder coating looking new! Use warm water and soap and wipe it with a clean cloth or paper towels. Don't use abrasive cleaners or scouring pads!
5. **Remove extra ash from the fire pot**, even if you don't want to clean it completely, at least once every 5 times you use it, remove the grates, the drain pan, and the heat baffle to remove the ash in and around the fire pot. You can use a shop vac for this job. Make sure that all the components are cold and the grill is unplugged and not switched on.

TROUBLESHOOTING FOR THE MOST COMMON PROBLEMS

Like with all pellet grills, you may experience some malfunctions with the Traeger grill.
The grill is not flaming up, the pellets don't get into the fire pit, it cracks with declining temperature. All the most common problem can be resolved by troubleshooting guide.
If you are not comfortable with fixing it yourself, you can call the customer service or contact your local Traeger dealer. Also remember that the warranty is valid for three years (in the U.S.A) But if you have a bit of DIY skills, most fixes are easy and you can find any parts that needs replacing on the Traeger website.

THE GRILL IS NOT STARTING UP

There are three main causes for which your Traeger grills might not be firing.

The first one is your hot rod is not heating up, the second one is your draft induction fan may not be spinning, and the third reason could be your auger is not feeding pellets to the fire pot.

The great thing about the hot rod is that it's super easy: it either works or it doesn't work.
The way that you can figure this out is by simply removing the grill grate, the drip tray, and the heat baffle.
Turn your grill on to the smoke setting and place your hand over the fire pot at a safe distance so you don't get your hand burn and feel if there's heat.
If you feel heat, you know that your hot rod should be working properly.
If your hot rod is not heating up, most likely you have some sort of wire damage.
Check for any fraying of the wires and the connector that connects to your controller, if you see any damage then you need to replace your hot rod.
The best way to get it replaced is either call 1-800 Traeger to the customer service or go to the website and order one online. You don't need to replace the entire fire pot, just the rod.

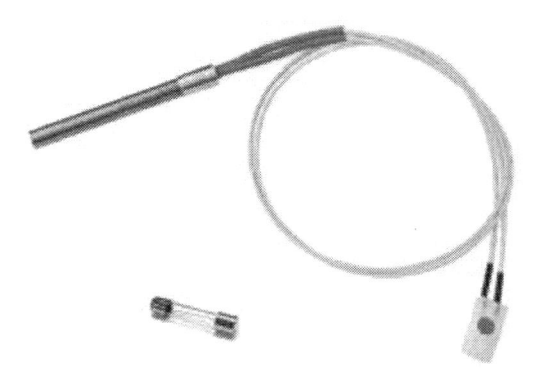

Another common reason why your grill may not be starting up properly is that the draft induction fan is not working.
Your fan is actually located underneath your hopper, it's horizontal so it's very easy to locate; it'll also have an orange wire coming off of it.

Sometimes the fan might not be spinning because you haven't used your grill for a while; there's grease and dirt or sand built up on it.
So, if you go down underneath your hopper and just give that fan a spin, that will help get it going again. You need a fan with a wood pellet grills because not only does it stoke the fire, but it also creates the convection inside the grill, which is ultimately what cooks your food.
When you install parts inside your grill, wires may get crossed up underneath the fan stopping it from spinning.
If your wires are blocking the fan, grab a couple zip ties, find the few other wires that are underneath your grill from your other parts, zip them together, and pull them out of the way. Your fan will be able to spin freely.

You should also check your auger, because it can also cause issues, when it's not actually feeding pellets to the fire pot.
The pellets are the fuel for your fire; without that you're not going to get any heat in your grill.
The most common cause for an auger jam is going to be wet pellets.
The pellets are extremely vulnerable to moisture, they'll expand rapidly and get held up inside the auger shaft not allowing your auger to spin pellets into the fire pot. Read below how to clear a jammed auger.

The auger motor is actually located in the hopper, it's a smaller fan and it's located vertically if you see that's not spinning you know that there's something wrong with your motor you can always go to the website to purchase a replacement or call 1-800 Traeger and talk to the customer service team.

HOW TO CLEAR AN AUGER JAM

We are going to explain in just a few steps how to remove an auger jam in the event that your auger stops spinning and is not feeding pellets into the fire-pot, one of the most common problems Traeger owners experience, especially if the pellets get wet and expand.

Step 1 The first thing we need to do is remove the four screws on the back side of your hopper, as well as the screws that hold your controller in place.
By removing the hopper, we can see the mechanics of the grill and work on the auger jam.

Step 2 Put the controller back through the mounting hole, the easiest way to do it is to pull it out of the hopper and then put it through sideways and wiggle its way into the mounting hole.

Step 3 The next thing we want to do is take off the hopper from the grill, it's mounted to the side of the grill with four screws, two in the front, two in the back.
When you remove that last screw, make sure that the hopper doesn't fall off. Just let your controller dangle down, it shouldn't be a problem when it's hanging by the wires. Now we are into the guts of the grill and we can work on our auger jam.

Step 4 There are a couple tools that you're going to need to get rid of your auger jam, one of them is going to be a **7/64 hex key**, a **pipe wrench**, a **flathead screwdriver** and a **Phillips head screwdriver**, as well as a **set of pliers**, a **hammer** to clean out the most stubborn jams, and something that has a flat edge on it.

Step 5 First thing we're going to do is remove the shear pin that is holding the auger motor to the auger shaft, you are going to need your hex key and the pliers to hold down the nut. This will then allow us to remove the motor completely from the shaft, and open the shaft.

Step 6 The next thing we want to do is remove the bushing and the screw, this can either be a flathead screw or a Phillips screw.
Once we get that out, we're going to try and move the auger. If we can't move it, this is when our pipe wrench is going to come in handy. After a couple cranks this will be a lot easier.

Step 7 Once you get the auger removed from the auger shaft, you can either use a hammer something with a flat edge to remove whatever is blocking your auger.
Sometimes the auger actually works really well, so you can just spin it push it in and out and it should help clear the jam, usually wet pellets.

Step 8 Once the auger shaft is cleaned out, use a vacuum to clear out the fire pot first of any excess pellets or objects. Then, clean the top of the auger and remove anything that may be inside of the auger shaft.

Step 9 Now that you have the auger shaft cleaned out, we're just going to put everything back together the same way that we did it.
First put the auger back into the auger shaft, you will set the bushing with the set screw and then you will attach the motor back to the auger and use the shear pin.

You should be back up and running; whether you have wet pellets or random other objects that have gone into your hopper into the auger shaft, this is how you fix an auger jam.

MAINTAINING TEMPERATURE

To get the temperature of a wood pellet grill on lockdown, it may be tricky.
Different wood pellet blends burn at different rates and temperatures but Traeger's temperature control devices regulate like a champ.

If your wood pellet grill has issues with maintaining temperatures, here are a few steps you can take to keep them steady.

Cooking with fire is like cooking with a convection oven, when the door or lid opens and heat escapes the internal temperatures may fluctuate.

How to maintain a Traeger's internal temperature:
Traeger temperature gauges and temperature controllers give precise readings of the internal grill temperature at the time you view it. Once you open it the internal temp can change.

1. It's always best to use Traeger pellets.
2. Make sure your pellets are dry. Moist or wet pellets will not burn evenly, they may not ignite and this may cause your wood-fired grill not to function properly.
3. A clean grill helps keep temperatures consistent, make sure your fire pot is clear of ash to keep air flow consistent
4. Clean the RTD temperature controller. It's on left of the inside of your grill next to the hopper.
5. Make sure your hopper is full so you have enough pellets to fuel into the fire. 6. Swap out your temperature controller to a newer model. The 2016 Digital Pro Temperature Controller has Advanced Grilling Logic which checks the internal temperature every 60 seconds and fuels the fire if there are any deviations from the set internal temperature. Swapping out your temperature gauge with this controller will ensure precision control.
7. Older grills may have corrosion or rust in the grill. If the fire pot has too big of holes, you have too much air flowing into the fire creating which can create varying temperatures. If this is the case, order a new fire pot (fire pot replacement) or upgrade your grill.

Remember, consistent temps create consistently delicious food.

CHOOSING THE RIGHT PELLET

Wood pellets are the fuel source of pellet grills. Essentially, they are compressed capsules of sawdust from repurposed wood. Lumber yards, for example, have a lot of scrap wood that is useless for most practical applications. Pellet grills found a use for this scrap by collecting and pressurizing it into a small wood pellet.

It's important to quickly note the difference between heating pellets and food grade hardwood pellets for smoking and grilling. Heating pellets can be made from wood that has chemicals and toxins in it – the kind of stuff you'd never ever want getting into your food. These pellets were designed for old school heating stoves and NOT for pellet grills. The type of pellets we're talking about are made from 100% all-natural hardwood that is dried out then ground to sawdust. The sawdust is pressurized at extreme heat to create compact pellets, which are then coated and held together.

Hardwood pellets are great because they impart bona fide wood fired flavor into your food. They also burn quite efficiently and ash at an extremely low rate. For reference, a 40-pound bag of wood pellets will typically produce only about half of a cup of ash.

Different types of wood impart different flavors onto your food. Some wood species work best with specific types of food, but half of the fun of outdoor cooking is experimenting! Don't be afraid to try a new wood flavor with your food next time you fire up the grill.
Also worth noting – you can blend pellets. Traeger sells their own proprietary pellet blend recipes, which are great, but nothing is stopping you from blending at home. If you want to soften the flavor of a stronger smoke or simply want to experiment, try different blends and see how they go.

It's hard to predict what's next in pellet flavors. Special blends have become marketable for many pellet makers, but a lot of cooks like creating their own blends. Other than new blends, the newest pellet "flavor" is charcoal. If you have a soft spot for traditional backyard grill flavor, this could be what you've been looking for. These black-colored pellets are best mixed with any regular wood pellet to enhance the smoke ring on your meat (charcoal's hotter combustion atmosphere aids in the creation of a more distinct smoke ring). Charcoal pellets also feature a hotter, cleaner burn than regular wood pellets.

WOOD PELLET REFERENCE CHART

Wood	Flavor Profile	Use With
Alder	Delicate and earthy, with a hint of sweetness	Fish, Shellfish, Beef, Pork, Lamb, Poultry, Veggies
Apple	Mild, subtle sweet and fruity flavor	Pork, Poultry, Lamb, Wild Game, Beef, Some Seafood
Cherry	Light and sweet. Delicate, not overpowering	Beef, Pork, Poultry, Wild Game, Some Seafood
Hickory	Sweet, yet strong flavor. Not overpowering. Versatile	Beef, Pork, Poultry, Fish, Wild Game
Maple	Mild and slightly sweet flavor	Beef, Pork, Poultry, Small Game Birds, Cheese, Veggies
Mesquite	Strong and earthy flavor. One of the hottest burning woods	Red meats, Dark Meats, Wild Game
Oak	Medium smoky flavor. Versatile. Milder than Hickory, stronger than Cherry	Beef, Pork, Poultry, Fish, Some Wild Game
Pecan	Sronger than most fruitwoods, but milder than Hickory and Mesquite	Beef, Pork, Poultry
Peach	Sweet, fruity flavor	Pork, Poultry, Small Game Birds

MOST POPULAR PELLET BLENDS

Wood	Brand(s)	Flavor profile	Use with
Apple Mash Blend	CookinPellets	Lightly sweet blend of apple mash and hard maple	Great with light-flavor foods like chicken, pork, muffins, and cold-smoked dishes.
BBQ Blend	Pit Boss	Sweet, savory, and tart blend of maple, hickory, and cherry	Good for all foods
Bourbon Brown Sugar	Cabela's	Seasoned oak blend of bourbon, smoke flavor, and sweetness	Good for beef, chicken, and pork
Pellet Pro exclusive charcoal blend	Smoke Daddy Inc.	Charcoal blended with red oak. Mix with any flavor of wood pellets and use to enhance smoke ring.	Good for all meats
Competition blend	Traeger	Blend of sweet, savory, and tart (maple, hickory, and cherry)	Good for pork, chicken, and beef
Perfect mix blend	CookinPellets	Blend of hickory, cherry, hard maple, and apple	Great on short cooks; for any foods
Texas blend	Green Mountain	Blend of oak, hickory, and mesquite	Good for all meats
Realtree big game blend	Traeger	Blend of hickory, red and white oak, and rosemary	Great for venison, pheasant, and game meats
Turkey pellet blend with brine kit	Traeger	Oak, hickory, maple, and rosemary	Turkey
Tennessee Whiskey Barrel	Big Poppa Smokers	Aged oak from Jack Daniels Whiskey	Good for most meats

HOW TO STORE YOUR PELLETS

How and where you store your pellets is key for taking care of your wood.
Follow our guide below and never worry about finding crumbly dust in your bag ever again.

1. Store pellets inside a dry area free from flooding, humidity, and mold. Garage or shed works best.

2. Do not leave the pellets in the bags they come in.

3. Grab one of Traeger's pellet storage metal buckets or an airtight container of your choice. The pellet lid must be airtight and shouldn't allow moisture to get in. You can also use a Rubbermaid tote.

The Traeger bucket is actually a great investment because it's weather resistant, allows for an easy pour, and has a filter that strains sawdust, plus 20 lb capacity to store exactly one bag of pellet.

TIP: Do not use zip bags. They're not actually airtight.

ACCESSORIES

You're off to a great start with your pellet grill, but there are a few other valuable tools that are well worthwhile to invest in. These tools appear throughout this cookbook – some are vital, and some simply elevate your repertoire.

Drip pans and bucket liners
Heavy-duty food service foil with an 18-inch width is the common choice to cover the drip pan in your pellet smoker. Recently, some grill manufacturers have started selling drip pan liners as well as disposable inserts to keep your drip bucket clean. It may seem like overprotection, but drippings and grease are exceptionally stubborn and better to throw out than wash down a sink. I recommend Drip EZ brand liners.

Probe Meat Thermometer – If your grill doesn't have probe thermometers built in, you 100% need to get one or two of them. They are crucial to almost any recipe, but especially for smoking recipes. Measuring your meat's internal temperature is the only way you can know when your food is safely cooked all the way through. It will also help you pull your food off of the cooker at your exact desired doneness.

BBQ Gloves – For your safety, it's best to have a pair of BBQ gloves just in case. Most of our recipes don't require BBQ gloves to safely handle your food, but some do. Plus, it never hurts to take extra caution when you're dealing with scorching hot temperatures.

Silicone Basting Brush – Many grill and smoker recipes utilize marinades that need to be brushed or basted onto your food. Basting brushes are quite affordable and a borderline necessity for any grilling tool box.

Cast Iron Skillet – The cast iron skillet is one of the most versatile pans in any kitchen, and since pellet grills can bake, roast, and braise, we'll use them on the pellet grill too.

Cold smoker tubes
Wood pellet grills are unable to sustain smoke production and temperatures under 120°F. If you are looking to do a lot of cold-smoking of cheese or just want to add extra smoke flavor, do what many pit masters do and use a specially made tube filled with pellets. These tubes can burn on top of the grill grate for hours without generating substantial heat. As a result, they can convert your grill into a cold smoker. The most popular brand is A-Maze-N.

… or Cold Smoker addition
The Trager markets a Cold Smoker addition, ideal to smoke fish or cheeses at low temperature. The results are amazing! It's an attachment for the right side of your grill that includes to porcelain-coated grill grates and an adjustable warming vent, that can be opened and shut to adjust the temperature of your smoke. It's a "sidecar" smoker that keeps the temperature extra-low allowing you to smoke lox style salmon, cheeses, hard boiled eggs, bacon, and even flavor steaks that can be hard seared later.

Electric knives
Electric knives can help you slice meats to your desired thickness. They're essential tools for cutting your brisket razor-thin.

Bear Claws
Not the pastry! "Bear" claws are handheld pronged forks allow you to pull apart whole roasts for such dishes as authentic pulled pork or carnitas.

Cedar planks
If you're looking to show off a bit, you can use cedar or other hardwood planks both to add flavor to smoked entrées and to make yourself look über-cool serving smoked fish right on a smoking board! This is a unique and traditional presentation for salmon, and the cedar adds a wonderful flavor above and beyond the wood pellet smoke flavor.

SMOKING, AND GRILLING, AND COOKING, AND BAKING ON YOUR TRAEGER

Before we can get to the fun part, i.e. the recipes, there are a few things that you must know to get the best out of your Traeger grill. In this chapter we will explore all the different techniques and cooking tips you will ever need.

Since the Traeger grill is so versatile, I quickly compiled a list of all the different techniques that you can apply to your wood pellet grill.

Besides smoking for which it is most famous for, there are a few other cooking methods or techniques that the pellet grill offers. We'll spend time on some of these throughout the book, whereas we'll just touch on others here.

The versatility of a pellet grill or smoker gives you options. No other grill on the market allows you to have so many methods for smoking foods. Mastering these techniques will not only make you look great in front of friends and family, but also help you cook outside on that day you don't want to heat the kitchen and dirty your clean stove.

BARBECUE
The actual definition of barbecue is as varied as the barbecues themselves. For our purposes, we will define barbecue as a method of cooking, either with direct or indirect heat, in which a hardwood-fired heat source is used. Barbecue is done at lower temperatures, usually below 400°F, separating it from grilling.

BAKE
Baking is one of my favorite things to do on the grill! Everything from pizza to brownies to apple pie can be cooked on your pellet grill. Giving that wood-fired smoky flavor to your baked goods might just be the flavor you have been missing.

The convection oven–style characteristics of a pellet grill make it perfect for baking. Because the air temperature is consistent throughout your chamber, baking can be done just as easily as in your kitchen oven.

Homemade wood-fired pizzas are always the go-to on the pellet grill, but you can do so much more, depending on your tastes and what local produce is in season. For instance, since I grew up in Oregon's Willamette Valley, grilled marionberry pies were a summer staple in our home. Wood-fired lasagna is a treat for any Italian food lover. Not sure what snack to grab for the kids? Fire up a pan of brownies!

BRAISE
Braising is a cooking method that uses both wet and dry cooking. In terms of a pellet grill, we braise primarily by cooking directly on the grill grate before placing the food into a liquid to complete its cooking. Multiple forms of dry cooking can be done before placing the item in liquid, including slow smoking. Wet cooking can be done both open and closed on your pellet grill or smoker. Shrimp, chili, and short ribs are wood-fired favorites for braising.

GRILL
Grilling is like barbecuing but at a higher temperature. When grilling, you cook meats quickly, never low and slow, but you'll still get that beautiful wood-fired flavor from your pellet grill. Grilling is for burgers, sausages, and more.

ROAST
Roasting is achieved by cooking your meat over high heat for a long period of time. It gives your meat an amazing crust while sealing in juices. Roast your Christmas prime rib or leg of lamb in your pellet grill and it'll be the hit of the party

THE MOST IMPORTANT INGREDIENT: TEMPERATURE

To be a pit master, you need to learn to cook by temperature, not by time. Time is for baking; temperature is for meat.
The internal temperature of whatever you're cooking is the most important thing to look at when pulling anything from the grill—not color, shade, or anything else. Using temperature will prevent you from undercooking or overcooking your meats. The guide in the next subchapter shows you the proper internal temperature for meats discussed throughout this book.

THE STALL
The stall happens on longer cooks and typically occurs between 165°F and 170°F. The stall refers to a long period of time that your meat stays within a small range of temperature.
To imagine the stall, think of your favorite football team. The game is tied; one second is left and the opposing team is driving, but fumbles on the one-yard line into the hands of a defensive tackle. That defensive lineman gets running, but at about the 70-yard line starts slowing down. Those next 30 yards take forever. That is the stall.
Even though you are going to get to the end of that cooking session and that All-Pro defensive tackle is going to make it to the end zone, you both have serious doubts. Just hunker down, grab another beer or two, and wait it out a couple hours.

THE TEXAS CRUTCH
If that second beer just isn't an option, this is where the Texas crutch comes in. The Texas crutch is a method of wrapping meant to decrease the cooking time while maintaining moisture. By wrapping your brisket or pork shoulder with aluminum foil or butcher paper, you allow the meat to retain its moisture, even with consistent or increasing temperature.
To use the Texas crutch, wait until your meat has hit the stall (165°F) and wrap it with either foil or butcher paper for the remainder of the cook and rest time. If you can wait longer than 165°F, wait until 170°F. The longer you leave the meat exposed to smoke, the better the smoke flavor but also the dryer the meat.
I really don't recommend going too high and too fast; this is low-and-slow smoked barbecue.
There are arguments for wrapping and not wrapping, but if you ever have trouble with dry meat, use the Texas crutch; it's a simple way of preventing your meat from losing moisture, and if you are already using the crutch, use it earlier in the process.

SOMEONE LIKES IT SMOKED

Smoking isn't just for preserving any more. These days, it's common to see smoked turkey and cheeses in supermarkets because people love the flavor. And, though brisket, ribs, and chicken are popular favorites, the good taste isn't limited to meats. Smoked vegetables, nuts, and even fruit are becoming mainstream delicacies.

There are two smoking methods used with pellet grills: hot smoking and cold smoking. These two methods refer to the air temperature at the time of smoking and give you substantially different results.
There are many recipes best suited either for hot smoking or cold smoking. The recipes in this book touch on both methods and specify which type of smoking to use.

COLD SMOKING
Cold smoking is just what it sounds like: smoking at a lower temperature. Cold smoking on a pellet grill is typically done at temperatures between 80°F and 120°F in a chamber separate from the actual heat source. Cold smokes can be short or long, depending on what you are smoking.
In many instances, cold smoking is used to preserve foods, such as for smoked fish, jerky, and poultry. Cold smoking has been used for thousands of years, all over the world, to preserve meats for times where hunting and fishing were less of an option to provide food for a family.

Cold smoking can also be used as a method of adding flavor. Cheeses and nuts are primary examples of this. Cold smoking cheeses - like Cheddar and Havarti - and nuts - like almonds and cashews - will add that subtle smoke flavor we all enjoy without actually cooking the foods.

Most pellet grills do not come with a standard cold smoke option, but it can be purchased separately. Traeger and Louisiana Grills offer cold-smoker attachments.

HOT SMOKING

Hot smoking is done above 120°F and is the smoking functionality built into every pellet grill and smoker. Hot smoking is done in the same chamber as the smoke source or, in our case, the fire.

CLASSIC LOW-AND-SLOW SMOKING

Low-and-slow smoking is classic Southern smoking, the most popular form of smoking in the United States and the rest of North America.

Low-and-slow smoking is done at temperatures between 180°F and 250°F, with the most common temperature being 225°F.

Low-and-slow smoking is what produces spectacular brisket and pulled pork. Just writing this has me imagining a plate full of sauced-up ribs, pulled pork, and brisket, with a heaping scoop of coleslaw on the side!

INGREDIENTS	SMOKING TEMPERATURE	TIME	INTERNAL TEMPERATURE	TYPE OF PELLETS
CHICKEN				
CHICKEN (BONELESS, SKINLESS)	350°F	25 to 30 minutes	170°F	Alder, pecan
CHICKEN CUT UP (LEGS/THIGHS/BREASTS)	250°F	1 hour 30 minutes to 2 hours	165°F	Cherry, pecan, oak, apple, maple
CHICKEN OR TURKEY (GROUND)	275°F	1 hour to 1 hour 30 minutes	160°F	Apple
CHICKEN WINGS	350°F	50 to 60 minutes	165°F	Hickory, oak
CHICKEN, WHOLE (3 TO 4 POUNDS)	250°F	45 minutes per pound	165°F	Cherry, pecan, oak, apple
CHICKEN HALVES	250°F	3 hours	165°F	Cherry
JERK CHICKEN LEG QUARTERS	275°F	1 hour 30 minutes	165°F	Mesquite and a few whole pimento (allspice) berries
TURKEY				
TURKEY (WHOLE)	250°F	30 minutes per pound	165°F	Apple
TURKEY LEGS	225°F	4 to 5 hours	165°F	Apple
PORK				
BABY BACK RIBS	225°F	5 hours 30 minutes to 6 hours	190°F	Hickory
BRATS	225°F	1 hour 30 minutes to 2 hours	160°F	Oak, pecan, hickory
PORK SHOULDER BOSTON BUTT (PULLED)	225°F	8 to 9 hours	205°F	Hickory
PORK SAUSAGE (GROUND)	225°F	2 hours	165°F	Apple
PORK CHOPS	325°F	45 to 50 minutes	160°F	Oak, hickory, apple
PORK LOIN ROAST	250°F	3 hours	160°F	Apple, hickory
PORK SPARE RIBS	250°F	6 hours	190°F	Mesquite, cherry
PORK TENDERLOIN	225°F	2 hours to 2 hours 30 minutes	160°F	Hickory, apple

BEEF				
BRISKET	225°F	1 hour to 1 hour 30 minutes	195°F to 205°F	Oak
CHUCK ROAST	225°F	1 hour per pound	120°F to 155°F	Oak, mesquite
HAMBURGERS	425°F	20 to 25 minutes	160°F	Oak
FILET MIGNON	450°F	12 to 14 minutes	120°F Rare 135°F Medium 155°F Well-done	Oak, pecan
FLANK STEAK	450°F	8 to 20 minutes	120°F Rare 135°F Medium 155°F Well-done	Any
FLAT IRON STEAK	450°F	8 to 20 minutes	120°F Rare 135°F Medium 155°F Well-done	Any
LONDON BROIL (TOP ROUND)	350°F	12 to 16 minutes	120°F Rare 135°F Medium 155°F Well-done	Any
PRIME RIB	450°F to sear, 300°F to smoke	20 minutes per pound	120°F Rare 135°F Medium 155°F Well-done	Oak, pecan
RIBEYE	450°F	8 to 20 minutes	120°F Rare 135°F Medium 155°F Well-done	Hickory, oak, mesquite
RUMP ROAST	225°F	1 hour per pound	120°F Rare 135°F Medium 155°F Well-done	Oak, mesquite
SHORT RIBS (BEEF)	225°F	3 to 4 hours	175°F	Oak, mesquite
SIRLOIN TIP ROAST	225°F	1 hour per pound	120°F Rare 135°F Medium 155°F Well-done	Oak, mesquite
T-BONE AND PORTERHOUSE STEAKS	165°F, 450°F	45 to 50 minutes	120°F Rare 135°F Medium 155°F Well-done	Hickory
TENDERLOIN (BEEF)	400°F	25 to 30 minutes	120°F Rare 135°F Medium 155°F Well-done	Oak, hickory, pecan
TEXAS SHOULDER CLOD	250°F	12 to 16 hours	195°F	Oak
TRI-TIP	425°F	45 minutes to 1 hour	120°F Rare 135°F Medium 155°F Well-done	Oak
FISH AND SEAFOOD				
FISH (HALIBUT, SEA BASS, SWORDFISH, TROUT, AND COD)	200°F to 225°F	1 hour 30 minutes to 2 hours	140°F	Alder, apple, cherry, oak
OYSTERS	225°F	15 to 20 minutes	To taste	Apple, cherry, oak
SALMON	250°F	1 to 2 hours	145°F	Alder
TUNA STEAKS	250°F	1 hour	125°F	Apple, cherry, oak

FRUIT AND VEGETABLES				
BELL PEPPERS	225°F	1 hour 30 minutes	Until tender	Maple
CAULIFLOWER	200°F to 250°F	45 minutes to 1 hour 30 minutes	Until tender	Maple
CORN ON THE COB	450°F	12 to 14 minutes	Until tender	Hickory, oak, pecan, mesquite
JALAPEÑO PEPPERS	250°F	1 hour to 1 hour 30 minutes	Until tender	Maple
ONIONS	250°F	2 hours	Until tender	Maple, mesquite
PEACHES	225°F	35 to 45 minutes	To taste	Maple
PINEAPPLE	250°F	1 hour to 1 hour 30 minutes	To taste	Maple
POTATOES	400°F	1 hour 15 minutes	Until tender	Maple, pecan
SWEET POTATOES, WHOLE	375°F	1 hour to 1 hour 30 minutes	Until crispy	Maple
SQUASH AND ZUCCHINI	225°F	1 hour	Until tender	Maple

FINAL STEPS

One thing that surprises most entry-level grillers is that the post-cook time is as important as the pre-cook time. Resting, carving, and pulling can make or break your meats.
Have you ever had that perfect piece of meat—but the moment you cut into it, all the juices spilled out over the cutting board and out of the meat? Sure you have; we all have. This happens when the meat doesn't rest properly. It can be easily prevented, once again, with patience.

RESTING
As rest times vary from recipe to recipe, I'll include specific rest times in the recipes, but there's more to resting than just time.
If you aren't already using a Texas crutch, start wrapping your meat in foil or butcher paper when you pull it off the grill. After the initial wrapping, wrap it in old towels or blankets and place it in a cooler. This will keep your meat warm and allow it to continue to cook.
Always include rest time in your food preparation. Don't cut yourself short. By allowing your meat to rest, you actually continue to cook the meat and raise its internal temperature.
Also, let's not make rest time a bad thing. I use meats with long rest times for parties! While my meat rests, I am doing one of three things: cleaning up for company, driving to the party, or getting my pregame on. Never let smoking or barbecuing be a limiting experience. Barbecue is about good times with good people and good food.

TENTING
Tenting is another form of letting your meat rest. In tenting, you use foil to create a tent above your meat. This process allows air to flow around the meat, preventing condensation, but also blocks the heat from rising, keeping your meat warm.
To create a tent, simply use a sheet of foil and fold it to build a triangular tent over your meat. (Be sure the foil is not touching the skin or meat directly.)
This is ideal for poultry and other meats with short rest times. Tent your Thanksgiving turkey while waiting for guests to arrive. If your steaks require rest time, tent them.

CARVING

Carving correctly ensures that your meat retains moisture and is easier to cut while eating.
When carving, be sure to have the right tools. A quality cutting board and a sharp knife are necessary. Other important tools include cutting gloves, a fork, and food serving gloves.
Sharpen your knives frequently at home or pay a professional to do it. Tough cuts and solid barks all need a sharp knife.
Also, if you are like me, you like using your hands and not utensils. Grab your gloves. It gets hot, greasy, and just unsafe in there. Get your gloves on when you cut or pull any meat.

KNOW YOUR MEATS

PORK

Pork has a salty flavor that cannot be mistaken. The fat content in pork, though it can get in the way at times, allows it to be both juicy and tender.
Pork goes extremely well with sweet flavors, and I refer to that a lot. Pick up some local honey; it supports the beekeepers, farmers, and markets in the area. Plus, local honey tastes better. Brown sugar is delicious with pork, too. And whenever I visit a buddy in Toronto, I always pick up some Canadian maple syrup in the duty-free shop on the way home to have on hand for pork recipes.

1. Head
2. Clear Plate
3. Back Fat
4. Boston Butt/Shoulder
5. Loin/Tenderloin
6. Ham
7. Cheek
8. Picnic Shoulder
9. Ribs
10. Bacon/Belly
11. Hock

RIBS
I am going to speak in general terms when dealing with pork ribs, both spare ribs and baby backs. In both cases you want to select a cut with a good amount of fat, but it should be consistent throughout. Too much fat, especially if it is only in certain places, can make for an unappetizingly fatty bite.

We are going to prep our ribs the way you see them at a competition, not at the local chain barbecue restaurant. These will have just the slightest pull to them just before the meat slips and falls off the bone. If you want the meat slipping and sliding off the bone, cook them a little longer.

Tips and techniques

Remove the membrane. That weird membrane on the back of ribs (sometimes called silverskin) can make them harder to pull off the bone and less tender. To get pit master-level results each time, remove the membrane.
Use mustard as a binder. Mustard works great as a binder for your rub on fatty meats such as ribs. Rub plain yellow mustard or another smooth mustard over your ribs before or after your rub. This will keep your rub on your meat and not all over your drip pan.
Use whatever liquid you like best (including beer or wine, but not liquor) for your spritz or your wrap. When watching a competition cook prep ribs with Mountain Dew, I asked why. "It's what my brother and I like and what we had, so we just started using it," he told me. Use what you like, or see what other pit masters are using and try that for a change. It's a great place to experiment.
Sauce it—just don't overdo it. Again, saucing is a total preference. At parties, I always have a plate of ribs with just a dry rub. Over the years, my ribs have gone from dry to heavily sauced, and now I just use a light sweet coating. As you will see in the recipes, we also have other ways to achieve sweetness.
Country-style ribs are ribs. Cook boneless country-style ribs the same way you would other ribs. The smoked flavor is great and they are extremely tender when done.

PORK SHOULDER

Pulled pork is something pit masters love. Not just because it's easy and good, but because it typically means leftovers for days. Sliders, nachos, and sandwiches are all day-two and day-three renditions of the pulled-pork-leftover week. A good-size pork shoulder could feed an army—or at least an army of kids just back from baseball, gymnastics, or soccer.
When selecting your pork shoulder—also called pork butt or Boston butt—it doesn't matter if you choose one with or without a bone. Some people will tell you it does, but it's a personal preference. However, do check the fat content. You want some fat or your pork will dry out but too much can be overly fatty, just like with ribs. The fat cap should be less than 1 inch deep.

Tips and techniques
Inject your pork shoulder for extra moisture and flavor. Using a tea inject your shoulder. A good shoulder will have a nice flavorful bark (see the next tip), but injecting will give it flavor everywhere.
Smoke your pork longer for a good "bark." Bark isn't just on trees or what your dog does. Bark is that amazingly tasty crust on the outside of a well-smoked meat. The bark develops when the meat and rub combine with uninterrupted smoke for a long period of time. A good pork shoulder will have a good, dark bark. To increase the amount of bark, smoke the pork longer, unwrapped.
Use your hands when pulling the meat— it's just easier. There are some new cool claws available that can be used for pulling pork. They keep your hands from getting hot and greasy. Fact is, though, with those the pull never really feels right. I have a pair of cheap cotton gloves I wear under food service gloves. The gloves keep my hands from burning, but let me pull the meat exactly as I like it.

TENDERLOINS

Pork tenderloins are among the simplest smoke preparations on the grill but they're always impressive. I smoke a couple of tenderloins for my family every couple of weeks and they never get tired of them. The pellet grill or smoker does an amazing job with tenderloins, ensuring a juicy result each time.
When selecting tenderloins, as with most pork, the key is fat content. I try to limit the fat content on my tenderloins. A pellet grill will work to keep them moist and will limit dried-out areas.

Tips and techniques
If you're lazy, just smoke them. I will tell you how in the recipe section, but this is one of my secret easy preparations. The Smoke setting of the pellet grill works great to get your meat to temperature while always keeping it moist.

Use a reverse sear. Searing is usually done first, before cooking the meat fully. When we do it last, after fully smoking the meat, we call it a reverse sear. If your grill has an open flame option, like a flame broiler, use that; otherwise, crank up your grill's temperature as high as it will go. After smoking the tenderloins until their internal temperature reaches 135°F to 140°F, sear them off at a higher temperature until they reach 145°F, about 3 to 5 minutes per side.

Pork tenderloins are a great candidate for marinating. A teriyaki-marinated pork tenderloin tastes amazing and the meat can take on the marinade flavor in as little as 30 minutes.

BEEF

When I think smoking and barbecue, my mind immediately goes to beef: large cuts of brisket and tri-tip, steaks over a flame. Fortunately, with today's grill technology, all of these are possible on a pellet grill.

But the dream of so many pit masters is that perfect Texas-style brisket. We have all spent hours researching how best to achieve it: Wrapped or unwrapped? Foil or butcher paper? How long should it take? We also want steaks that even the owner of the best steakhouse would pay for—the smoke and the butter and the fire, all infused with the smell of searing meat. That's what we aim for in our backyards.

This is why I think "beef" when I think smoking and barbecue.

Selecting beef is made easier by its grade. We'll go into this here, as well as some other tips to make you a master of low-and-slow meat cooking.

1. Neck
2. Chuck
3. Rib
4. Short Loin
5. Sirloin
6. Tenderloin
7. Top Sirloin
8. Rump Cap
9. Round
10. Brisket
11. Shoulder Clod
12. Short Plate
13. Flank

BRISKET

In my experience, brisket tends to be the gold standard, and among the most difficult to cook, on the pellet grill. Many look at the perfect brisket with reverence and hope for the day when they'll successfully achieve it. Discussions fill message boards on the bend test, the pull test, and the like. The problem with this line of thinking around brisket? Well, it's actually not that difficult to make! Brisket, just like anything else, can be perfected with practice and patience.

When selecting the perfect brisket—and I am referring to a full brisket, with both the point and flat cuts (usually separated at most butchers) intact—the key is not too much fat. If you buy a brisket with a huge fat cap, you are just going to cut it off. Also, I suggest spending the extra money on the highest grade of brisket available to you. A cheap brisket can equal a tough brisket. Brisket is not a cheap cut anyway, so spend the money for the best cut.

Tips and techniques
Get rid of that fat cap. A huge fat cap is just not appetizing if you leave it on when you smoke your brisket. Use a boning knife or whatever knife you have available and cut the fat cap down to about ¼ inch. Trimming the fat cap will decrease the fattiness of your brisket, but leaving it partially there will keep the meat moist.

Wrap. Don't wrap. You choose. I will give you instructions in the recipe section, but for the most part, wrapping is a preference. Both aluminum foil and butcher paper can be used for wrapping—again, it is all about preference. The one thing I will say about wrapping, however, is don't do it until after the stall , 165°F to 170°F. Wrapping too early cuts down on your bark development and your brisket won't be as smoky.

If you don't wrap the meat, spritz it or use a water pan. Spritzing with liquid, like apple juice or plain water, will ensure your brisket stays moist. A water pan can be used in a pellet grill just like you would in any other type of grill, but be careful not to spill it. Simply fill a metal pan with water and place it inside the grill. If you have a flat drain pan, the water pan will sit there perfectly.

TRI-TIP
If pork ribs are my number one dish, tri-tip is my number two. I have spent many weekends working to perfect my tri-tip. I have used pellet grills, charcoal Kamados, and wood chip smokers, all in the quest to make the best tri-tip possible. Fortunately for us, my best tri-tip has come off a pellet grill.

Tri-tip is a lean meat that packs amazing flavor. When cooked properly, a tri-tip can smoke as well as any meat, but with a beautiful pink, juicy center. Eating a great smoked tri-tip is like eating only the best part of the best cooked steak.

As with other meats and cuts of meat, go lean on your tri-tip. It should have good, consistent marbling (the flecks of white fat seen in each cut of meat).

Tips and techniques
Tri-tip is best with a reverse sear. This can be done over a flame broiler or with a skillet. Giving your tri-tip a reverse sear seals in the juices after you have pumped in all that smoky flavor. I smoke my tri-tip similarly to other meats—to an internal temperature between 135°F and 140°F—then sear it over the flame broiler. If your grill does not have a flame broiler, use a cast-iron skillet on the grill. Simply heat the skillet to a temperature above 350°F, add the tri-tip and about 1 tablespoon of butter, and cook for 5 to 7 minutes per side, until it reaches an internal temperature of 145°F, flipping it once.

Tri-tip is cut against the grain, and the grain on tri-tip runs two different ways. Pay attention to the grain and you will be fine.

Tri-tip is another amazing leftover meat. Au jus sandwiches, tacos, and stroganoff are all day-two tri-tip meals my family and I enjoy regularly.

RIBS
I make beef ribs significantly less often than pork, and this is by no fault of the cows. Although I enjoy beef ribs, my wife does not, and that means their beefy goodness tends to elude me.

Beef back ribs can be amazing, but they can also be a lot of work for next to nothing. Make sure you select meaty beef ribs. Many beef ribs are cut far too close to the bone, leaving little meat, only what exists between the bones.

Tips and techniques
Try them dry rubbed. Try making beef ribs without a sauce. Sauce complements beef differently than pork and the sweetness doesn't always hit the spot. Use some of your favorite beef rubs to make your ribs stand out.

Use Worcestershire sauce for your spritz for extra flavor. I use a mix of about one part Worcestershire sauce to three parts water.

Peppered ribs are awesome. Black pepper is great with beef. Use freshly ground black pepper on your beef ribs for amazing flavor.

PRIME RIB
Prime rib is one of those cuts packed with its own flavor. Every holiday season, prime rib orders fill the local butcher and we all try to replicate the flavor of the meat we had at the company party. But again, the great thing about

being a pellet grill owner is now your dish will be better than the party version. (Unfortunately, that might mean your pals will start asking you to cater!)
The grade of meat decides what rib roast you choose for prime rib. Only choose prime grade rib with a generous amount of fat, as good marbling on the meat will help keep it moist and tender.

Tips and techniques
Prime rib can be done both at low heat and high heat. Most prime rib is roasted, but don't let that prevent you from smoking it.
Horseradish isn't necessary, but have some on the side. Horseradish is traditionally served with prime rib but you might find that, after the meat is cooked on the pellet grill, it just doesn't need horseradish as much.

POULTRY

Poultry is a central part of our food culture and history. From the Thanksgiving turkey to chicken noodle soup for the common cold, poultry is everywhere. Little did you know, however, that it played a large part in the spread of the pellet grill.
Think back to the first meal you had from a pellet grill. Things are changing slowly, but I would still guess 70 percent of you would say some sort of chicken. From the development of their first grills, Traeger barbecued chicken became a way to spread the pellet grill gospel from Mount Angel, Oregon to the rest of the country. Traeger chicken was served at local festivals, sporting events, and the supermarket. We had Traeger barbecue chicken before and after high school football games, while watching the Fourth of July show at Kennedy High School, and later at the Oregon Garden in Silverton. "That was all something very intentional by Randy," said Brian Traeger, former CEO of Traeger Pellet Grills, referring to his older brother. "Randy was our head of marketing at that time. He knew how well it would do."

1. Head
2. Neck
3. Back
4. Tail
5. Tenderloin
6. Wing
7. Breast
8. Drumstick
9. Thigh

WHOLE CHICKEN

At my parents' home, it was whole chicken with Traeger chicken rub or barbecue rub. Surprisingly, I still love this preparation today. Cooking chicken is actually an excellent way to learn to use a pellet grill. Whole chicken can be smoked before roasting as well, giving it extra flavor. I frequently smoke chickens and have even used them to test ideas for my Thanksgiving turkey.

Tips and techniques

Rub your chicken with oil as well as seasoning. This helps work in the rub, but also produces a more golden skin.
Injecting a whole chicken with liquid can change it from pedestrian to something that can only be described as amazing. Use a tea made from your favorite seasoning or even butter to inject your chicken with before cooking. Injecting adds flavor and keeps your chicken moist.
When you rub your chicken, get the rub between the skin and the breast meat. Just be careful not to rip the skin much when doing this. As someone who loves white meat but won't eat the skin, I can tell you this is a great way to add flavor.

CHICKEN WINGS

If you are a classic chicken wings fan like me, mark this page and get your highlighter ready. Wings are the best. I bring wings to my tailgate parties and I cook them at home when the guys come over to watch the game. I know I am getting stereotypical, but I love wings and that is typically the time I like to enjoy them.
Wings cooked on a pellet grill or smoker are perfect for one reason: smoke. Where every bar in town has Buffalo wings or sweet and spicy wings, you now have smoky Buffalo wings and smoky sweet and spicy wings—and smoky is just better.

Tips and techniques

If you don't already have some favorite sauces, learn to make some or get some. Wings are good dry, but they're better with sauce. I have a barbecue and a Buffalo-style sauce I turn to regularly.
This is another instance where cast iron is good. Use a small cast-iron pot to keep your sauce warm. This is also where you can mix things up. We all know that premade sauces aren't always the best, so make yours on the grill.
Try making sweet-and-sour wings. Use an Asian- or Thai-style rub for the wings. Once they reach an internal temperature of 165°F to 170°F, coat them in a sweet-and-sour sauce and finish for 10 minutes more at 300°F.
Experiment with dry rubs. Wings are small and cheap. If you mess up a batch, just strip off the skin and use the meat for sandwiches. There are tons of rubs out there to experiment with. I enjoy picking up rubs and shakes everywhere I travel. Wings are a perfect vehicle for testing new spices.

TURKEY

That perfect Thanksgiving turkey will make you the holiday hero of your family. The days of oven-cooked turkey or experimenting with dangerous fryers are over. The pellet grill or smoker is perfect for making that smoky yet moist golden bird.
I take any opportunity to make turkey throughout the year. I enjoy the flavor of turkey slightly more than chicken and the pellet grill does such a good job of making it an easy process.
When selecting turkey, don't get one that is already brined. You'll make it extra salty by brining it again or injecting it. Read the outside of the package; the ingredients will let you know if there is salt or any other solution already added.

Tips and techniques

Baste your turkey with butter. This is certainly not the healthiest way of cooking it, but it is the tastiest, in my opinion. Just leave the stick on your side table and rub the turkey with it as it cooks and becomes more golden.
Use your thermometer. Those built-in ones, the little red buttons, just don't work in a grill or smoker.
Don't put a stuffed turkey on the grill. Unfortunately, it's hard to make sure your turkey and stuffing are done at the same time—and I'm sorry, but moist turkey is too good to waste on even the best stuffing.

TURKEY DRUMSTICKS

There really isn't much to selecting a turkey drumstick, but if I were to make one rule, it would be to go big. Bigger is better, right?

Tips and techniques

Just like with whole chicken, rub some seasoning under the skin. Rubbing seasoning under the skin allows the meat to take on the flavor better.
For turkey legs, go a little higher on your cooking temperature (400°F+). The dark meat doesn't dry out as easily as white meat does and it helps brown the skin a little more.
All poultry can be cooked similarly. Cooking suggestions in the poultry sections apply to both chicken and turkey. The flavors and cooking styles are similar.

LAMB

Lamb is a meat I had little interest in learning to cook when I was younger. The gaminess of the meat was a challenge for me to conquer and I took suggestion after suggestion, all with little or no luck in the end. Luckily for the lamb industry, my tastes have changed as I have gotten older.
Lamb greets fresh herbs with open arms. I seriously suggest having a small herb garden at home, not just for lamb, but for all your grilling. Fresh herbs take so well to meat and it's hard to beat the price. Mint and rosemary are what I suggest with lamb, but thyme and basil are two herbs you must have in your garden as well.

1. Head
2. Tongue
3. Cheek
4. Neck
5. Shoulder
6. Rib
7. Loin
8. Sirloin
9. Leg
10. Breast
11. Flank
12. Fore Shank
13. Hind Flank

LAMB CHOPS
I suggest using rib chops, as they are the most tender, but loin or shoulder chops are great, too. (Shoulder chops are so tasty.)

Tips and techniques

Lamb chops are perfect with a reverse sear. Again, I like this best on a grill that has some kind of open flame option, but if yours doesn't, grab your cast-iron skillet instead and sear the chops at 400°F for about 2 minutes per side.
Mince your herbs for lamb chops and rub them into your meat. I like to use olive oil to help me rub the herbs all over the chops, not just in one area.
Go slightly overboard on the black pepper. The pepper gives your lamb a little kick.

LEG OF LAMB
A leg of lamb can be roasted, smoky perfection. The wood-fired flame gives it that old-world taste and packs it with moist flavor.
Cooking your leg of lamb on a pellet grill or smoker will wow your friends. Most of us are used to leg of lamb from an oven and the comparison just isn't possible. The pellet grill fills your meat with that hardwood smokiness that your oven can't touch.
When selecting your leg, try not to go too lean. The fat in the leg, like most other meats, will work to keep the meat from drying out while roasting. Bone in or out is totally a preference. Although bone-in may give slightly more flavor, it is definitely more difficult to cut.

Tips and techniques
Smoke lamb leg before roasting. Smoking the leg will allow it to absorb more smoke flavor. Give it at least 1 hour to smoke.
Cook lamb over an open flame. I like cooking lamb and other meats with a more game-like flavor over the open flame, slightly charring it, to give it an earthier flavor. On grills without an open flame, push the meat to the edges of the grill; just be careful to avoid any grease missing the drain pan.
Garlic also complements lamb well. I believe garlic complements everything well, and my breath typically tells this story, but it's especially true with lamb. Chop some and stuff or coat your leg with enough to keep vampires away for weeks.

RACK OF LAMB
If you can find it, get an already trimmed rack of lamb to save precious prep time.

Tips and techniques
I feel like a broken record, but sear the rack over an open flame, if possible. Once seared, continue smoking it. This will seal in those juices and flavor.
Smoke rack of lamb over a bed of rosemary. The lamb will take on the woodsy, aromatic rosemary flavor.
Another way of searing the rack is in individual cuts. Smoke the rack to an internal temperature of 135°F and cut each rib. Reverse-sear the ribs in a cast-iron pan with butter and fresh rosemary.

FISH

If I could, I would spend all my time cooking seafood. I love seafood. Salmon, oysters, tuna, halibut, calamari. . . The beauty of seafood is that there is a lot of it. There is a larger variety of creatures in the vast oceans than anywhere else on the planet—land or air—and the flavor varieties are just as vast. Among my favorite flavors are the Cajun flavor of Louisiana and the Baja flavor of Southern California. Being able to travel only enhances my love of seafood; I pick up a seafood rub at every coastal destination I visit.

SALMON
The wood-fired flavor is a natural pairing with salmon. Salmon was and is a central part of the diet of indigenous people in the Pacific Northwest, who set the precedent for the processes used to smoke salmon today.
When selecting salmon, always choose wild over farmed for better flavor and because it's typically fresh, not frozen.

Tips and techniques
Use a cedar plank for smoking and barbecuing salmon. Cooking with a cedar plank allows the wood's flavor and moisture to be passed directly to the salmon. Cedar planks are so common today you can find them at many local grocery stores, or even Walmart.

If you do grill salmon directly on the grate, oil the grates beforehand. Even on porcelain grates, fish skin likes to stick and it stinks the second time you cook it.

Hit the meat of the fish with an open flame after smoking. Only do this if you can and for a very short amount of time. Also, be careful that your salmon doesn't flake apart while doing this. A big spatula is key here.

Use mayonnaise or Dijon mustard to keep salmon moist. Applying a thin coat of mayonnaise or mustard to your salmon before cooking it will keep the fish from drying out, and I swear it won't taste weird at all.

TUNA

Tuna is similar to most seafood. Try for fresh, if you can. Avoid anything that looks dried out or like it may have freezer burn.

Tips and techniques

Try a reverse sear on tuna for a slight smoke flavor. I don't smoke tuna steaks as long as other fish—less than 30 minutes.

Dill is amazing on tuna, like it is on most seafood. I use dill weed a lot on seafood, but it is best on tuna steaks. Sprinkle on a generous amount for great flavor.

Be careful not to overcook the fish. Tuna can go from amazing to cat food really fast if you're not careful. They're steaks; treat them as such. Err on the side of rare, especially if using sushi-grade tuna. You can always put it back on the grill if it's not done enough for whomever is eating it.

SHRIMP

Shrimp is not only one of my favorite seafoods, but also one of my favorite foods, period. There are so many ways to prepare shrimp that I am never let down. I have spent hours cooking shrimp on and off pellet grills, and if you know how long shrimp takes (not very long), hours of experience equal tons of shrimp.

From blackened to barbecued, there are many spectacular ways of preparing shrimp and the pellet grill only adds to the variety.

Try to find fresh, never-frozen shrimp and always choose full-size shrimp, not the little salad guys.

Tips and techniques

My favorite shrimp is Cajun or Creole Louisiana-style shrimp, but there are all kinds of ways to prepare shrimp on your pellet grill. Just like any other meat we cook, never feel bound to any one style of cooking. Experimenting makes us all better pitmasters.

Lemon is a great complement to shrimp. Use it in the cooking or after for squeezing.

Grill baskets are worth their price and great for cooking shrimp. Pick one up and cook your shrimp over a direct flame or straight on the grill.

OYSTERS

In the shell is how we will usually prepare oysters on the pellet grill or smoker. I aim for medium-size, because they're easy to deal with and eat.

Tips and techniques

I have said it before, but a quality pair of gloves is a must. If you are going to prepare oysters on your grill, you will likely be handling hot shells—not a job for bare hands.

Peek at your oysters often, but quickly. Drying out the oysters is what you want to avoid, so you must keep tabs on them closely, but the lid needs to be closed to cook them.

Speaking of needing your lid to be closed to cook, this may be the job for a smoker. Vertical pellet smokers often have a window, making jobs like this much easier.

PANTRY ESSENTIALS

Barbecue is defined differently by different people. It's a verb. It's a noun. It's a sauce. It's a type of cooking. It's even considered a flavor of potato chip! When it comes to barbecue recipes, it is often the smoke, temperatures, and cook times that create the secret ingredient. There are only a few pantry must-haves; here's what you'll find in ours.

- **Allspice:** The dried black pimento berry is the key flavor behind jerk seasoning.
- **Black pepper:** For the most vibrant flavor, always grind fresh.
- **Bouillon cubes:** I use these to tuck concentrated umami flavor into tight spaces, like corned beef.
- Cajun seasoning
- Cayenne pepper
- **Celery salt and celery seed:** The distinct flavor of these spices adds a natural punch of smoke ring–enhancing nitrite. Use them as alternatives to curing salts like Morton Tender Quick. Keep both spices on hand to control the saltiness in your rubs.
- **Chili powder:** The trick to winning a chili cook-off is using the freshest—preferably homemade—chili powder.
- **Coffee:** Great in rubs. I recommend stocking microground instant coffees, such as Starbucks' Via brand.
- **Coriander (cilantro) seeds:** Coriander is the seed of the cilantro plant, but its flavor is not like the cilantro leaf; it tastes a bit like unsweetened Froot Loops cereal. Whole or crushed seeds round out the flavor of robust pork rubs.
- Cumin, ground
- Garlic, powdered
- Ginger, powdered
- Mustard, dry
- **Onions, dried:** Dried onions can easily be rehydrated and used for steaming small burgers or as a condiment. They can also add strong flavor to rubs and marinades.
- Paprika, sweet and smoked
- **Red pepper flakes:** A little bit goes a long way, but it kicks up flavor.
- **Salt, curing:** Morton Tender Quick is a venerable brand. Also known as pink salt, Prague powder, or Insta Cure, curing salt will also artificially enhance a smoke ring.
- **Salt, kosher:** Stick to your favorite name brand to control recipe consistency.
- **Sugar, turbinado:** This is also known as raw sugar.

Just a few tips about sugar:
Not all sugar is created equal (no pun intended). Most barbecue smoking rub and sauce recipes call for brown sugar because it adds a deeper flavor to the meat. While you can use regular light or dark brown sugar (which is really just white sugar with added molasses), many pit masters prefer turbinado sugar (a.k.a. raw sugar) because its larger crystals add a welcome texture to robust rubs. Bonus: It's less processed and stands up well to heat.

Sugars and sweet sauces are normally added at the very end of high-heat grilling for caramelization, but because you'll typically stick with low-and-slow temperatures when smoking, adding them earlier shouldn't be a problem. Word of caution: Sugar has a scorch point (when it burns) of just above 330°F, so you'll want to watch out for that when using your wood pellet grill's higher heat settings.

Sauce it up!
Some pit master purists don't allow sauces at their tables. I understand this, because it can sometimes seem like a crime to cover up the pure wood smoke flavors you achieve with pellet power. Still, sauces have joys of their own. Here are a few sauce ingredients staples:

Ketchup: You probably have a favorite brand—just watch out for the quality and quantity of sugar. Many cheaper ketchups contain high-fructose corn syrup (sometimes labeled as corn sugar) in their ingredients. Try to stick with a brand that doesn't contain this processed ingredient.

Mustard: In smoking prep, you can use mustard as a no-fuss adherent for rubs. Keep it simple and stick with cheap yellow table mustard, unless otherwise directed in a recipe. It's also the base for South Carolina–style sauces.

Vinegar: Apple cider vinegar provides a tart punch to a sauce recipe. It plays a starring role in North Carolina–style barbecue sauces.

Worcestershire sauce: Only use high-quality brands, because the punch behind its flavor comes from anchovies; generics often skip the fish.

COOKOUT TIPS

With proper planning and plenty of time, you can consolidate a menu and cook several recipes at once. Here are a few tips to maximize your pellet-powered cookout:

1. Orchestrate a detailed **timeline** for your smoking day. This should culminate with the reveal of your centerpiece meat as your friends and family are just getting settled in. Don't forget to account for the meat's resting time.
2. **Serve it hot.** Take care with the resting process and be sure you still serve your dish hot. Hot food pulls in more senses like smell. For example, nothing is better than hot pizza—even cheap pizza! That steaming slice on the ride home is as good as it gets. Hot food gets people's attention on a primal level.
3. Use **secondary grill shelves as a staging area for appetizers** with shorter cook times. Quick-cooking veggies can be added last and will hold until serving.
4. **Avoid peeking** and allow for extra cook time when adding cold food alongside items already cooking in the pellet grill.
5. Allow for good smoke flow across your entire grate surface. **Avoid crowding the food,** and leave 1 to 2 inches of space surrounding food pieces.
6. Rib racks are affordable and can save large amounts of cook space. They are a must if you regularly smoke ribs for a crowd.
7. Say yes when somebody asks, "Is there something I can do to help?" One of the greatest assists can be a help with cleanup. Be ready if they ask, "Is there anything we can bring?" Some ideas include chips, condiments, ice, or a cooler of beverages. Most guests enjoy contributing, so make them feel good!
8. Because wood pellet grill smokers offer high temperatures in addition to low, you can make some things quickly or in advance, such as appetizers, smoked nuts and cheeses, and desserts. Of course, when cooking for a really large crowd, it might help if you cook or finish a couple of side dishes in the oven or have a neighbor bring over an extra grill.

A FEW FINAL TIPS

Sweet finish: Hold sweet sauces until the end of your cook because sugar burns quickly. Consider cutting out the sugar or just serving sauce as an optional side. There's an old saying, "Taste the flavor in the meat when the sauce is on the side."

Back to the grind: Eliminate boring black pepper shakers. Grinding your own fresh whole black peppercorns will add next-level flavor, guaranteed.

Convection: The convection oven–like qualities of your pellet grill are unique in the barbecue world. The even heat and circulation may reduce cook times for recipes designed for other types of smokers.

Tongs, not forks: You don't want to pierce, puncture, or prick the exterior surface of your barbecue, especially sausage and poultry, because that will drain out those fabulous and flavorful juices from the meat. Use that long barbecue fork for a tent spike instead. Seriously, jam it into the ground and use it to secure your tailgating tent! Just don't use it on meat and drain those flavorful juices if you don't have to.

Fire safety: Have a dedicated fire extinguisher on hand that is rated for grease fires as well as wood, and be ready to use it. Most competitions require you to have one at your cook site, and they're not expensive.

Shut it down: Remember to shut down your pellet grill using Traeger's recommended process. This method will burn out excess pellets so your grill's fire pot is empty and safely ready for the next cook.

MEAT RECIPES

BEEF

eep in the heart of Texas, the barbecue focus is pure beef. Of course, everything's bigger in Texas, so the stars of the show are hunks of beef brisket, massive shoulder clod, and Flintstones-esque beef ribs. The beef and smoke flavors alone are so delicious, there's no real need for additional sauce or seasonings—just salt and pepper. In fact, some legendary Texas joints, like Kreuz Market in Lockhart, prohibit sauce! The same thinking applies at great steakhouses, where top-quality beef needs only salt, pepper, and smoke.

If you can't get to the Lone Star State, don't worry. Beef roams well beyond Texas. In California, the Santa Maria–style tri-tip is the defining protein on the grill.

A FEW WORDS ABOUT QUALITY

Neighborhood butcher shops are hard to come by these days. The butcher at your supermarket can help, but you may have to seek out one of today's mail-order options to find what you need. Cuts that are best to smoke low and slow include brisket, shoulder clod, prime rib, beef ribs, and tri-tip.

Even the brisket has different "cuts" to it. The point and the flat are the brisket's two distinct muscle sections. The "flat" is a grainy slab of muscle fibers that is typically served sliced pencil-thin against the grain. The "point" is an attached group of muscle fibers that has no uniform grain and is considerably fattier than the flat. Serious barbecue joints will allow you to choose point or flat, and some even dice the point to serve as "burnt ends."

These days when I buy beef, I look for attributes like organic, hormone-free, and grass-fed, and for breeds like Wagyu. The cost of quality beef for barbecue continues to rise, and compared to chicken and pork, it can be downright expensive. But nothing tastes better than beef after a low-and-slow cook on a smoker. If it's good beef, all you really need to add is salt and pepper, but experimenting with different spices is rewarding as well.

Of course, most people shop at big grocery stores where it's difficult to find high-quality beef. Fortunately, today's trend of to-your-door delivery opens up a world of options, but you still need to watch out for shady steak salesmen who have moved from selling out of the back of an unmarked truck to Internet sales. The best beef providers include Snake River Farms (my favorite for brisket), ButcherBox (grass-fed), and Allen Brothers (high-end steaks), and they change every so often.

You have likely heard the saying "fat is flavor," and that is especially true when it comes to beef for the barbecue. There's actually a grading system that will give you a quick rating of a cut's features, including juiciness, tenderness, and flavor. To be honest, it's all simply about fat content, without regard to any of the attributes (like hormone-free) I mentioned earlier. You'll probably only ever see the grades "Choice" and "Select" in supermarket chains, but here's the full list to broaden your horizons:

PRIME: This is the high-quality beef served in great steakhouses. You probably would want to avoid it if you are following a low-fat diet.

CHOICE: This is what you'll find most often in supermarkets. Because fat content is relative and you can usually see fat marbling through the packaging, Choice beef really comes off as more of a marketing term. It simply means meat that has less fat than what is labeled as Prime.

SELECT: It doesn't sound like it, but Select could be a positive if you seek a lean and low-fat source of protein.

STANDARD: You may find Standard in stores, but it will more likely just be "ungraded." Beware of misleading packaging that says Choice or Prime without USDA attribution.

OTHER: Cutter, Utility, and Canner labels denote lower quality. Stay away, because these cuts are nothing you want for barbecue.

NOTE: In some recipes I refer to the marinades, rubs, and spritzes in the next chapter. You may use those, choose another rub, or make your own versions.

TEXAS SMOKED BRISKET

The perfect brisket is the telltale sign of a great pit master. The most experienced grillers are well versed in the art of brisket and spend most of their time on the pit smoking this difficult cut. Though I would never suggest doing brisket as your first cook on a brand-new grill, there is no reason to be intimidated by it. The Traeger makes this cut all the easier to turn out perfectly.

Ingredients
1 (12-pound) full packer brisket
2 tablespoons yellow mustard
1 batch Espresso Brisket Rub
Worcestershire Mop and Spritz, for spritzing

Preparation time: 15 minutes
Smoking time: 16 to 20 hours
Temperature: 225°F
Portions: 12 to 15
Recommended pellets: Hickory, Oak, Mesquite
Recommended sides: Roasted vegetables, collard greens, garlic mashed potatoes

Instructions
1. Supply your Traeger with wood pellets and follow the start-up procedure. Preheat the grill, with the lid closed, to 225°F.
2. Using a boning knife, carefully remove all but about ½ inch of the large layer of fat covering one side of your brisket.
3. Coat the brisket all over with mustard and season it with the rub. Using your hands, work the rub into the meat. Pour the mop into a spray bottle.
4. Place the brisket directly on the grill grate and smoke until its internal temperature reaches 195°F, spritzing it every hour with the mop.
5. Pull the brisket from the grill and wrap it completely in aluminum foil or butcher paper. Place the wrapped brisket in a cooler, cover the cooler, and let it rest for 1 or 2 hours.
6. Remove the brisket from the cooler and unwrap it.
7. Separate the brisket point from the flat by cutting along the fat layer and slice the flat. The point can be saved for burnt ends (see Sweet Heat Burnt Ends), or sliced and served as well.

Secret tip: Your brisket temperature might "stall" for a few hours around 160°F. Don't worry! This is perfectly natural. Don't panic and crank up the heat or deviate from the recipe.

MESQUITE SMOKED BRISKET

To wrap or not to wrap? That is the age-old question that has plagued pitmasters for years. Wrapping, or the Texas crutch, allows your brisket to retain so much more moisture than when it is cooked unwrapped. The downside of the crutch is that it may not allow for that beautiful bark, if you wrap it too early. I tend to prefer unwrapped, so as not to miss any of that barky goodness, but I have wrapped my briskets many times to achieve that moist, bendable result. If you haven't smoked many briskets, I recommend mastering the unwrapped Texas Smoked Brisket first, to learn what the proper bark looks like, before wrapping it as we do here.

Ingredients
1 (12-pound) full packer brisket
2 tablespoons yellow mustard (you can also use soy sauce)
Salt
Freshly ground black pepper

Preparation time: 15 minutesSmoking time: 12 to 16 hours
Temperature: 225°F and 350°F
Portions: 8 to 12
Recommended pellets: Mesquite
Recommended sides: Roasted vegetables, collard greens, garlic mashed potatoes

Instructions
1. Supply your Traeger with wood pellets and follow the start-up procedure. Preheat the grill, with the lid closed, to 225°F.
2. Using a boning knife, carefully remove all but about ½ inch of the large layer of fat covering one side of your brisket.
3. Coat the brisket all over with mustard and season it with salt and pepper.
4. Place the brisket directly on the grill grate and smoke until its internal temperature reaches 160°F and the brisket has formed a dark bark.
5. Pull the brisket from the grill and wrap it completely in aluminum foil or butcher paper.
6. Increase the grill's temperature to 350°F and return the wrapped brisket to it. Continue to cook until its internal temperature reaches 190°F.
7. Transfer the wrapped brisket to a cooler, cover the cooler, and let the brisket rest for 1 or 2 hours.
8. Remove the brisket from the cooler and unwrap it.
9. Separate the brisket point from the flat by cutting along the fat layer, and slice the flat. The point can be saved for burnt ends (see Sweet Heat Burnt Ends), or sliced and served as well.

Secret tip: Wrapping your brisket too early can cause you to miss the bark that is so desired by the world's best pitmasters. Be very aware not only of how a good bark should look, but also how you like it. Always determine the best time to wrap the meat based on looks, not temperature.

SWEET HEAT BURNT ENDS

If there are two things that describe barbecue country perfectly, they are the amazing smoked meats and amazingly hot weather. You can have both smoke and heat in these burnt ends. I love spicy foods. Five Monkeys and Sweet Baby Ray's Sweet 'n Spicy sauces have the perfect amount of sweet, but punch you in the mouth with just the right amount of spicy, so as to not overpower the meat.

Ingredients

1 (6-pound) brisket point
2 tablespoons yellow mustard
1 batch Sweet Brown Sugar Rub
2 tablespoons honey
1 cup barbecue sauce
2 tablespoons light brown sugar

Preparation time: 30 minutes Smoking time: 6 hours
Temperature: 225°F and 350°F
Portions: 8 to 10
Recommended pellets: Mesquite
Recommended sides: Grilled asparagus and The Ultimate BBQ sauce

Instructions
1. Supply your Traeger with wood pellets and follow the start-up procedure. Preheat the grill, with the lid closed, to 225°F.
2 Using a boning knife, carefully remove all but about ½ inch of the large layer of fat covering one side of your brisket point.
3. Coat the point all over with mustard and season it with the rub. Using your hands, work the rub into the meat.
4. Place the point directly on the grill grate and smoke until its internal temperature reaches 165°F.
5. Pull the brisket from the grill and wrap it completely in aluminum foil or butcher paper.
6. Increase the grill's temperature to 350°F and return the wrapped brisket to it. Continue to cook until its internal temperature reaches 185°F.
7. Remove the point from the grill, unwrap it, and cut the meat into 1-inch cubes. Place the cubes in an aluminum pan and stir in the honey, barbecue sauce, and brown sugar.
8. Place the pan in the grill and smoke the beef cubes for 1 hour more, uncovered. Remove the burnt ends from the grill and serve immediately.

Secret tip: If making burnt ends from either of the previous full packer recipes, start this recipe at step 7.

REVERSE-SEARED TRI-TIP

Tri-tip is the king of beef cuts, in my opinion, mainly because of its taste. It's good in standard sandwiches, au jus sandwiches, beef stroganoff, or all by itself with a nice helping of horseradish on the side.

Ingredients
1½ pounds tri-tip roast
1 batch Espresso Brisket Rub

Preparation time: 10 minutes Smoking time: 2 to 3 hours
Temperature: 180°F and 450°F
Portions: 4
Recommended pellets: Oak
Recommended sides: Garlic mashed potatoes

Instructions
1. Supply your Traeger with wood pellets and follow the start-up procedure. Preheat the grill, with the lid closed, to 180°F.
2. Season the tri-tip roast with the rub. Using your hands, work the rub into the meat.
3. Place the roast directly on the grill grate and smoke until its internal temperature reaches 140°F.
4. Increase the grill's temperature to 450°F and continue to cook until the roast's internal temperature reaches 145°F. This same technique can be done over an open flame or in a cast-iron skillet with some butter.
5. Remove the tri-tip roast from the grill and let it rest 10 to 15 minutes, before slicing and serving.

Secret tip: Use flavored salts or smoked salts to add a different flavor to your tri-tip.

SMOKED TRI-TIP

This tri-tip is significantly different than the Reverse-Seared Tri-Tip and most other recipes in this book, in that we don't worry about temperature. Our goal with this tri-tip is to get as much smoky flavor in it as we can.

Ingredients
1½ pounds tri-tip roast
Salt
Freshly ground black pepper
2 teaspoons garlic powder
2 teaspoons lemon pepper
½ cup apple juice

Preparation time: 25 minutes Smoking time: 5 hours
Temperature: 180°F and 375°F
Portions: 4
Recommended pellets: Hickory
Recommended sides: Garlic mashed potatoes

Instructions
1. Supply your Traeger with wood pellets and follow the start-up procedure. Preheat the grill, with the lid closed, to 180°F.
2. Season the tri-tip roast with salt, pepper, garlic powder, and lemon pepper. Using your hands, work the seasoning into the meat.
3. Place the roast directly on the grill grate and smoke for 4 hours.
4. Pull the tri-tip from the grill and place it on enough aluminum foil to wrap it completely.
5. Increase the grill's temperature to 375°F.
6. Fold in three sides of the foil around the roast and add the apple juice. Fold in the last side, completely enclosing the tri-tip and liquid. Return the wrapped tri-tip to the grill and cook for 45 minutes more.
7. Remove the tri-tip roast from the grill and let it rest for 10 to 15 minutes, before unwrapping, slicing, and serving.

SANTA MARIA TRI-TIP

In California, the Santa Maria–style tri-tip is legendary. The pit masters of the Santa Maria Valley in central California focus on the triangular-shaped roast from the lower area of the sirloin. Unlike brisket, this beef is typically wood-fired over a live fire of red oak, using a unique and very cool grill grate that can be raised and lowered to adjust the heat. Also unlike brisket, this is best served medium-rare with an herb-heavy dry rub.

Ingredients
2 teaspoons sea salt
2 teaspoons freshly ground black pepper
2 teaspoons onion powder
2 teaspoons garlic powder
2 teaspoons dried oregano
1 teaspoon cayenne pepper
1 teaspoon ground sage
1 teaspoon finely chopped fresh rosemary

1 (1½ – to 2-pound) tri-tip bottom sirloin

Preparation time: 15 minutes
Smoking time: 45 minutes to 1 hour
Temperature: 425°F
Portions: 4
Recommended pellets: Oak
Recommended sides: Pinquito beans with salsa

Instructions
1. Supply your Traeger with wood pellets and follow the start-up procedure. Preheat the grill, with the lid closed, to 425°F.
2. In a small bowl, combine the salt, pepper, onion powder, garlic powder, oregano, cayenne pepper, sage, and rosemary to create a rub.
3. Season the meat all over with the rub and lay it directly on the grill.
4. Close the lid and smoke for 45 minutes to 1 hour, or until a meat thermometer inserted in the thickest part of the meat reads 120°F for rare, 130°F for medium-rare, or 140°F for medium, keeping in mind that the meat will come up in temperature by about another 5°F during the rest period.
5. Remove the tri-tip from the heat, tent with aluminum foil, and let rest for 15 minutes before slicing against the grain.

Secret tip: In California, the traditional side dish for tri-tip is savory pinquito beans, along with salsa. The pinquito is in the same family as the pinto bean but is harder to find. Search online for specialty food shops that offer a variety of heirloom beans

PULLED BEEF

Oregon has its fair share of food trucks and among my favorite things to get from them are shredded beef burritos. Shredded beef is a solid step above steak, in my opinion, and makes the perfect burrito.

Ingredients
1 (4-pound) top round roast
2 tablespoons yellow mustard
1 batch Espresso Brisket Rub
½ cup beef broth

Preparation time: 25 minutes
Smoking time: 12 to 14 hours
Temperature: 225°F and 350°F
Portions: 5 to 8
Recommended pellets: Competition Blend
Recommended sides: Black beans, corn tortillas, avocado slices, or guacamole

Instructions
1. Supply your Traeger with wood pellets and follow the start-up procedure. Preheat the grill, with the lid closed, to 225°F.
2. Coat the top round roast all over with mustard and season it with the rub. Using your hands, work the rub into the meat.
3. Place the roast directly on the grill grate and smoke until its internal temperature reaches 160°F and a dark bark has formed.
4. Pull the roast from the grill and place it on enough aluminum foil to wrap it completely.
5. Increase the grill's temperature to 350°F.

6. Fold in three sides of the foil around the roast and add the beef broth. Fold in the last side, completely enclosing the roast and liquid. Return the wrapped roast to the grill and cook until its internal temperature reaches 195°F.
7. Pull the roast from the grill and place it in a cooler. Cover the cooler and let the roast rest for 1 or 2 hours.
8. Remove the roast from the cooler and unwrap it. Pull apart the beef using just your fingers. Serve immediately.

Secret tip: It's not done until it's done. Let the meat rest, 2 to 3 hours on a big cut of meat. If it burns your hands, you haven't let it rest long enough.

SMOKED ROAST BEEF

A classic roast beef tastes amazing. Something about the roast makes it the perfect comfort food. Pair this roast beef with your favorite roasted vegetables. All the veggies can be cooked on a pellet grill and always taste better wood-fired.

Ingredients
1 (4-pound) top round roast
1 batch Espresso Brisket Rub
1 tablespoon butter

Preparation time: 10 minutes
Smoking time: 12 to 14 hours
Temperature: 180°F and 450°F
Portions: 5 to 8
Recommended pellets: Mesquite
Recommended sides: Roasted vegetables, collard greens, garlic mashed potatoes

Instructions
1. Supply your Traeger with wood pellets and follow the start-up procedure. Preheat the grill, with the lid closed, to 180°F.
2. Season the top round roast with the rub. Using your hands, work the rub into the meat.
3. Place the roast directly on the grill grate and smoke until its internal temperature reaches 140°F. Remove the roast from the grill.
4. Place a cast-iron skillet on the grill grate and increase the grill's temperature to 450°F. Place the roast in the skillet, add the butter, and cook until its internal temperature reaches 145°F, flipping once after about 3 minutes.
5. Remove the roast from the grill and let it rest for 10 to 15 minutes, before slicing and serving.

Secret tip: Substitute any beef roast you like for this recipe. As with just about every other recipe here, it is all about cooking to temperature, not time, so adjust as needed.

SMOKED BEEF RIBS

Beef ribs are huge and flavorful, and your pellet grill keeps them from drying out.

Ingredients
2 (2- or 3-pound) racks beef ribs
2 tablespoons yellow mustard
1 batch Sweet and Spicy Cinnamon Rub

Preparation time: 25 minutes
Smoking time: 4 to 6 hours

Temperature: 225°F

Portions: 4 to 8
Recommended pellets: Mesquite
Recommended sides: Corn fritters, collard greens

Instructions
1. Supply your Traeger with wood pellets and follow the start-up procedure. Preheat the grill, with the lid closed, to 225°F.
2. Remove the membrane from the backside of the ribs. This can be done by cutting just through the membrane in an X pattern and working a paper towel between the membrane and the ribs to pull it off.
3. Coat the ribs all over with mustard and season them with the rub. Using your hands, work the rub into the meat.
4. Place the ribs directly on the grill grate and smoke until their internal temperature reaches between 190°F and 200°F.
5. Remove the racks from the grill and cut them into individual ribs. Serve immediately.

Secret tip: Coat your ribs with a thin layer of your favorite barbecue sauce and finish for 10 minutes more at 300°F.

BRAISED SHORT RIBS

There is nothing short about short ribs. Anyone who has had short ribs knows they are huge and packed with huge flavor. You'll notice we're cooking to time here rather than temperature; pitmasters tend to do this more when braising meats.

Ingredients
4 beef short ribs
Salt
Freshly ground black pepper
½ cup beef broth

Preparation time: 25 minutes
Smoking time: 4 hours
Temperature: 180°F and 375°F
Portions: 2 to 4
Recommended pellets: Hickory
Recommended sides: Mashed potatoes, glazed carrots

Instructions
1. Supply your Traeger with wood pellets and follow the start-up procedure. Preheat the grill, with the lid closed, to 180°F.
2. Season the ribs on both sides with salt and pepper.
3. Place the ribs directly on the grill grate and smoke for 3 hours.
4. Pull the ribs from the grill and place them on enough aluminum foil to wrap them completely.
5. Increase the grill's temperature to 375°F.
6. Fold in three sides of the foil around the ribs and add the beef broth. Fold in the last side, completely enclosing the ribs and liquid. Return the wrapped ribs to the grill and cook for 45 minutes more. Remove the short ribs from the grill, unwrap them, and serve immediately.

Secret tip: Adding herbs to your wrap, such as rosemary or thyme, can contribute some fresh, delicious flavor to the short ribs.

PERFECT ROAST PRIME RIB

Whether it's for your holiday party or just because Sundays are for smoking, prime rib is one of the best cuts out there. Because prime rib is typically very high-quality meat, it will cost you a little extra, but it will be worth it.

Ingredients
1 (3-bone) rib roast
Salt
Freshly ground black pepper
1 garlic clove, minced

Preparation time: 15 minutes
Smoking time: 4 or 5 hours
Temperature: 360°F
Portions: 8 to 12
Recommended pellets: Apple
Recommended sides: Herbed potatoes

Instructions
1. Supply your Traeger with wood pellets and follow the start-up procedure. Preheat the grill, with the lid closed, to 360°F.
2. Season the roast all over with salt and pepper and, using your hands, rub it all over with the minced garlic.
3. Place the roast directly on the grill grate and smoke for 4 or 5 hours, until its internal temperature reaches 145°F for medium-rare.
4. Remove the roast from the grill and let it rest for 15 minutes, before slicing and serving.

Secret tip: This same recipe can be used for a 5- or 7-bone rib roast. Just increase the smoking time and the garlic, as desired.

PASTRAMI

As a Traeger owner and someone who smokes all their meats, corned beef isn't actually on the menu, as corned beef is boiled, not smoked. Even though smoking corned beef is technically making pastrami, that doesn't stop me from parading some awesome pastrami as corned beef each St. Patrick's Day.

Ingredients
1 (8-pound) corned beef brisket
2 tablespoons yellow mustard
1 batch Espresso Brisket Rub
Worcestershire Mop and Spritz, for spritzing

Preparation time: 15 minutes
Smoking time: 12 to 16 hours
Temperature: 225°F

Portions: 6 to 8
Recommended pellets: Oak
Recommended sides: Whole-wheat sandwich, coleslaw, pickles, and potato chips

Instructions
1. Supply your Traeger with wood pellets and follow the start-up procedure. Preheat the grill, with the lid closed, to 225°F.

2. Coat the brisket all over with mustard and season it with the rub. Using your hands, work the rub into the meat. Pour the mop into a spray bottle.
3. Place the brisket directly on the grill grate and smoke until its internal temperature reaches 195°F, spritzing it every hour with the mop.
4. Pull the corned beef brisket from the grill and wrap it completely in aluminum foil or butcher paper. Place the wrapped brisket in a cooler, cover the cooler, and let it rest for 1 or 2 hours.
5. Remove the corned beef from the cooler and unwrap it. Slice the corned beef and serve.

Secret tip: If you have trouble with dry corned beef, try wrapping it. When the corned beef reaches an internal temperature between 160°F and 165°F, wrap it. Increase the cooking temperature to 350°F and return the wrapped brisket to the grill until its internal temperature reaches 195°F.

SMOKED NEW YORK STEAKS

A nice seared steak is hard to beat. Adding smoke to your steak makes it even better. If you can use an open flame to reverse-sear your steaks, you'll have all the more wood-fired flavor, but a cast-iron skillet also works perfectly to lock in juices and flavor.

Ingredients
4 (1-inch-thick) New York steaks
2 tablespoons olive oil
Salt
Freshly ground black pepper

Preparation time: 15 minutes
Smoking time: 1 to 2 hours
Temperature: 180°F and 375°F
Portions: 4
Recommended pellets: Oak
Recommended sides: Garlic mashed potatoes

Instructions
1. Supply your Traeger with wood pellets and follow the start-up procedure. Preheat the grill, with the lid closed, to 180°F.
2. Rub the steaks all over with olive oil and season both sides with salt and pepper.
3. Place the steaks directly on the grill grate and smoke for 1 hour.
4. Increase the grill's temperature to 375°F and continue to cook until the steaks' internal temperature reaches 145°F for medium-rare.
5. Remove the steaks and let them rest 5 minutes, before slicing and serving.

Secret tip: When cooking steaks, be aware of hot spots on your grill, and use them to your advantage. Even though the hot spots on a pellet grill are minimal, they exist. I place those steaks that I want more done in the hottest areas of the grill. Using the hot spots allows me to have all my meat done at the same time, but cooked to everyone's liking.

THE PERFECT T-BONES

T-bone is the quintessential steak. Take a look at your phone's set of emojis—there's a T-bone there. We relate T-bones with barbecue for good reason: They're great. T-bones pack amazing flavor and have a generous amount of marble. So, if you are going to be a barbecue pitmaster, you'd better learn how to cook the best steaks on the best grill.

Ingredients
4 (1½- to 2-inch-thick) T-bone steaks
2 tablespoons olive oil
1 batch Espresso Brisket Rub or Chili-Coffee Rub

Preparation time: 10 minutes
Smoking time: 30 minutes
Temperature: 500°F
Portions: 4
Recommended pellets: Competition Blend
Recommended sides: Garlic mashed potatoes

Instructions
1. Supply your Traeger with wood pellets and follow the start-up procedure. Preheat the grill, with the lid closed, to 500°F.
2. Coat the steaks all over with olive oil and season both sides with the rub. Using your hands, work the rub into the meat.
3. Place the steaks directly on a grill grate and smoke until their internal temperature reaches 135°F for rare, 145°F for medium-rare, and 155°F for well-done. Remove the steaks from the grill and serve hot.

Secret tip: Any of these steak recipes are essentially interchangeable and can be used for just about any cut. If you ever find yourself in a bind, pick up your favorite steaks and use this recipe—you can't go wrong.

REVERSE-SEARED STEAKS

Of all the foods that the pellet grill has ruined for me (meaning I don't like them cooked any other way!), steaks are at the top of the list. The wood-fired flavor is just something you won't find in even the best restaurants. The great thing about these amazing wood-fired steaks is that the grill does all the work. By allowing the smoke to fully absorb into the beef, you'll give yourself a special treat that can't be beat.

Ingredients
4 (4-ounce) sirloin steaks
2 tablespoons olive oil
Salt
Freshly ground black pepper
4 tablespoons butter

Preparation time: 15 minutes
Smoking time: 1 or 2 hours
Temperature: 180°F and 450°F
Portions: 4
Recommended pellets: Oak
Recommended sides: Garlic mashed potatoes

Instructions

1. Supply your Traeger with wood pellets and follow the start-up procedure. Preheat the grill, with the lid closed, to 180°F.
2. Rub the steaks all over with olive oil and season both sides with salt and pepper.
3. Place the steaks directly on the grill grate and smoke until their internal temperature reaches 135°F. Remove the steaks from the grill.
4. Place a cast-iron skillet on the grill grate and increase the grill's temperature to 450°F.
5. Place the steaks in the skillet and top each with 1 tablespoon of butter. Cook the steaks until their internal temperature reaches 145°F, flipping once after 2 or 3 minutes. (I recommend reverse-searing over an open flame rather than in the cast-iron skillet, if your grill has that option.) Remove the steaks and serve immediately.

Secret tip: If cooking with cast iron, add some fresh rosemary leaves to the butter for that extra herby flavor.

ASIAN STEAK SKEWERS

You can organize skewers to your preference but we recommend a ratio of 1 beef piece per 1 red onion piece.

Ingredients
1 1/2 lbs top sirloin steak
6 garlic cloves, minced
1 red onion
1/3 cup sugar
3/4 cup soy sauce
1 tbsp ground ginger
1/4 cup sesame oil
3 tbsp sesame seeds
1/4 cup vegetable oil
Bamboo skewers

Preparation time: 10 minutes
Smoking time: 1 hour and 20 minutes
Temperature: 180°F and 450°F
Portions: 6
Recommended pellets: Hickory
Recommended sides: Steamed or fried rice

Instructions
1. Cut sirloin steak into cubes, about 1 inch.
2. Cut red onion into chunks similar in size to the sirloin steak cubes.
3. In a bowl, combine and whisk soy sauce, sesame oil, vegetable oil, minced garlic, sugar, ginger, and sesame seeds.
4. Add steak to sauce bowl and toss to coat until steak is covered in the sauce.
5. Marinate for at least 1 hour in a refrigerator (if you are in a rush it's ok to skip this part, but you'll sacrifice a little bit of flavor).
6. Preheat pellet grill to 350°F.
7. Thread marinated beef and red onion pieces onto bamboo skewers.
8. Grill the skewers, turning after about 4 minutes. Cook for 8 minutes total or until meat reaches your desired doneness.

Secret tip: Garnish your skewers with lime or green onion.

TRADITIONAL TOMAHAWK STEAK

The giant Tomahawk is one of the most visually impressive steaks money can buy. Featuring a thick chunk of ribeye at one end, they usually have at least 6-8 inches of bone handle – perhaps the ultimate meat lollipop.

Ingredients
1 tomahawk ribeye steak (2 1/2 to 3 1/2 lbs)
5 garlic cloves, minced
2 tbsp kosher salt
1 bundle fresh thyme
2 tbsp ground black pepper
8 oz butter stick
1 tbsp garlic powder
1/8 cup olive oil

Preparation time: 45 minutes
Smoking time: 1 or 2 hours
Temperature: 180°F and 450°F
Portions: 4 to 6
Recommended pellets: Hickory, Oak
Recommended sides: Garlic mashed potatoes

Instructions
1. Mix rub ingredients (salt, black pepper, and garlic powder) in a small bowl. Use this mixture to season all sides of the ribeye steak generously. You can also substitute your favorite steak seasoning. After applying seasoning, let the steak rest at room temperature for at least 30 minutes.
2. While the steak rests, preheat your pellet grill to 450°F - 550°F for searing
3. Sear the steak for 5 minutes on each side. Halfway through each side (so after 2 1/2 minutes), rotate the steak 90° to form grill marks on the tomahawk
4. After the tomahawk steak has seared for 5 minutes on each side (10 minutes total), move the steak to a raised rack
5. Adjust your pellet grill's temperature to 250°F and turn up smoke setting if applicable. Leave the lid open for a moment to help allow some heat to escape
6. Stick your probe meat thermometer into the very center of the cut to measure internal temperature.
7. Place butter stick, garlic cloves, olive oil, and thyme in the aluminum pan. Then place the aluminum pan under the steak to catch drippings. After a few minutes, the steak drippings and ingredients will mix together
8. Baste the steak with the aluminum pan mixture every 10 minutes until the tomahawk steak reaches your desired doneness
9. Once the steak reaches its desired doneness, remove from the grill and place on a cutting board or serving dish. The steak should rest for 10-15 minutes before cutting/serving.

Secret tip: Measure internal temperature at the center most point of the loin (i.e. the furthest point away from the outside of your steak. Your steak will spend roughly 45 minutes total on the grill. It might be more or might be less depending on your doneness preferences and how large your tomahawk cut is. Your steak is ready to come off the grill when it reaches the target internal temperature, regardless of how long it's been on there.

PEPPERED BEEF TENDERLOIN

Classy and delicious.

Ingredients
2 1/2 lb center cut beef tenderloin, trimmed and tied if uneven
2 tbsp unsalted butter, room temperature

6 tbsp peppercorns, mixed colors
1 tbsp kosher salt
1 cup parsley, chopped
Horseradish sauce, on the side
4 tbsp Dijon mustard

Preparation time: 25 minutes
Smoking time: 1 hour and 15 minutes
Temperature: 450°F
Portions: 6
Recommended pellets: Hickory, Maple, Cherry
Recommended sides: Garlic mashed potatoes and collard greens

Instructions
1. Coarsely grind peppercorn mixture into a bowl. Add parsley, mustard, butter, and salt. Mix until thoroughly combined
2. Rub spiced butter mixture generously and thoroughly on all sides of the tenderloin. Coat completely and roll tenderloin in bowl if necessary to soak up as much seasoning as possible.
3. Preheat pellet grill to 450°F4. Place tenderloin on an elevated rack (important) and roast. Use a probe meat thermometer to measure internal temperature. Cook until the center of the tenderloin reaches a temperature of 130°F. This typically takes 30-45 minutes but could be more or less depending on the size of your tenderloin
5. Once tenderloin reaches desired doneness, remove from grill and allow to rest for at least 15 minutes6. Move tenderloin to a cutting board and slice. Try to catch as many juices as possible. Garnish with additional parsley

Secret tip: If preparing tenderloin in advance, wrap in plastic wrap and refrigerate for 4- 24 hours after step 2.

KOREAN STYLE BBQ PRIME RIBS

Ingredients
3 lbs beef short ribs
2 tbsp sugar
3/4 cup water
1 tbsp ground black pepper
3 tbsp white vinegar
2 tbsp sesame oil
3 tbsp soy sauce
6 cloves garlic, minced
1/3 cup light brown sugar
1/2 yellow onion, finely chopped

Preparation time: 15 minutes
Smoking time: 8 hours
Temperature: 225°F
Portions: 5
Recommended pellets: Apple, Pecan, Maple, Cherry, Hickory
Recommended sides: Green salad and Kimchi

Instructions
1. Combine soy sauce, water, and vinegar in a bowl. Mix and whisk in brown sugar, white sugar, pepper, sesame oil, garlic, and onion. Whisk until the sugars have completely dissolved

2. Pour marinade into large bowl or baking pan with high sides. Dunk the short ribs in the marinade, coating completely. Cover marinaded short ribs with plastic wrap and refrigerate for 6 to 12 hours3. Preheat pellet grill to 225°F.
4. Remove plastic wrap from ribs and pull ribs out of marinade. Shake off any excess marinade and dispose of the contents left in the bowl.
5. Place ribs on grill and cook for about 6-8 hours, until ribs reach an internal temperature of 203°F. Measure using a probe meat thermometer
6. Once ribs reach temperature, remove from grill and allow to rest for about 20 minutes. Slice, serve, and enjoy!

BACON-SWISS CHEESESTEAK MEATLOAF

Meatloaf is a favorite comfort food for the baby boomer generation. It gained popularity during the Great Depression as a way to stretch dinner budgets by utilizing leftovers and affordable ground beef. Meatloaf made on a smoker becomes even more comforting when it takes on the flavor of your favorite wood smoke.

Ingredients
1 tablespoon canola oil
2 garlic cloves, finely chopped
1 medium onion, finely chopped
1 poblano chile, stemmed, seeded, and finely chopped
2 pounds extra-lean ground beef
2 tablespoons Montreal steak seasoning
1 tablespoon A.1. Steak Sauce
½ pound bacon, cooked and crumbled
2 cups shredded Swiss cheese
1 egg, beaten
2 cups breadcrumbs
½ cup Tiger Sauce

Preparation time: 15 minutes
Smoking time: 2 hours
Temperature: 225°F
Portions: 4
Recommended pellets: Hickory and mesquite
Recommended sides: Roasted Brussel sprouts and bacon

Instructions
1. On your stove top, heat the canola oil in a medium sauté pan over medium-high heat. Add the garlic, onion, and poblano, and sauté for 3 to 5 minutes, or until the onion is just barely translucent
2. Supply your smoker with wood pellets and follow the manufacturer's specific start-up procedure. Preheat, with the lid closed, to 225°F.
3. In a large bowl, combine the sautéed vegetables, ground beef, steak seasoning, steak sauce, bacon, Swiss cheese, egg, and breadcrumbs. Mix with your hands until well incorporated, then shape into a loaf.
4. Put the meatloaf in a cast iron skillet and place it on the grill. Close the lid and smoke for 2 hours, or until a meat thermometer inserted in the loaf reads 165°F.
5. Top with the meatloaf with the Tiger Sauce, remove from the grill, and let rest for about 10 minutes before serving.

Secret tip: Montreal steak seasoning is a coarse and distinct seasoning made of dehydrated garlic, paprika, granulated onion, coriander, and plenty of chunky sea salt and pepper. It is considered the perfect complement to steak. The varieties in the supermarket spice section are all good, but you can easily grind your own blend. Be sure to use whole peppercorns and sea salt to control your desired coarseness.

LONDON BROIL

You'll often see meats labeled "London broil" at the market, but it's actually more of a style of steak than a type, marinated and grilled rare in the center, and sliced into strips against the grain. The actual cut is typically top round steak or flank steak. Tenderizing it with a meat mallet and marinating it for several hours helps the cheap cut of meat achieve higher status among steaks.

Ingredients
1 (1½- to 2-pound) London broil or top round steak
¼ cup soy sauce
2 tablespoons white wine
2 tablespoons extra-virgin olive oil
¼ cup chopped scallions
2 tablespoons packed brown sugar
2 garlic cloves, minced
2 teaspoons red pepper flakes
1 teaspoon freshly ground black pepper

Preparation time: 15 minutes + 4 hours marinating

Smoking time: 12 to 16 minutes
Temperature: 350°F
Portions: 4
Recommended pellets: Apple mash blend
Recommended sides: Garlic mashed potatoes

Instructions
1. Using a meat mallet, pound the steak lightly all over on both sides to break down its fibers and tenderize. You are not trying to pound down the thickness
2. In a medium bowl, make the marinade by combining the soy sauce, white wine, olive oil, scallions, brown sugar, garlic, red pepper flakes, and black pepper
3. Put the steak in a shallow plastic container with a lid and pour the marinade over the meat. Cover and refrigerate for at least 4 hours.
4. Remove the steak from the marinade, shaking off any excess, and discard the marinade
5. Supply your smoker with wood pellets and follow the manufacturer's specific start-up procedure. Preheat, with the lid closed, to 350°F6. Place the steak directly on the grill, close the lid, and smoke for 6 minutes. Flip, then smoke with the lid closed for 6 to 10 minutes more, or until a meat thermometer inserted in the meat reads 130°F for medium-rare
7. Let the steak rest for about 10 minutes before slicing and serving. The meat's temperature will rise by about 5 degrees while it rests
Secret tip: To attain a hearty char, make "reverse sear." Cook as directed in step 6 until you are 5°F under the desired final internal target temperature. Then boost the grill to a high setting—such as 400°F to 450°F—to finish with a quick sear on both sides (about 1 minute per side).

TEXAS SHOULDER CLOD

Beef shoulder clod is an affordable cut of beef made famous in select Texas smokehouses. The connective tissue requires a long, slow cook in order to break down to succulence. This massive hunk of beef feeds a crowd, but you can size down as needed. If you're cooking for 16 hours with a set-it-and-forget-it wood pellet grill smoker, you'll want to plan ahead. Have a beer and prepare a side dish. That should occupy half of your time, but you'll still have a few hours for a good book, gaming, or (if you're not careful) household chores.

Ingredients
½ cup sea salt
½ cup freshly ground black pepper
1 tablespoon red pepper flakes
1 tablespoon minced garlic
1 tablespoon cayenne pepper
1 tablespoon smoked paprika
1 (13- to 15-pound) beef shoulder clod

Preparation time: 15 minutes
Smoking time: 12 to 16 hours
Temperature: 250°F
Portions: 16 to 20
Recommended pellets: Oak
Recommended sides: Twice-Smoked Potatoes

Instructions
1. In a small bowl, combine the salt, pepper, red pepper flakes, minced garlic, cayenne pepper, and smoked paprika to create a rub. Generously apply it to the beef shoulder.
2. Supply your smoker with wood pellets and follow the manufacturer's specific start-up procedure. Preheat, with the lid closed, to 250°F.
3. Put the meat on the grill grate, close the lid, and smoke for 12 to 16 hours, or until a meat thermometer inserted deeply into the beef reads 195°F. You may need to cover the clod with aluminum foil toward the end of smoking to prevent overbrowning.
4. Let the meat rest for about 15 minutes before slicing against the grain and serving.

Secret tip: Whole clod is hard to find. With more than five muscle groups coming together, at 15 pounds, it is often sold in smaller parts. It is also known as chuck arm pot roast, boneless shoulder cutlet, or arm chuck.

CHEESEBURGER HAND PIES

Sometimes an idea sounds too good not to try. Consider this a poor man's beef Wellington . . . or maybe more of an upscale Hot Pocket. I tried using filo dough and piecrust dough before settling on rectangular sheets of pizza dough as the way to go. I got the best results using Pillsbury refrigerated pizza dough. Be sure to start with chilled dough, as it will make for much easier handling.

Ingredients
½ pound lean ground beef
1 tablespoon minced onion
1 tablespoon steak seasoning
1 cup shredded Monterey Jack and Colby cheese blend
8 slices white American cheese, divided
2 (14-ounce) refrigerated prepared pizza dough sheets, divided
2 eggs, beaten with 2 tablespoons water (egg wash), divided

24 hamburger dill pickle chips
2 tablespoons sesame seeds
6 slices tomato, for garnish
Ketchup and mustard, for serving

Preparation time: 35 minutes
Smoking time: 10 minutes
Temperature: 325°F
Portions: 4
Recommended pellets: Hickory
Recommended sides: Sweet potato chips

Instructions
1. Supply your smoker with wood pellets and follow the manufacturer's specific start-up procedure. Preheat, with the lid closed, to 325°F.
2. On your stove top, in a medium sauté pan over medium-high heat, brown the ground beef for 4 to 5 minutes, or until cooked through. Add the minced onion and steak seasoning.
3. Toss in the shredded cheese blend and 2 slices of American cheese, and stir until melted and fully incorporated.
4. Remove the cheeseburger mixture from the heat and set aside.
5. Make sure the dough is well chilled for easier handling. Working quickly, roll out one prepared pizza crust on parchment paper and brush with half of the egg wash.
6. Arrange the remaining 6 slices of American cheese on the dough to outline 6 hand pies.
7. Top each cheese slice with ¼ cup of the cheeseburger mixture, spreading slightly inside the imaginary lines of the hand pies.
8. Place 4 pickle slices on top of the filling for each pie.
9. Top the whole thing with the other prepared pizza crust and cut between the cheese slices to create 6 hand pies.
10. Using kitchen scissors, cut the parchment to further separate the pies, but leave them on the paper.
11. Using a fork dipped in egg wash, seal the edges of the pies on all sides. Baste the tops of the pies with the remaining egg wash and sprinkle with the sesame seeds.
12. Remove the pies from the parchment paper and gently place on the grill grate. Close the lid and smoke for 5 minutes, then carefully flip and smoke with the lid closed for 5 more minutes, or until browned.
13. Top with the sliced tomato and serve with ketchup and mustard.

PORK

Unless you're in Texas, most people think of pork when they think of barbecue. The "other white meat" is chock-full of marbled fat and succulence, and the sweet meat (still technically considered red meat) absorbs smoke wonderfully. Pork barbecue has a long and storied history. Christopher Columbus noted in his writings that the Taíno people of the Caribbean cooked in a style featuring a grid of green sticks over indirect campfire heat that they deemed "barbacoa."

HOW TO GET A SMOKIN' PORK

There's no barbecue feast quite as fine as one that includes a whole hog. Although there are competition-size trailer-bound wood pellet smokers, most of the ones sold these days can only handle smaller cuts. Pork shoulder remains the slow-smoking leader in the South. In fact, to many Southerners, barbecue is synonymous with pulled or chopped smoked pork butt. You should also know that the butt is really the shoulder of the pig, and the rear or hindquarter is the ham. Wood pellet grills are often built to resemble large offset smokers and can usually accommodate any individual cut from the massive whole shoulder to the pork belly, hams, and ribs. After you run through all of those big cuts, there's still plenty of pork to work with, from sausage to tenderloin. Some of my favorite selections, like rib tips and cracklings, are sometimes considered scraps!

There are dozens of ways to prepare pork. From going big with a whole hog to curing bacon, the task can be as big or as small as your imagination desires. I love the way a spicy brine saturates a good pork chop. If you have a large roast, you can rub it, inject it, and later wrap it in aluminum foil. One ultimate goal for roasts and ribs is to build a beautiful bark. The dark-brown crust can be enhanced by steady smoke, the right rub, intermittent basting, and layering sauce over the course of the cook.

When it comes to a Boston butt, the technique of pulling apart the softened meat fibers into long strands is known as "pulled pork." Pulled pork is usually comprised of a small pork shoulder, but if you are serving a group, one technique for increasing the amount of lean white meat is to mix in the meat of an uncured whole ham or pork loin.

The big trick to pulled pork is that you'll need to achieve higher internal temperatures to achieve that pull-apart texture. Sure, the USDA says it's "done" when you hit 160°F, but in order to break down the collagen and intramuscular fat in a big pork roast, you need to top 200°F. It is only then that your temperature probe will slide into the meat with little to no resistance. Serving on a bun or white bread is optional.

If you're looking for a technique to produce fall-off-the-bone ribs, simply remember the 3-2-1 method: Smoke your ribs for 3 hours, wrap them in foil and cook for 2 more hours, and then smoke them unwrapped for 1 hour to firm up the bark. It's a long process, but good things come to those who wait.

Finally, one of the most popular techniques for making spare ribs is to neatly trim them "St. Louis–style," a term for a full rack of spare ribs that is shaped into a tidy elongated rectangle. This makes for a nice presentation, but there's nothing wrong with that meat you may have trimmed off in the process. It has a name, too: rib tips. You can cook the rib tips along with the full slabs to help track cooking.

Pork barbecue is one of the most popular meats for low-and-slow smoking on a pellet smoker. Here are a few more tips to up your pork barbecue game:

- The convection-like heating of Traeger can benefit from a water pan. Nestle a pan filled with water or juice in a corner of your grill to add a bit of moisture to long cooks (as with ribs).
- Pork chops edged with a succulent layer of fat tend to curl up during grilling. Avoid the curl by scoring the fatty rim with a few cuts.
- Great flavor starts with high-quality meat. Consider antibiotic-free, heritage, and premium breeds, such as Kurobuta.
- Better ribs start at the market. Look for meaty slabs, and avoid racks with spots of exposed bones, also known as "shiners."
- Pulled pork and ribs need to hit internal temperatures that are much higher than USDA recommendations. Target 205°F for butts to achieve pull-apart tenderness. Invest in a quality instant-read electric meat thermometer, if you don't already have one on your Traeger.
- You'll want to remove the tough membrane on the back side of pork ribs **before** cooking to allow for better smoke and spice penetration. Enlist the help of a sheet of paper towel to grip the membrane and give it a good hard tug to peel it off those ribs.
- Pork ribs come with their own natural "pop-up" thermometer. Look for the ends of the bones to extrude from the meat as a telltale sign of doneness.

BABY BACK RIBS

Ingredients
2 full slabs baby back ribs, back membranes removed
1 cup prepared table mustard
1 cup Pork Rub
1 cup apple juice, divided
1 cup packed light brown sugar, divided
1 cup of The Ultimate BBQ Sauce, divided

Preparation time: 15 minutes
Smoking time: 5 to 6 hours
Temperature: 150°F and 225°F
Portions: 12 to 15
Recommended pellets: Hickory, Competition blend
Recommended sides: Herb potato salad, corn on a cob

Instructions
1. Supply your Traeger with wood pellets and follow the manufacturer's specific start-up procedure. Preheat, with the lid closed, to 150° to 180°F, or to the "Smoke" setting.
2. Coat the ribs with the mustard to help the rub stick and lock in moisture.
3. Generously apply the rub
4. Place the ribs directly on the grill, close the lid, and smoke for 3 hours5. Increase the temperature to 225°F.
6. Remove the ribs from the grill and wrap each rack individually with aluminum foil, but before sealing tightly, add ½ cup apple juice and ½ cup brown sugar to each package
7. Return the foil-wrapped ribs to the grill, close the lid, and smoke for 2 more hours.
8. Carefully unwrap the ribs and remove the foil completely. Coat each slab with ½ cup of barbecue sauce and continue smoking with the lid closed for 30 minutes to 1 hour, or until the meat tightens and has a reddish bark. For the perfect rack, the internal temperature should be 190°F.

Secret tip: Instant-read digital thermometers are a must for outdoor cooking, but using the thermometer on ribs can be tricky. To get an accurate reading, avoid probing too close to the bones. An easy trick is to use a toothpick to probe ½ inch into the meat between the ends of two bones. If the toothpick slides in with very little resistance, the ribs are ready to serve.

MAPLE BABY BACKS

Ingredients
2 (2- or 3-pound) racks baby back ribs
2 tablespoons yellow mustard
1 batch Sweet Brown Sugar Rub
½ cup plus 2 tablespoons maple syrup, divided
2 tablespoons light brown sugar
1 cup Pepsi or other non-diet cola
¼ cup The Ultimate BBQ Sauce

Preparation time: 25 minutes
Smoking time: 4 hours
Temperature: 180°F and 300°F
Portions: 4 to 6
Recommended pellets: Maple
Recommended sides: Collard greens, herbed potato salad, corn with basil butter and flaky salt

Instructions
1. Supply your smoker with wood pellets and follow the manufacturer's specific start-up procedure. Preheat the grill, with the lid closed, to 180°F.
2. Remove the membrane from the backside of the ribs. This can be done by cutting just through the membrane in an X pattern and working a paper towel between the membrane and the ribs to pull it off.
3. Coat the ribs on both sides with mustard and season them with the rub. Using your hands, work the rub into the meat.
4. Place the ribs directly on the grill grate and smoke for 3 hours.
5. Remove the ribs from the grill and place them, bone-side up, on enough aluminum foil to wrap the ribs completely. Drizzle 2 tablespoons of maple syrup over the ribs and sprinkle them with 1 tablespoon of brown sugar. Flip the ribs and repeat the maple syrup and brown sugar application on the meat side.
6. Increase the grill's temperature to 300°F.
7. Fold in three sides of the foil around the ribs and add the cola. Fold in the last side, completely enclosing the ribs and liquid. Return the ribs to the grill and cook for 30 to 45 minutes.
8. Remove the ribs from the grill and unwrap them from the foil.
9. In a small bowl, stir together the barbecue sauce and remaining 6 tablespoons of maple syrup. Use this to baste the ribs. Return the ribs to the grill, without the foil, and cook for 15 minutes to caramelize the sauce.
10. Cut into individual ribs and serve immediately.

Secret tip: For ribs that fall off the bone, increase the temperature to 375°F while the wrapped ribs are cooking. You'll get the most tender ribs you have ever eaten.

SIMPLE SMOKED BABY BACKS

Baby back ribs are so good because they are naturally so darn tender! And being this tender means they're more forgiving than their more flavorful cousin, the spare rib. Because of their tenderness and their ability to take on so much flavor, you can get to four to six hours of amazing smoky goodness. This method will pack your ribs full of wood-fired taste!

Ingredients
2 (2- or 3-pound) racks baby back ribs
2 tablespoons yellow mustard
1 batch Pork Rub

Preparation time: 25 minutes
Smoking time: 4 to 6 hours
Temperature: 225°F
Portions: 4 to 8
Recommended pellets: Hickory
Recommended sides: Collard greens, herbed potato salad, corn with basil butter and flaky salt

Instructions
1. Supply your smoker with wood pellets and follow the manufacturer's specific start-up procedure. Preheat the grill, with the lid closed, to 225°F.
2. Remove the membrane from the backside of the ribs. This can be done by cutting just through the membrane in an X pattern and working a paper towel between the membrane and the ribs to pull it off.
3. Coat the ribs on both sides with mustard and season them with the rub. Using your hands, work the rub into the meat.
4. Place the ribs directly on the grill grate and smoke until their internal temperature reaches between 190°F and 200°F.
5. Remove the racks from the grill and cut into individual ribs. Serve immediately.

Secret tip: Sear your ribs for 1 or 2 minutes over an open flame or in a cast-iron skillet before pulling them off the grill.

SMOKED SPARE RIBS

Spare ribs are the tastier of the two types of bone-in pork ribs and most professional cooks tend to use spare ribs for this reason. After smoking spare ribs on your pellet grill or smoker, you will understand the difference. Because spare ribs are the less tender of the two, it's important to ensure they get to a higher temperature for proper tenderness.

Ingredients
2 (2- or 3-pound) racks spare ribs
2 tablespoons yellow mustard
1 batch Sweet Brown Sugar Rub
¼ cup The Ultimate BBQ Sauce

Preparation time: 25 minutes
Smoking time: 4 to 6 hours
Temperature: 225°F and 300°F
Portions: 4 to 8
Recommended pellets: Hickory
Recommended sides: Collard greens, herbed potato salad, corn with basil butter and flaky salt

Instructions
1. Supply your smoker with wood pellets and follow the manufacturer's specific start-up procedure. Preheat the grill, with the lid closed, to 225°F.
2. Remove the membrane from the backside of the ribs. This can be done by cutting just through the membrane in an X pattern and working a paper towel between the membrane and the ribs to pull it off.
3. Coat the ribs on both sides with mustard and season with the rub. Using your hands, work the rub into the meat.
4. Place the ribs directly on the grill grate and smoke until their internal temperature reaches between 190°F and 200°F.
5. Baste both sides of the ribs with barbecue sauce.
6. Increase the grill's temperature to 300°F and continue to cook the ribs for 15 minutes more.
7. Remove the racks from the grill, cut them into individual ribs, and serve immediately.

Secret tip: If your ribs aren't as tender as you'd like, increase the internal temperature to which you cook them. A higher internal temperature yields more tender ribs.

SWEET SMOKED COUNTRY RIBS

Country ribs are like boneless wings: awesome. Country ribs are boneless rib meat, which means you can have that extra IPA while eating them and not worry about being a sticky mess.

Ingredients
2 pounds country-style ribs
1 batch Sweet Brown Sugar Rub
2 tablespoons light brown sugar
1 cup Pepsi or other cola
¼ cup The Ultimate BBQ Sauce

Preparation time: 25 minutes
Smoking time: 4 hours
Temperature: 180°F and 300°F
Portions: 12 to 15
Recommended pellets: Apple
Recommended sides: Collard greens, herbed potato salad, corn with basil butter and flaky salt

Instructions
1. Supply your smoker with wood pellets and follow the manufacturer's specific start-up procedure. Preheat the grill, with the lid closed, to 180°F.
2. Sprinkle the ribs with the rub and use your hands to work the rub into the meat.
3. Place the ribs directly on the grill grate and smoke for 3 hours.
4. Remove the ribs from the grill and place them on enough aluminum foil to wrap them completely. Dust the brown sugar over the ribs.
5. Increase the grill's temperature to 300°F.
6. Fold in three sides of the foil around the ribs and add the cola. Fold in the last side, completely enclosing the ribs and liquid. Return the ribs to the grill and cook for 45 minutes.
7. Remove the ribs from the foil and place them on the grill grate. Baste all sides of the ribs with barbecue sauce. Cook for 15 minutes more to caramelize the sauce.
8. Remove the ribs from the grill and serve immediately.

Secret tip: Use juice rather than soda when you wrap the meat. Apple juice is the most popular choice.

CLASSIC PULLED PORK

This is pulled pork that is so authentic, your friends will think you picked it up at the local barbecue joint. Use it in tacos, sliders, and sandwiches and you'll still have leftovers for days. Little did you know that classic pulled pork can be made on your pellet grill—with minimal effort.

Ingredients
1 (6- to 8-pound) bone-in pork shoulder
2 tablespoons yellow mustard
1 batch Pork Rub

Preparation time: 15 minutes

Smoking time: 16 to 20 hours
Temperature: 225°F
Portions: 8 to 12
Recommended pellets: Hickory
Recommended sides: Sweet jalapeno cornbread, buttermilk hush puppies, shredded apple carrot salad, black bean and corn salad

Instructions
1. Supply your smoker with wood pellets and follow the manufacturer's specific start-up procedure. Preheat the grill, with the lid closed, to 225°F.
2. Coat the pork shoulder all over with mustard and season it with the rub. Using your hands, work the rub into the meat.
3. Place the shoulder on the grill grate and smoke until its internal temperature reaches 195°F.
4. Pull the shoulder from the grill and wrap it completely in aluminum foil or butcher paper. Place it in a cooler, cover the cooler, and let it rest for 1 or 2 hours.
5. Remove the pork shoulder from the cooler and unwrap it. Remove the shoulder bone and pull the pork apart using just your fingers. Serve immediately as desired. Leftovers are encouraged.

Secret tip: Use a foil baking pan and aluminum foil rather than a foil or butcher paper wrap. The pan gives you an easy way to contain the meat while pulling, and is the perfect place for leftovers.
Where did you put the thermometer in your pork shoulder? It should go in the middle, otherwise you aren't reading the actual temperature and you're going to pull it too early.

RUB-INJECTED PORK SHOULDER

Injecting your pork shoulder will pack it with moisture and flavor. Injecting meat ensures that flavor touches all portions of it, not just the outside bark; you also keep your meat from drying out. Injecting pork shoulders creates the moistest pulled pork you have ever tasted.

Ingredients
1 (6- to 8-pound) bone-in pork shoulder
2 cups Tea Injectable made with Pork Rub
2 tablespoons yellow mustard
1 batch Pork Rub

Preparation time: 15 minutes
Smoking time: 16 to 20 hours
Temperature: 225°F and 350°F
Portions: 8 to 12
Recommended pellets: Apple
Recommended sides: Sweet jalapeno cornbread, buttermilk hush puppies, shredded apple carrot salad, black bean and corn salad

Instructions
1. Supply your smoker with wood pellets and follow the manufacturer's specific start-up procedure. Preheat the grill, with the lid closed, to 225°F.
2. Inject the pork shoulder throughout with the tea injectable.
3. Coat the pork shoulder all over with mustard and season it with the rub. Using your hands, work the rub into the meat.
4. Place the shoulder directly on the grill grate and smoke until its internal temperature reaches 160°F and a dark bark has formed on the exterior.
5. Pull the shoulder from the grill and wrap it completely in aluminum foil or butcher paper.
6. Increase the grill's temperature to 350°F.

7. Return the pork shoulder to the grill and cook until its internal temperature reaches 195°F.
8. Pull the shoulder from the grill and place it in a cooler. Cover the cooler and let the pork rest for 1 or 2 hours.
9. Remove the pork shoulder from the cooler and unwrap it. Remove the shoulder bone and pull the pork apart using just your fingers. Serve immediately.

Secret tip: For a different flavor, use your favorite store brand of pork rub to make the tea and season the pork, or try Sweet and Spicy Cinnamon Rub.

MAPLE-SMOKED PORK CHOPS

Honestly, because they're such small cuts, I sometimes look at pork chops as the black sheep of the family that brings us ribs, pulled pork, and bacon. In reality, pork chops bring their own flavor to the table and are great alongside potatoes. Smoking your pork chops will give them a little extra something you don't expect from these small cuts.

Ingredients
1 (12-pound) full packer brisket
2 tablespoons yellow mustard
1 batch Espresso Brisket Rub
Worcestershire Mop and Spritz, for spritzing

Preparation time: 10 minutes
Smoking time: 55 minutes
Temperature: 180°F and 350°F
Portions: 4
Recommended pellets: Maple
Recommended sides: Garlic mashed potatoes, twice smoked potatoes, garlicky brussels sprouts.

Instructions
1. Supply your smoker with wood pellets and follow the manufacturer's specific start-up procedure. Preheat the grill, with the lid closed, to 180°F.
2. Season the pork chops on both sides with salt and pepper.
3. Place the chops directly on the grill grate and smoke for 30 minutes.
4. Increase the grill's temperature to 350°F. Continue to cook the chops until their internal temperature reaches 145°F.
5. Remove the pork chops from the grill and let them rest for 5 minutes before serving.

Secret tip: Reverse-sear your pork chops rather than cooking them at 350°F. Place the chops in a cast-iron skillet or over an open flame and cook for about 2 minutes per side until they reach an internal temperature of 145°F to give your meat a different flavor and texture. Give it a try, especially if you're a pellet grill veteran.

APPLE-SMOKED PORK TENDERLOIN

Smoked pork tenderloins are a head turner. Pellet grill manufacturers, including Pit Boss, use smoked tenderloins to attract potential grill buyers. Joe Traeger said that, along with chicken, they used tenderloin to sell customers on the grill because they barbecued so well.
Smoked tenderloin is tasty yet easy to make, allowing the griller to step away and not have to worry about it burning or drying out. Smoke pork tenderloin at your next big game party or tailgate. You will never miss the action and always end up with amazing pork.

Ingredients
2 (1-pound) pork tenderloins
1 batch Pork Rub

Preparation time: 15 minutes
Smoking time: 4 to 5 hours
Temperature: 180°F
Portions: 4 to 6
Recommended pellets: Apple
Recommended sides: Roasted garlic parmesan fingerling potatoes

Instructions
1. Supply your smoker with wood pellets and follow the manufacturer's specific start-up procedure. Preheat the grill, with the lid closed, to 180°F.
2. Generously season the tenderloins with the rub. Using your hands, work the rub into the meat.
3. Place the tenderloins directly on the grill grate and smoke for 4 or 5 hours, until their internal temperature reaches 145°F.
4. Remove the tenderloins from the grill and let them rest for 5 to 10 minutes before thinly slicing and serving.

Secret tip: Being a pit master is all about making great taste look easy. Pork tenderloin is a simple dish to master and it never disappoints. The convection-style cooking of a pellet grill and smoker produces the juiciest pork loins you have ever had. This dish is the definition of set-and-forget, so you might want to pick up your Wi-Fi controller for this one.

TERIYAKI PORK TENDERLOIN

Ingredients
2 (1-pound) pork tenderloins
1 batch Quick and Easy Teriyaki Marinade
Smoked salt

Preparation time: 30 minutes
Smoking time: 1½ to 2 hours
Temperature: 180°F and 300°F
Portions: 12 to 15
Recommended pellets: Cherry
Recommended sides: Sesame ginger roasted broccoli

Instructions
1. In a large zip-top bag, combine the tenderloins and marinade. Seal the bag, turn to coat, and refrigerate the pork for at least 30 minutes—I recommend up to overnight.
2. Supply your smoker with wood pellets and follow the manufacturer's specific start-up procedure. Preheat the grill, with the lid closed, to 180°F.
3. Remove the tenderloins from the marinade and season them with smoked salt.
4. Place the tenderloins directly on the grill grate and smoke for 1 hour.
5. Increase the grill's temperature to 300°F and continue to cook until the pork's internal temperature reaches 145°F.
6. Remove the tenderloins from the grill and let them rest for 5 to 10 minutes, before thinly slicing and serving.

Secret tip: Don't be afraid to try out your favorite teriyaki marinade here.

BARBECUED TENDERLOIN

Tenderloin is such a versatile cut. It can be long-smoked, letting the flavors seep into the meat over time, or it can be grilled at high temperature, sealing in all those tasty juices—and everything in between. Barbecuing your tenderloin on a pellet grill creates an awesome brown crust and seals in all the moisture.

Ingredients
2 (1-pound) pork tenderloins
1 batch Sweet and Spicy Cinnamon Rub

Preparation time: 5 minutes
Smoking time: 30 minutes
Temperature: 225°F
Portions: 4 TO 6
Recommended pellets: Cherry
Recommended sides: Roasted garlic parmesan fingerling potatoes

Instructions
1. Supply your smoker with wood pellets and follow the manufacturer's specific start-up procedure. Preheat the grill, with the lid closed, to 350°F.
2. Generously season the tenderloins with the rub. Using your hands, work the rub into the meat.
3. Place the tenderloins directly on the grill grate and smoke until their internal temperature reaches 145°F.
4. Remove the tenderloins from the grill and let them rest for 5 to 10 minutes, before thinly slicing and serving.

Secret tip: Tongs or a pigtail work great when cooking tenderloins. Rather than fighting the meat from rolling off your spatula, just use the tongs or pigtail to grab your pork tenderloin off the grill.

PORK BELLY BURNT ENDS

Ingredients
1 (3-pound) skinless pork belly (if not already skinned, use a sharp boning knife to remove the skin from the belly), cut into 1½- to 2-inch cubes
1 batch Sweet Brown Sugar Rub
½ cup honey
1 cup The Ultimate BBQ Sauce
2 tablespoons light brown sugar

Preparation time: 30 minutes
Smoking time: 6 hours
Temperature: 250 °F
Portions: 8 to 10
Recommended pellets: Maple
Recommended sides: Walnut, Celery, Chicory & Apple Salad

Instructions
1. Supply your smoker with wood pellets and follow the manufacturer's specific start-up procedure. Preheat the grill, with the lid closed, to 250°F.
2. Generously season the pork belly cubes with the rub. Using your hands, work the rub into the meat.
3. Place the pork cubes directly on the grill grate and smoke until their internal temperature reaches 195°F.
4. Transfer the cubes from the grill to an aluminum pan. Add the honey, barbecue sauce, and brown sugar. Stir to combine and coat the pork.

5. Place the pan in the grill and smoke the pork for 1 hour, uncovered. Remove the pork from the grill and serve immediately.

APPLE-SMOKED BACON

Bacon is among the best things you can cook on your grill. That smoky flavor will give you the best bacon ever. Sunday mornings will never be the same, so put away your skillet. I know you're asking, "How hard can bacon be?" The truth is, it isn't—but that's the problem. It allows even the best grillers to become careless.

Ingredients
1 (1-pound) package thick-sliced bacon

Preparation time: 5 minutes
Smoking time: 20 to 30 minutes
Temperature: 275 °F
Portions: 4 to 6
Recommended pellets: Apple
Recommended sides: Eggs and whole wheat toast

Instructions
1. Supply your smoker with wood pellets and follow the manufacturer's specific start-up procedure. Preheat the grill, with the lid closed, to 275°F.
2. Supply your smoker with wood pellets and follow the manufacturer's specific start-up procedure. Preheat the grill, with the lid closed, to 275°F.

Secret tip: Place a baking sheet or aluminum pan on the drain pan to catch the grease and keep it from burning on the pan.

CAJUN DOUBLE-SMOKED HAM

You might not think of smoking your pre-smoked ham, but this is the only way to serve it. Going low and slow helps break down the meat and allows that pellet smoke to penetrate it completely. This technique will wow your family and friends at that next holiday get-together.

Ingredients
1 (5- or 6-pound) bone-in smoked ham
1 batch Cajun Rub
3 tablespoons honey

Preparation time: 20 minutes
Smoking time: 4 or 5 hours
Temperature: 225°F
Portions: 12 to 15
Recommended pellets: Apple
Recommended sides: Garlic Mashed Potatoes With Parmesan Cheese, Cauliflower Gratin, Sweet Potato Casserole

Instructions
1. Supply your smoker with wood pellets and follow the manufacturer's specific start-up procedure. Preheat the grill, with the lid closed, to 225°F.

2. Generously season the ham with the rub and place it either in a pan or directly on the grill grate. Smoke it for 1 hour.
3. Drizzle the honey over the ham and continue to smoke it until the ham's internal temperature reaches 145°F.
4. Remove the ham from the grill and let it rest for 5 to 10 minutes, before thinly slicing and serving.

Secret tip: Use your favorite pork or sweet rub with ham. Also, be aware of any other flavors the ham might have already been cooked with and try to work with them. Our Sweet and Spicy Cinnamon Rub complements any fruit-smoked ham perfectly.

SMOKED HAM

Fresh ham is amazing. I don't know why so few of us eat it, but it is, hands down, one of the best cuts out there. The flavor is so different, less packaged, than pre-smoked hams.

Ingredients
1 (10-pound) fresh ham, skin removed
2 tablespoons olive oil
1 batch Rosemary-Garlic Lamb Seasoning

Preparation time: 15 minutes
Smoking time: 5 or 6 hours
Temperature: 180°F and 375°F
Portions: 12 to 15
Recommended pellets: Maple
Recommended sides: Roasted asparagus, Garlic Mashed Potatoes With Parmesan Cheese

Instructions
1. Supply your smoker with wood pellets and follow the manufacturer's specific start-up procedure. Preheat the grill, with the lid closed, to 180°F.
2. Rub the ham all over with olive oil and sprinkle it with the seasoning.
3. Place the ham directly on the grill grate and smoke for 3 hours.
4. Increase the grill's temperature to 375°F and continue to smoke the ham until its internal temperature reaches 170°F.
5. Remove the ham from the grill and let it rest for 10 minutes, before carving and serving.

Secret tip: Using a boning knife, score your ham in a crosshatch pattern, creating roughly 1-inch squares and cutting about ½ inch into the surface of the meat before smoking. This allows more smoke to penetrate the meat, but also holds onto any glaze you might use in the process.

BBQ BREAKFAST GRITS

Finally, barbecue has made its way to the breakfast table. This is another opportunity to get creative with leftover pulled pork. Smoked pulled pork freezes well, and so does this casserole. Pull it out when you have company, and they'll be impressed.

Ingredients
2 cups chicken stock
1 cup water
1 cup quick-cooking grits
3 tablespoons unsalted butter
2 tablespoons minced garlic
1 medium onion, chopped
1 jalapeño pepper, stemmed, seeded, and chopped
1 teaspoon cayenne pepper
2 teaspoons red pepper flakes
1 tablespoon hot sauce
1 cup shredded Monterey Jack cheese
1 cup sour cream
Salt
Freshly ground black pepper
2 eggs, beaten

⅓ cup half-and-half
3 cups leftover pulled pork (preferably smoked)

Preparation time: 20 minutes
Smoking time: 30 to 40 minutes
Temperature: 350°F
Portions: 12 to 15
Recommended pellets: Hickory

Instructions
1. Supply your smoker with wood pellets and follow the manufacturer's specific start-up procedure. Preheat, with the lid closed, to 350°F.
2. On your kitchen stove top, in a large saucepan over high heat, bring the chicken stock and water to a boil.
3. Add the grits and reduce the heat to low, then stir in the butter, garlic, onion, jalapeño, cayenne, red pepper flakes, hot sauce, cheese, and sour cream. Season with salt and pepper, then cook for about 5 minutes.
4. Temper the beaten eggs (see Tip below) and incorporate into the grits. Remove the saucepan from the heat and stir in the half-and-half and pulled pork.
5. Pour the grits into a greased grill-safe 9-by-13-inch casserole dish or aluminum pan.
6. Transfer to the grill, close the lid, and bake for 30 to 40 minutes, covering with aluminum foil toward the end of cooking if the grits start to get too brown on top.

Secret tip: Tempering eggs is a technique for adding them to already hot ingredients without ending up with scrambled eggs. The trick is to combine things slowly. Beat your eggs in a separate bowl and slowly bring up their temperature by mixing in small amounts of slightly cooled grits mixture until you can finally add them to the saucepan.

LIP-SMACKIN' PORK LOIN

The pork loin differs a bit from the pricier, smaller, and more tender pork tenderloin, but both cuts cook nicely on a wood pellet grill thanks to the grill's steady and dependable low temperature. It used to be that most pork got overcooked due to a fear of trichinosis, but these days, that disease is extremely rare. Plus, trichinae (the parasites that cause it) are killed at 137°F. Pork loin and pork tenderloin can now safely be served rare and are great sources of lean, healthy protein.

Ingredients
¼ cup finely ground coffee
¼ cup paprika
¼ cup garlic powder
2 tablespoons chili powder
1 tablespoon packed light brown sugar
1 tablespoon ground allspice
1 tablespoon ground coriander
1 tablespoon freshly ground black pepper
2 teaspoons ground mustard
1½ teaspoons celery seeds
1 (1½- to 2-pound) pork loin roast

Preparation time: 10 minutes
Smoking time: 3 hours
Temperature: 250°F
Portions: 8
Recommended pellets: Hickory, Apple
Recommended sides: Sweet onion bake

Instructions

1. Supply your smoker with wood pellets and follow the manufacturer's specific start-up procedure. Preheat, with the lid closed, to 250°F.
2. In a small bowl, combine the ground coffee, paprika, garlic powder, chili powder, brown sugar, allspice, coriander, pepper, mustard, and celery seeds to create a rub, and generously apply it to the pork loin roast.
3. Place the pork loin on the grill, fat-side up, close the lid, and roast for 3 hours, or until a meat thermometer inserted in the thickest part of the meat reads 160°F.
4. Let the pork rest for 5 minutes before slicing and serving.

PINEAPPLE-PEPPER PORK KEBABS

If the only meat on a stick you've ever tried is a corn dog, it's time I broaden your horizons. Kebabs are an easy way to mix different flavors on the grill, and they've been around for a long time. The first known use of the word "kebab" was in 1377; it is widely thought to have originated in Turkey.

Ingredients

1 (20-ounce) bottle hoisin sauce
½ cup Sriracha
¼ cup honey
¼ cup apple cider vinegar
2 tablespoons canola oil
2 teaspoons minced garlic
2 teaspoons onion powder
1 teaspoon ground ginger
1 teaspoon salt
1 teaspoon freshly ground black pepper
2 pounds thick-cut pork chops or pork loin, cut into 2-inch cubes
10 ounces fresh pineapple, cut into chunks
1 red onion, cut into wedges
1 bag mini sweet peppers, tops removed and seeded
12 metal or wooden skewers (soaked in water for 30 minutes if wooden)

Preparation time: 20 minutes
Smoking time: 1 to 4 hours
Temperature: 450°F
Portions: 12 to 15
Recommended pellets: Apple, Cherry
Recommended sides: Roasted potatoes

Instructions

1. In a small bowl, stir together the hoisin, Sriracha, honey, vinegar, oil, minced garlic, onion powder, ginger, salt, and black pepper to create the marinade. Reserve ¼ cup for basting.
2. Toss the pork cubes, pineapple chunks, onion wedges, and mini peppers in the remaining marinade. Cover and refrigerate for at least 1 hour or up to 4 hours.
3. Supply your smoker with wood pellets and follow the manufacturer's specific start-up procedure. Preheat, with the lid closed, to 450°F.
4. Remove the pork, pineapple, and veggies from the marinade; do not rinse. Discard the marinade.
5. Use the double-skewer technique to assemble the kebabs (see Tip below). Thread each of 6 skewers with a piece of pork, a piece of pineapple, a piece of onion, and a sweet mini pepper, making sure that the skewer goes through the left side of the ingredients. Repeat the threading on each skewer two more times. Double-skewer the kebabs by sticking another 6 skewers through the right side of the ingredients.
6. Place the kebabs directly on the grill, close the lid, and smoke for 10 to 12 minutes, turning once. They are done when a meat thermometer inserted in the pork reads 160°F.

Secret tip: Double-skewering your kebabs keeps the meat from spinning on the grill and allows for better overall maneuverability.

JALAPEÑO-BACON PORK TENDERLOIN

The pork loin and the pork tenderloin are both fantastic meats for absorbing smoke flavors on the grill. But did you know they are really separate cuts from different parts of the hog? The tenderloin is quite a bit smaller than the loin, which is often covered in a layer of fat. Tenderloins may have a bit of silverskin to remove but are otherwise lean and delicious. For this dish, the pork can be served on the rare side and pink in the center.

Ingredients
¼ cup yellow mustard
2 (1-pound) pork tenderloins
¼ cup Pork Rub
8 ounces cream cheese, softened
1 cup grated Cheddar cheese
1 tablespoon unsalted butter, melted
1 tablespoon minced garlic
2 jalapeño peppers, seeded and diced
1½ pounds bacon
Preparation time: 25 minutes
Smoking time: 2 hours and 30 minutes
Temperature: 225°F and 375°F
Portions: 4 to 6
Recommended pellets: Hickory, Apple
Recommended sides: Garlic Mashed Potatoes With Parmesan Cheese

Instructions
1. Slather the mustard all over the pork tenderloins, then sprinkle generously with the dry rub to coat the meat.
2. Supply your smoker with wood pellets and follow the manufacturer's specific start-up procedure. Preheat, with the lid closed, to 225°F.
3. Place the tenderloins directly on the grill, close the lid, and smoke for 2 hours.
4. Remove the pork from the grill and increase the temperature to 375°F.
5. In a small bowl, combine the cream cheese, Cheddar cheese, melted butter, garlic, and jalapeños.
6. Starting from the top, slice deeply along the center of each tenderloin end to end, creating a cavity.
7. Spread half of the cream cheese mixture in the cavity of one tenderloin. Repeat with the remaining mixture and the other piece of meat.
8. Securely wrap one tenderloin with half of the bacon. Repeat with the remaining bacon and the other piece of meat.
9. Transfer the bacon-wrapped tenderloins to the grill, close the lid, and smoke for about 30 minutes, or until a meat thermometer inserted in the thickest part of the meat reads 160°F and the bacon is browned and cooked through.
10. Let the tenderloins rest for 5 to 10 minutes before slicing and serving.

Secret tip: A bacon wrap adds a nice amount of self-basting fat to the lean tenderloin in this recipe. If you want to amp up the table conversation, try encasing the pork with a bacon weave. It's double the bacon, and double the fun. Start with a flat surface and 8 cold strips of bacon lying close together vertically. Then weave 8 more strips horizontally under and over the vertical strips. It takes a few tries to get right, but it looks amazing. You can hide ragged edges in the seam on the bottom of the small roast.

COUNTRY PORK ROAST

The pork loin roast is one of my favorite cuts of the pig because, like a blank canvas, there are a lot of ways to prepare it. You can even add it to pulled Boston butt to increase the white meat mix. And the loin is nice and lean, a good choice if you are watching your waistline.

Ingredients
1 (28-ounce) jar or 2 (14.5-ounce) cans sauerkraut
3 Granny Smith apples, cored and chopped
¾ cup packed light brown sugar
3 tablespoons Greek seasoning
2 teaspoons dried basil leaves
Extra-virgin olive oil, for rubbing
1 (2- to 2½-pound) pork loin roast

Preparation time: 20 minutes
Smoking time: 3 hours
Temperature: 250°F
Portions: 8
Recommended pellets: Hickory, Apple
Recommended sides: Southern Slaw

Instructions
1. Supply your smoker with wood pellets and follow the manufacturer's specific start-up procedure. Preheat, with the lid closed, to 250°F.
2. In a large bowl, stir together the sauerkraut, chopped apples, and brown sugar.
3. Spread the sauerkraut-apple mixture in the bottom of a 9-by-13-inch baking dish.
4. In a small bowl, mix together the Greek seasoning and dried basil for the rub.
5. Oil the pork roast and apply the rub, then place it fat-side up in the baking dish, on top of the sauerkraut.
6. Transfer the baking dish to the grill, close the lid, and roast the pork for 3 hours, or until a meat thermometer inserted in the thickest part of the meat reads 160°F.
7. Remove the pork roast from the baking dish and let rest for 5 minutes before slicing.
8. To serve, divide the sauerkraut-apple mixture among plates and top with the sliced pork.

PICKLED-PEPPER PORK CHOPS

Use the zesty jalapeño juice to fire things up before the chops even touch the grill. You could use pickle juice instead for a low-heat option.

Ingredients
4 (1-inch-thick) pork chops
½ cup pickled jalapeño juice or pickle juice
¼ cup chopped pickled (jarred) jalapeño pepper slices
¼ cup chopped roasted red peppers
¼ cup canned diced tomatoes, well-drained
¼ cup chopped scallions
2 teaspoons poultry seasoning
2 teaspoons salt
2 teaspoons freshly ground black pepper
Preparation time: 15 minutes + at least 4 hours to marinate

Smoking time: 45 to 50 minutes
Temperature: 325°F

Portions: 4
Recommended pellets: Hickory, Oak
Recommended sides: Bread fresh from your Traeger

Instructions
1. Pour the jalapeño juice into a large container with a lid. Add the pork chops, cover, and marinate in the refrigerator for at least 4 hours or overnight, supplementing with or substituting pickle juice as desired.
2. In a small bowl, combine the chopped pickled jalapeños, roasted red peppers, tomatoes, scallions, and poultry seasoning to make a relish. Set aside.
3. Remove the pork chops from the marinade and shake off any excess. Discard the marinade. Season both sides of the chops with the salt and pepper.
4. Supply your smoker with wood pellets and follow the manufacturer's specific start-up procedure. Preheat, with the lid closed, to 325°F.
5. b
6. To serve, divide the chops among plates and top with the pickled pepper relish.

Secret tip: Keep thinner chops from curling up by strategically making a few small cuts in the rim of fat surrounding the meat.

SOUTHERN SUGAR-GLAZED HAM

Cooking a big, fat ham on your wood pellet grill is an easy way to create that Norman Rockwell vibe for your next holiday feast. It's easy because whole bone-in hams come fully cured and cooked—just add smoke. Pound for pound, it makes for one of the simplest, most elegant, and most affordable celebratory meals.

Ingredients
1 (12- to 15-pound) whole bone-in ham, fully cooked
¼ cup yellow mustard
1 cup pineapple juice
½ cup packed light brown sugar
1 teaspoon ground cinnamon
½ teaspoon ground cloves

Preparation time: 30 minutes
Smoking time: 5 hours
Temperature: 275°F
Portions: 12 to 15
Recommended pellets: Apple, Cherry
Recommended sides: Sweet potato casserole, green bean casserole

Instructions
1. Supply your smoker with wood pellets and follow the manufacturer's specific start-up procedure. Preheat, with the lid closed, to 275°F.
2. Trim off the excess fat and skin from the ham, leaving a ¼-inch layer of fat. Put the ham in an aluminum foil–lined roasting pan.
3. On your kitchen stove top, in a medium saucepan over low heat, combine the mustard, pineapple juice, brown sugar, cinnamon, and cloves and simmer for 15 minutes, or until thick and reduced by about half.
4. Baste the ham with half of the pineapple–brown sugar syrup, reserving the rest for basting later in the cook.
5. Place the roasting pan on the grill, close the lid, and smoke for 4 hours.
6. Baste the ham with the remaining pineapple–brown sugar syrup and continue smoking with the lid closed for another hour, or until a meat thermometer inserted in the thickest part of the ham reads 140°F.
7. Remove the ham from the grill, tent with foil, and let rest for 20 minutes before carving.

Secret tip: A boneless ham will work with this method, too; however, cuts cooked bone-in tend to have more flavor.

STUFFED PORK CROWN ROAST

Take the grilling throne with this stuffed pork crown roast recipe. Brush on the homemade marinade, load up the middle of the crown with your favorite stuffing, and infuse it all with wood-fired flavor.

Ingredients
10 Pound Crown Roast of Pork, 12-14 ribs
1 Cup apple juice or cider
2 Tablespoon apple cider vinegar
2 Tablespoon Dijon mustard
1 Tablespoon brown sugar
2 Clove garlic, minced
2 Tablespoon Thyme or Rosemary, fresh
1 Teaspoon salt
1 Teaspoon coarse ground black pepper, divided
1/2 Cup olive oil
8 Cup Your Favorite Stuffing, Prepared According to the Package Directions, or Homemade

Preparation time: 1 hour
Smoking time: 3 hours
Temperature: 325°F
Portions: 2 to 4
Recommended pellets: Apple, Hickory, Cherry
Recommended sides: Collard greens, garlic mashed potatoes

Instructions
1. Set the pork on a flat rack in a shallow roasting pan. Cover the end of each bone with a small piece of foil.
2. Make the marinade: Bring the apple cider to a boil over high heat and reduce by half. Remove from the heat, and whisk in the vinegar, mustard, brown sugar, garlic, thyme, and salt and pepper. Slowly whisk in the oil.
3. Using a pastry brush, apply the marinade to the roast, coating all surfaces. Cover it with plastic wrap and allow it to sit until the meat comes to room temperature, about 1 hour.
4. When ready to cook, set grill temperature to High and preheat, lid closed for 15 minutes.
5. Arrange the roasting pan with the pork on the grill grate. Roast for 30 minutes.
6. Reduce the heat to 325°F. Loosely fill the crown with the stuffing, mounding it at the top. Cover the stuffing with foil. (Alternatively, you can bake the stuffing in a separate pan alongside the roast.)
7. Roast the pork for another 1-1/2 hours. Remove the foil from the stuffing and continue to roast until the internal temperature of the meat is 150°F, about 30 minutes to an hour. Make sure the temperature probe doesn't touch bone or you will get a false reading.
8. Remove roast from grill and allow to rest for 15 minutes. Remove the foil covering the bones, but leave the butcher's string on the roast until ready to carve. Transfer to a warm platter.
9. To serve, carve between the bones. Enjoy!

Secret tip: You can brush the marinade on the roast and return it, covered, to the refrigerator until ready to cook. Let the meat warm to room temperature before putting it on the grill.

BACON STUFFED SMOKED PORK LOIN

If you're nuts about bacon, try this deliciously tender walnut & craisin stuffed pork loin.

Ingredients
3 Pound Pork Loin, Butterflied
As Needed Pork Rub
1/4 Cup Walnuts, Chopped
1/3 Cup Craisins
1 Tablespoon Oregano, fresh
1 Tablespoon fresh thyme
6 Pieces Asparagus, fresh
6 Slices Bacon, sliced
1/3 Cup Parmesan cheese, grated
As Needed Bacon Grease

Preparation time: 20 minutes
Smoking time: 1 hour
Temperature: 180°F and 350°F
Portions: 4 to 6
Recommended pellets: Hickory
Recommended sides: Roasted potatoes

Instructions
1. Lay down 2 large pieces of butcher's twine on your work surface. Place butterflied pork loin perpendicular to twine.
2. Season the inside of the pork loin with the pork rub.
3. On one end of the loin, layer in a line all of the ingredients, beginning with the chopped walnuts, craisins, oregano, thyme, and asparagus.
4. Add bacon and top with the parmesan cheese.
5. Starting at the end with all of the fillings, carefully roll up the pork loin and secure on both ends with butcher's twine.
6. Roll the pork loin in the reserved bacon grease and season the outside with more Pork Rub.
7. When ready to cook, set temperature to 180°F and preheat, lid closed for 15 minutes. Place stuffed pork loin directly on the grill grate and smoke for 1 hour.
8. Remove the pork loin; increase the temperature to 350°F and allow to preheat.
9. Place the loin back on the Traeger and grill for approximately 30 to 45 minutes or until the temperature reads 135°F on an instant-read thermometer.
10. Move the pork loin to a plate and tent it with aluminum foil. Let it rest for 15 minutes before slicing and serving. Enjoy!

SMOKED PORCHETTA WITH ITALIAN SALSA VERDE

We've got a delicious Traeger take on a classic Italian dish. Pork loin is wrapped with pork belly, layered with a citrus and herb blend, smoked over applewood to golden brown crispy perfection and served with a fresh Italian salsa verde.

Ingredients
3 Tablespoon dried fennel seed
2 Tablespoon red pepper flakes
2 Tablespoon sage, minced
1 Tablespoon rosemary, minced
3 Clove garlic, minced
As Needed lemon zest
As Needed orange zest
To Taste salt and pepper
6 Pound Pork Belly, skin on

As Needed salt and pepper
1 Whole shallot, thinly sliced
6 Tablespoon parsley, minced
2 Tablespoon freshly minced chives
1 Tablespoon Oregano, fresh
3 Tablespoon white wine vinegar
1/2 Teaspoon kosher salt
3/4 Cup olive oil
1/2 Teaspoon Dijon mustard
As Needed fresh lemon juice

Preparation time: 30 minutes
Smoking time: 3 hours
Temperature: 225°F
Portions: 8 to 12
Recommended pellets: Apple
Recommended sides: Garlic mashed potatoes

Instructions

1. Prepare herb mixture: In a medium bowl, mix together fennel seeds, red pepper flakes, sage, rosemary, garlic, citrus zest, salt and pepper.
2. Place pork belly skin side up on a clean work surface and score in a crosshatch pattern. Flip the pork belly over and season flesh side with salt, pepper and half of the herb mixture.
3. Place trimmed pork loin in the center of the belly and rub with remaining herb mixture. Season with salt and pepper.
4. Roll the pork belly around the loin to form a cylindrical shape and tie tightly with kitchen twine at 1" intervals.
5. Season the outside with salt and pepper and transfer to refrigerator, uncovered and let air dry overnight.
6. When ready to cook, start the Traeger grill and set to Smoke.
7. Fit a rimmed baking sheet with a rack and place the pork on the rack seam side down.
8. Place the pan directly on the grill grate and smoke for 1 hour.
9. Increase the grill temperature to 325 degrees F and roast until the internal temperature of the meat reaches 135 degrees, about 2 1/2 hours. If the exterior begins to burn before the desired internal temperature is reached, tent with foil.
10. Remove from grill and let stand 30 minutes before slicing.
11. To make the Italian salsa verde: Combine shallot, parsley, chives, vinegar, oregano and salt in a medium bowl. Whisk in olive oil then stir in mustard and lemon juice.
12. Drizzle slices with Italian salsa verde and enjoy!

CHICKEN AND POULTRY

Both backyard chefs and hard-core competition barbecue teams like wood pellet grills for their ability to smoke fowl, such as chicken and turkey, to perfection. By cooking low and slow with hardwood pellet smoke, the skin of your poultry gets plenty of time for the fat to render (and with duck there's plenty of flavorful fat). As the poultry smokes, it also bastes itself slowly. Plus, the more delicate meat showcases subtle fruitwood smoke flavors nicely. When you see pink, don't panic. As long as the juices run clear and you verify with a good thermometer that your bird is not bleeding, it's smokin'!

One of the best things about smoking poultry is the price. Pound for pound, there is no protein more affordable than chicken leg quarters. But even if you pay a bit more for the breast meat, you won't be disappointed. The smoke flavor takes the healthy, sometimes boring boneless breast to heavenly new hickory heights!

Turkey, chicken, and duck each have their own power cuts, but they are all a perfect match for your wood pellet grill:

Breast meat is like a blank canvas for flavors. It's delicate, lean, and clean, and is the top choice for many health-conscious diners. Note that the breast is also the easiest to dry out, so smoke with care.

Thighs are a favorite on smokers because, unlike breasts, they take much longer to dry out. Thighs are actually difficult to overcook. That, along with their relatively inexpensive price, makes them an easy choice for feeding a crowd.

The drumsticks or legs are Mother Nature's food on a stick! They are a top cookout choice, especially when kids are at the table.

Wings have come a long way. They used to be a budget cut of meat but over the years have become a tailgate obsession. If you are feeding a large group, be sure to separate whole wings into wingettes (the "flat" two-bone section) and the drumettes. It's interesting to observe that everyone has a personal preference.

You should also consider smoking the **whole bird**, although it's technically the opposite of a cut. A roast turkey or chicken makes for a table centerpiece that is as beautiful as it is delicious. Just take care not to overcook the breast meat before the thighs are done.

TECHNIQUES

Your wood pellet grill will handle most of the hard work for poultry, but there are a few techniques you might want to try in your attempt to reach pit master perfection. The main techniques for turkey and chicken include brining, injecting, seasoning, and dry brining.

For **brining**, use what many people consider to be a universal ratio of salt to water: one gallon of water mixed with one cup of kosher salt. You may initially use hot water to dissolve the salt and/or sugar (if you're using that), but always keep the meat and brine solution chilled to prevent food contamination.

When **injecting**, take care to insert the injector needle into the meat via the interior of the cavity and rib cage. This way, you won't pierce or blemish the outer skin, so it will hold in juices just as the food gods intended.

When **seasoning** the whole bird or most individual cuts, I make an effort to carefully peel back the skin and rub seasonings underneath it and into the muscles in all parts of the bird. It takes a little extra effort, but by doing this you'll get salt and real flavor into the meat. Poultry skin—especially thick turkey skin—is akin to a wetsuit. You want to season it, but the seasoning won't penetrate the skin.

Dry **brining** is a technique that I use to help create a crisp chicken skin you can bite through. It involves rubbing a dry seasoning, mostly salt, over and under the skin of the bird. Then you let it dry uncovered in the refrigerator for four hours before blotting completely dry with paper towels and cooking. The final result is a well-seasoned, crispy treat.

Two turkeys are better than one
You know you normally have half a turkey left over anyway, so why bust your grill with a 20-pound turkey when you could smoke two 12-pound birds? This way, you get twice the drumsticks and double the smoky surface area, and you'll dramatically reduce your cook time.

SPATCHCOCKING
Another way to trim your poultry is by using a butterflying technique called spatchcocking. This can be a slippery task, but it's definitely not complicated. Simply use a heavy pair of kitchen shears to cut out the spine of the bird. You'll scissor completely through the skin up and down each side of the spine. Then open and flatten the full carcass skin-side up on the grill grate, cracking or splitting the small breast bone in the middle. The bigger the bird, the tougher the task; just take care to start and finish with thoroughly sanitized scissors and hands. The newfound surface area will now allow the bird to absorb twice the smoke flavor. It will be easier to carve, and it looks extra cool on the grate of your wood pellet grill.

To Skin or Not to Skin?
Skin is always a consideration when dealing with poultry. My suggestion is to leave it on. The heat from a wood pellet fire easily blasts through rubbery skin; however, poultry skin can often get a leathery texture when it's slow-smoked. To promote crisp skin, use the dry brining technique. With a little extra time, you can finally achieve crispy skin on your bird!

CLEANING
Do you need to wash your bird? These days, many barbecue gurus say it is not necessary, because having raw poultry come in additional contact with your cleaning area will invite increased danger of bacterial contamination. Call me squeamish, but I always wash the exterior and interior of poultry before seasoning. It's also a great time to remove any extras stuffed inside the cavity, like gizzards and giblets. (If your bird has one of those pop thermometers, you can leave it in and use it, as your wood pellet grill temperature will be controlled much like a home oven.)

RULES TO GRILL BY
Here are a few pro tips to perfect your smoked poultry skills:

1. Since we do much of our meat shopping in supermarkets, you'll want to read the packaging for any indication that the bird may have been pre-brined or enhanced with salt water. Added salt water is not a bad thing, but doing this will simply help you know if you're paying by the pound for chicken or for chicken swelled with heavy liquid and other preservatives. Plus, you'll be able to more precisely control your recipe's salt quantity.

2. Poultry is more prone to contamination than other meats such as beef. Use extra care to avoid foodborne pathogens such as salmonella by regularly washing your hands while cooking and after handling raw meat. Also, make sure to keep raw poultry (and any residual liquid) away from ready-to-serve smoked meats. Sanitize everything that comes into contact with raw poultry before reusing it, including the sink, counter, cutting board, knives, and utensils.

3. So much of barbecue and grilling prep is done outdoors during the summer months. That's an atmosphere ripe for bacteria growth. Be sure you keep your marinating meat cold. Always marinate in the refrigerator and never reuse marinades.

4. The only real way to know if your bird is safely cooked is to break out a meat thermometer and take the internal temperature of the thickest part of the meat. Avoid probing next to bone or out through the other side of the cut. An internal temperature of 165°F is a must.

5. As mentioned previously, thick turkey and chicken skin won't allow seasoning to penetrate. Make a plan to carefully season under the skin using your fingers. It's easier to do than you think; just put the skin back in place once you're done.

BEER CAN—SMOKED CHICKEN

The hardest thing about this recipe and technique is keeping your balance. Not because you're probably drinking beer while you're cooking, but because it's important to balance your chicken on the beer can carefully, using the legs to create a sturdy tripod. Your injection will add more flavor than any of the liquid in the can. Try to inject from the inside of the cavity of the bird to keep the outer skin unblemished.

Ingredients
8 tablespoons (1 stick) unsalted butter, melted
½ cup apple cider vinegar
½ cup Cajun seasoning, divided
1 teaspoon garlic powder
1 teaspoon onion powder
1 (4-pound) whole chicken, giblets removed
Extra-virgin olive oil, for rubbing
1 (12-ounce) can beer
1 cup apple juice
½ cup extra-virgin olive oil

Preparation time: 30 minutes
Smoking time: 3 to 4 hours
Temperature: 250°F
Portions: 3 to 4
Recommended pellets: Hickory, Oak, Apple, Pecan
Recommended sides: Roasted vegetables, collard greens, garlic mashed potatoes

Instructions
1. In a small bowl, whisk together the butter, vinegar, ¼ cup of Cajun seasoning, garlic powder, and onion powder.
2. Use a meat-injecting syringe to inject the liquid into various spots in the chicken. Inject about half of the mixture into the breasts and the other half throughout the rest of the chicken.
3. Rub the chicken all over with olive oil and apply the remaining ¼ cup of Cajun seasoning, being sure to rub under the skin as well.
4. Drink or discard half the beer and place the opened beer can on a stable surface.
5. Place the bird's cavity on top of the can and position the chicken so it will sit up by itself. Prop the legs forward to make the bird more stable, or buy an inexpensive, specially made stand to hold the beer can and chicken in place.
6. Supply your smoker with wood pellets and follow the manufacturer's specific start-up procedure. Preheat, with the lid closed, to 250°F.
7. In a clean 12-ounce spray bottle, combine the apple juice and olive oil. Cover and shake the mop sauce well before each use.
8. Carefully put the chicken on the grill. Close the lid and smoke the chicken for 3 to 4 hours, spraying with the mop sauce every hour, until golden brown and a meat thermometer inserted in the thickest part of the thigh reads 165°F. Keep a piece of aluminum foil handy to loosely cover the chicken if the skin begins to brown too quickly.
9. Let the meat rest for 5 minutes before carving.

Secret tip: The mop sauce helps keep the bird moist, but you are not limited to using apple juice. Apple cider vinegar, orange juice, or a mix of both would also work nicely. But be careful: The more sugar you add to the mop, the more you'll need to watch out for burning.

BUFFALO CHICKEN WRAPS

The origin of Buffalo sauce goes back to 1964, to the Anchor Bar in Buffalo, New York. It is really the easiest sauce to make. It's simply hot sauce and melted butter.

Ingredients
2 teaspoons poultry seasoning
1 teaspoon freshly ground black pepper
1 teaspoon garlic powder
1 to 1½ pounds chicken tenders
4 tablespoons (½ stick) unsalted butter, melted
½ cup hot sauce (such as Frank's RedHot)
4 (10-inch) flour tortillas
1 cup shredded lettuce
½ cup diced tomato
½ cup diced celery
½ cup diced red onion
½ cup shredded Cheddar cheese
¼ cup blue cheese crumbles
¼ cup prepared ranch dressing
2 tablespoons sliced pickled jalapeño peppers (optional)

Preparation time: 30 minutes

Smoking time: 20 minutes
Temperature: 350°F
Portions: 4
Recommended pellets: Hickory, Oak
Recommended sides: Cheesy baked asparagus

Instructions
1. Supply your smoker with wood pellets and follow the manufacturer's specific start-up procedure. Preheat, with the lid closed, to 350°F.
2. In a small bowl, stir together the poultry seasoning, pepper, and garlic powder to create an all-purpose rub, and season the chicken tenders with it.
3. Arrange the tenders directly on the grill, close the lid, and smoke for 20 minutes, or until a meat thermometer inserted in the thickest part of the meat reads 170°F.
4. In another bowl, stir together the melted butter and hot sauce and coat the smoked chicken with it.
5. To serve, heat the tortillas on the grill for less than a minute on each side and place on a plate.
6. Top each tortilla with some of the lettuce, tomato, celery, red onion, Cheddar cheese, blue cheese crumbles, ranch dressing, and jalapeños (if using).
7. Divide the chicken among the tortillas, close up securely, and serve.

Secret tip: Only add hot sauce—that is, hot in temperature—to hot food, or in the case of this recipe, warmed hot sauce. The "warm sauce on hot meat" rule helps keep meat from seizing up and becoming tough. Plus, the risk of foodborne germs is generally reduced if the sauce has been heated through.

ROASTED WHOLE CHICKEN

As I mentioned earlier, the pellet grill world was built on barbecued chicken. Chicken prepared on a pellet grill spread throughout the Northwest, bringing with it faithful followers. The moist, evenly cooked chicken you can make on a pellet grill or smoker is unmatched. Where other grills need a rotisserie to achieve such even cooking, the pellet grill does it with ease.

Ingredients
1 whole chicken
2 tablespoons olive oil
1 batch Chicken Rub

Preparation time: 15 minutes
Smoking time: 1 to 2 hours
Temperature: 375°F
Portions: 6 to 8
Recommended pellets: Hickory
Recommended sides: Corn on the cob, garlic bread, and baked beans

Instructions
1. Supply your smoker with wood pellets and follow the manufacturer's specific start-up procedure. Preheat the grill, with the lid closed, to 375°F.
2. Coat the chicken all over with olive oil and season it with the rub. Using your hands, work the rub into the meat.
3. Place the chicken directly on the grill grate and smoke until its internal temperature reaches 170°F.
4. Remove the chicken from the grill and let it rest for 10 minutes, before carving and serving.

Secret tip: If you like crispier skin, increase the grill's temperature to 450°F for the last 10 minutes of cooking.

SMOKED WHOLE CHICKEN

Ingredients
1 whole chicken
2 cups Tea Injectable (using Not-Just-for-Pork Rub)
2 tablespoons olive oil
1 batch Chicken Rub
2 tablespoons butter, melted

Preparation time: 25 minutes
Smoking time: 4 hours
Temperature: 225°F
Portions: 6 to 8
Recommended pellets: Hickory

Instructions
1. Supply your smoker with wood pellets and follow the manufacturer's specific start-up procedure. Preheat the grill, with the lid closed, to 180°F.
2. Inject the chicken throughout with the tea injectable.
3. Coat the chicken all over with olive oil and season it with the rub. Using your hands, work the rub into the meat.
4. Place the chicken directly on the grill grate and smoke for 3 hours.
5. Baste the chicken with the butter and increase the grill's temperature to 375°F. Continue to cook the chicken until its internal temperature reaches 170°F.
6. Remove the chicken from the grill and let it rest for 10 minutes, before carving and serving.

Secret tip: Basting with butter can be done at any time in the smoking process. I have been known to baste a single chicken with almost an entire stick of butter. I know it is probably not the best choice health-wise, but it sure is tasty.

SKINNY SMOKED CHICKEN BREASTS

Chicken breasts are great cuts for the health conscious in your life and are fantastic cooked on a wood pellet grill. Packed with protein but lower in calories and fat, they offer great taste with little guilt. Without the skin, boneless, skinless breasts can dry out, but that isn't a problem on your pellet grill, which works spectacularly to pack your chicken breasts with all sorts of wood-fired flavor.

Ingredients
2½ pounds boneless, skinless chicken breasts
Salt
Freshly ground black pepper

Preparation time: 15 minutes
Smoking time: 1 hour, 25 minutes
Temperature: 180°F and 325°F
Portions: 4 to 6
Recommended pellets: Competition Blend
Recommended sides: Garlic mashed potatoes

Instructions
1. Supply your smoker with wood pellets and follow the manufacturer's specific start-up procedure. Preheat the grill, with the lid closed, to 180°F.
2. Season the chicken breasts all over with salt and pepper.

3. Place the breasts directly on the grill grate and smoke for 1 hour.
4. Increase the grill's temperature to 325°F and continue to cook until the chicken's internal temperature reaches 170°F. Remove the breasts from the grill and serve immediately.

Secret tip: For a slightly sweet and tangy version, lightly coat the breasts with your favorite barbecue sauce during the last 10 minutes of cooking.

WOOD-FIRED CHICKEN BREASTS

For those of us who prefer white meat over dark, chicken breasts are it. Chicken breasts are typically low cost and low effort. Wood-fired chicken breasts have just enough smoke flavor to make them the hit for dinner this week and not break the bank if you want to have them twice.

Ingredients
2 (1-pound) bone-in, skin-on chicken breasts
1 batch Chicken Rub

Preparation time: 10 minutes
Smoking time: 45 minutes
Temperature: 350°F
Portions: 2 to 4
Recommended pellets: Apple
Recommended sides: Green salad, potato wedges

Instructions
1. Supply your smoker with wood pellets and follow the manufacturer's specific start-up procedure. Preheat the grill, with the lid closed, to 350°F.
2. Season the chicken breasts all over with the rub. Using your hands, work the rub into the meat.
3. Place the breasts directly on the grill grate and smoke until their internal temperature reaches 170°F. Remove the breasts from the grill and serve immediately.

Secret tip: Potato wedges go great with chicken breasts and can be cooked on the grill at the same time. Cut a potato into eighths and rub the pieces with oil, salt, and pepper, then put the wedges on the grill at the same time as the breasts. They will finish right around the same time.

CHICKEN TENDERS

Ingredients
1 pound boneless, skinless chicken breast tenders
1 batch Chicken Rub

Preparation time: 15 minutes
Smoking time: 1 hour, 20 minutes
Temperature: 180°F and 300°F
Portions: 2 to 4
Recommended pellets: Pecan
Recommended sides: Roasted vegetables, collard greens, garlic mashed potatoes

Instructions

1. Supply your smoker with wood pellets and follow the manufacturer's specific start-up procedure. Preheat the grill, with the lid closed, to 180°F.
2. Season the chicken tenders with the rub. Using your hands, work the rub into the meat.
3. Place the tenders directly on the grill grate and smoke for 1 hour.
4. Increase the grill's temperature to 300°F and continue to cook until the tenders' internal temperature reaches 170°F. Remove the tenders from the grill and serve immediately.

Secret tip: Chicken tenders take well to a marinade. Try the Quick and Easy Teriyaki Marinade or a Buffalo sauce to marinate your tenders for a few hours before cooking. They will take on a great amount of flavor in a short time.

BUFFALO WINGS

Buffalo wings are the ultimate snack for the game, poker night, or just a Friday night at home. Wings have a large following, so much so that restaurant chains exist dedicated solely to this small piece of meat. This spicy treat can come in many forms and can be easily cooked to perfection on your pellet grill. The next time it's your job to pick up the wings for the big game, don't worry; you have it covered.

Ingredients
1 pound chicken wings
1 batch Chicken Rub
1 cup Frank's Red-Hot Sauce, Buffalo wing sauce, or similar

Preparation time: 15 minutes
Smoking time: 35 minutes
Temperature: 300°F
Portions: 2 to 3
Recommended pellets: Hickory

Instructions
1. Supply your smoker with wood pellets and follow the manufacturer's specific start-up procedure. Preheat the grill, with the lid closed, to 300°F.
2. Season the chicken wings with the rub. Using your hands, work the rub into the meat.
3. Place the wings directly on the grill grate and smoke until their internal temperature reaches 160°F.
4. Baste the wings with the sauce and continue to smoke until the wings' internal temperature reaches 170°F.

Secret tip: Want some extra kick with your wings? Use a spicy rub, such as the Sweet and Spicy Cinnamon Rub, instead of the chicken rub. I enjoy extra-spicy wings and this is just the way to get them.

SWEET AND SPICY SMOKED WINGS

Ingredients
1 pound chicken wings
1 batch Sweet and Spicy Cinnamon Rub
1 cup barbecue sauce

Preparation time: 20 minutes
Smoking time: 1 hour, 25 minutes
Temperature: 325°F and 250°F
Portions: 2 to 4

Recommended pellets: Competition Blend

Instructions
1. Supply your smoker with wood pellets and follow the manufacturer's specific start-up procedure. Preheat the grill, with the lid closed, to 325°F.
2. Season the chicken wings with the rub. Using your hands, work the rub into the meat.
3. Place the wings directly on the grill grate and cook until they reach an internal temperature of 165°F.
4. Transfer the wings into an aluminum pan. Add the barbecue sauce and stir to coat the wings.
5. Reduce the grill's temperature to 250°F and put the pan on the grill. Smoke the wings for 1 hour more, uncovered. Remove the wings from the grill and serve immediately.

Secret tip: If you can find them, use drumettes rather than full wings. Drumettes are the part of the wing that looks like a drumstick. They tend to have the most meat and are easier to eat.

SMOKED DRUMSTICKS

Drumsticks are dark meat that holds the wood-fired flavor well. One of the great characteristics of drumsticks is actually their greasiness, which helps keep them moist. Overcooking drumsticks is nearly impossible, as the fatty meat keeps itself moist.

Ingredients
1 pound chicken drumsticks
2 tablespoons olive oil
1 batch Sweet and Spicy Cinnamon Rub

Preparation time: 15 minutes
Smoking time: 25 minutes
Temperature: 350°F
Portions: 2 to 4
Recommended pellets: Mesquite
Recommended sides: Potato salad with bacon

Instructions
1. Supply your smoker with wood pellets and follow the manufacturer's specific start-up procedure. Preheat the grill, with the lid closed, to 350°F.
2. Coat the drumsticks all over with olive oil and season with the rub. Using your hands, work the rub into the meat.
3. Place the drumsticks directly on the grill grate and smoke until their internal temperature reaches 170°F. Remove the drumsticks from the grill and serve immediately.

Secret tip: Use a wing rack when cooking drumsticks. A wing rack hangs your drumsticks perfectly while cooking, making it easier to baste them.

SMOKED QUARTERS

Chicken quarters are awesome because they are nearly impossible to dry out on a pellet grill. I have seen chicken quarters covering grate after grate on commercial pellet grills, manned by the most inexperienced cooks, and they never dry out. Though quarters are easy, you can definitely kick them up with a little extra smoke.

Ingredients
4 chicken quarters

2 tablespoons olive oil
1 batch Chicken Rub
2 tablespoons butter

Preparation time: 15 minutes
Smoking time: 2 hours
Temperature: 180°F and 375°F
Portions: 2 to 4
Recommended pellets: Hickory
Recommended sides: Garlic mashed potatoes

Instructions
1. Supply your smoker with wood pellets and follow the manufacturer's specific start-up procedure. Preheat the grill, with the lid closed, to 180°F.
2. Coat the chicken quarters all over with olive oil and season them with the rub. Using your hands, work the rub into the meat.
3. Place the quarters directly on the grill grate and smoke for 1½ hours.
4. Baste the quarters with the butter and increase the grill's temperature to 375°F. Continue to cook until the chicken's internal temperature reaches 170°F.
5. Remove the quarters from the grill and let them rest for 10 minutes before serving.

Secret tip: Inject your quarters using a Tea Injectable or butter, such as the Garlic Butter Injectable, for more moisture and flavor. Though poultry leg meat is juicier than other cuts, it can still dry out.

SMOKING DUCK WITH MANDARIN GLAZE

Duck is a notoriously fatty bird. The low, slow cook time here allows for maximum smoke and fat rendering. In fact, you'll need to break my usual rule of not piercing poultry skin! With duck, you'll be poking the skin (not the meat), with a fork to allow for easier rendering. Before you start, trim off and reserve as much of that extra fat in the cavity, on the skin, and around the neck of the duck as possible. Render it later for delicacies such as duck-fat fries.

Ingredients
1 quart buttermilk
1 (5-pound) whole duck
¾ cup soy sauce
½ cup hoisin sauce
½ cup rice wine vinegar
2 tablespoons sesame oil
1 tablespoon freshly ground black pepper
1 tablespoon minced garlic
Mandarin Glaze, for drizzling

Preparation time: 20 minutes + overnight brining

Smoking time: 4 hours
Temperature: 250°F
Portions: 4
Recommended pellets: Cherry, Pecan
Recommended sides: Duck fat roasted potatoes

Instructions
1. With a very sharp knife, remove as much fat from the duck as you can. Refrigerate or freeze the fat for later use.

2. Pour the buttermilk into a large container with a lid and submerge the whole duck in it. Cover and let brine in the refrigerator for 4 to 6 hours.
3. Supply your smoker with wood pellets and follow the manufacturer's specific start-up procedure. Preheat, with the lid closed, to 250°F.
4. Remove the duck from the buttermilk brine, then rinse it and pat dry with paper towels.
5. In a bowl, combine the soy sauce, hoisin sauce, vinegar, sesame oil, pepper, and garlic to form a paste. Reserve ¼ cup for basting.
6. Poke holes in the skin of the duck and rub the remaining paste all over and inside the cavity.
7. Place the duck on the grill breast-side down, close the lid, and smoke for about 4 hours, basting every hour with the reserved paste, until a meat thermometer inserted in the thickest part of the meat reads 165°F. Use aluminum foil to tent the duck in the last 30 minutes or so if it starts to brown too quickly.
8. To finish, drizzle with glaze.

Secret tip: I love the flavor of hoisin sauce, but if you don't want to buy a jar just for this recipe, feel free to use teriyaki sauce instead

EASY RAPID-FIRE ROAST CHICKEN

The beauty of the wood pellet grill is that it can smoke either low and slow or hot and fast with the flip of a switch. This is a time-saving recipe for roast chicken—it's almost as easy as buying a cooked rotisserie chicken at the market, but better.

Ingredients
1 (4-pound) whole chicken, giblets removed
Extra-virgin olive oil, for rubbing
3 tablespoons Greek seasoning
Juice of 1 lemon
Butcher's string

Preparation time: 10 minutes
Smoking time: 1 to 2 hours
Temperature: 450°F
Portions: 4
Recommended pellets: Apple, Pecan
Recommended sides: Roasted vegetables, collard greens, garlic mashed potatoes

Instructions
1. Supply your smoker with wood pellets and follow the manufacturer's specific start-up procedure. Preheat, with the lid closed, to 450°F.
2. Rub the bird generously all over with oil, including inside the cavity.
3. Sprinkle the Greek seasoning all over and under the skin of the bird, and squeeze the lemon juice over the breast.
4. Tuck the chicken wings behind the back and tie the legs together with butcher's string or cooking twine.
5. Put the chicken directly on the grill, breast-side up, close the lid, and roast for 1 hour to 1 hour 30 minutes, or until a meat thermometer inserted in the thigh reads 165°F.
6. Let the meat rest for 10 minutes before carving.

Secret tip: The seasoning possibilities are endless here. Try Cajun, chipotle, Italian, or adobo seasoning, or create your own.

CINCO DE MAYO CHICKEN ENCHILADAS

Cinco de Mayo celebrates the Mexican victory over French forces during the 1862 Battle of Puebla. These days, we mark the occasion with parties, tequila, and, of course, great food. Adding some mesquite smoke makes this an enchilada bake you'll want to go back to more than just one day a year.

Ingredients
6 cups diced cooked chicken
3 cups grated Monterey Jack cheese, divided
1 cup sour cream
1 (4-ounce) can chopped green chiles
2 (10-ounce) cans red or green enchilada sauce, divided
12 (8-inch) flour tortillas
½ cup chopped scallions
¼ cup chopped fresh cilantro

Preparation time: 15 minutes
Smoking time: 45 minutes
Temperature: 350°F
Portions: 6
Recommended pellets: Mesquite

Instructions
1. Supply your smoker with wood pellets and follow the manufacturer's specific start-up procedure. Preheat, with the lid closed, to 350°F.
2. In a large bowl, combine the cooked chicken, 2 cups of cheese, the sour cream, and green chiles to make the filling.
3. Pour one can of enchilada sauce in the bottom of a 9-by-13-inch baking dish or aluminum pan.
4. Spoon ⅓ cup of the filling on each tortilla and roll up securely.
5. Transfer the tortillas seam-side down to the baking dish, then pour the remaining can of enchilada sauce over them, coating all exposed surfaces of the tortillas.
6. Sprinkle the remaining 1 cup of cheese over the enchiladas and cover tightly with aluminum foil.
7. Bake on the grill, with the lid closed, for 30 minutes, then remove the foil.
8. Continue baking with the lid closed for 15 minutes, or until bubbly.
9. Garnish the enchiladas with the chopped scallions and cilantro and serve immediately.

Secret tip: Red enchilada sauce is made with red chiles and tomato. Some people prefer a green enchilada sauce, made from green chiles and tomatillos. If you're hunting for heat, you'll want to go green, and if you like it extra-spicy, add jalapeños to the blend.

MINI TURDUCKEN ROULADE

Turducken is a Cajun specialty. Sure, you could start with a 30-pound turkey and de-bone all the birds, or you can make things much easier by using boneless breasts like I do here. This makes for an easy mini roulade, a French word meaning a dish cooked in the form of a roll with a soft filling. If you still think it's too much trouble, call your butcher. You can occasionally find a raw turducken roast at the grocery store, where all the work has been done for you, or you can order one online.

Ingredients
1 (16-ounce) boneless turkey breast
1 (8-to 10-ounce) boneless duck breast
1 (8-ounce) boneless, skinless chicken breast
Salt

Freshly ground black pepper
2 cups Italian dressing
2 tablespoons Cajun seasoning
1 cup prepared seasoned stuffing mix
8 slices bacon
Butcher's string

Preparation time: 20 minutes
Smoking time: 2 hours
Temperature: 275°F
Portions: 6
Recommended pellets: Oak, Cherry
Recommended sides: Sweet potato fries, Watermelon berry bowl

Instructions
1. Butterfly the turkey, duck, and chicken breasts, cover with plastic wrap and, using a mallet, flatten each ½ inch thick.
2. Season all the meat on both sides with a little salt and pepper.
3. In a medium bowl, combine the Italian dressing and Cajun seasoning. Spread one-fourth of the mixture on top of the flattened turkey breast.
4. Place the duck breast on top of the turkey, spread it with one-fourth of the dressing mixture, and top with the stuffing mix.
5. Place the chicken breast on top of the duck and spread with one-fourth of the dressing mixture.
6. Supply your smoker with wood pellets and follow the manufacturer's specific start-up procedure. Preheat, with the lid closed, to 275°F.
7. Tightly roll up the stack, tie with butcher's string, and slather the whole thing with the remaining dressing mixture.
8. Wrap the bacon slices around the turducken and secure with toothpicks, or try making a bacon weave (see the technique for this in the Jalapeño-Bacon Pork Tenderloin recipe).
9. Place the turducken roulade in a roasting pan. Transfer to the grill, close the lid, and roast for 2 hours, or until a meat thermometer inserted in the turducken reads 165°F. Tent with aluminum foil in the last 30 minutes, if necessary, to keep from overbrowning.
10. Let the turducken rest for 15 to 20 minutes before carving. Serve warm.

SMOKE-ROASTED CHICKEN THIGHS

Chicken thighs are an easy win on the grill for several reasons. They are fatty and delicious, super affordable, and almost impossible to overcook and dry out. Many pit masters keep the seasoning simple by using their favorite salad dressing as a marinade.

Ingredients
3 pounds chicken thighs
2 teaspoons salt
2 teaspoons freshly ground black pepper
2 teaspoons garlic powder
2 teaspoons onion powder
2 cups prepared Italian dressing

Preparation time: 5 minutes + 1 hour to marinate

Smoking time: 1 to 2 hours
Temperature: 250°F
Portions: 12 to 15

Recommended pellets: Pecan, Oak
Recommended sides: Roasted potatoes

Instructions
1. Place the chicken thighs in a shallow dish and sprinkle with the salt, pepper, garlic powder, and onion powder, being sure to get under the skin.
2. Cover with the Italian dressing, coating all sides, and refrigerate for 1 hour.
3. Supply your smoker with wood pellets and follow the manufacturer's specific start-up procedure. Preheat, with the lid closed, to 250°F.
4. Remove the chicken thighs from the marinade and place directly on the grill, skin-side down. Discard the marinade.
5. Close the lid and roast the chicken for 1 hour 30 minutes to 2 hours, or until a meat thermometer inserted in the thickest part of the thighs reads 165°F. Do not turn the thighs during the smoking process.

Secret tip: Competition barbecue pit masters obsess over chicken thigh preparation. They take great effort to remove and trim the underside of the skin. It's a meticulous process of surgically shaving with a razor blade and delicately scraping. Then they replace the skin and, to smoke, they divide the chicken pieces among the cups of a muffin pan to ensure that they're uniformly shaped with bite-through consistency. You won't need to go through that much trouble to impress your guests, but do take some extra time to trim off excess fat and allow for a bit of seasoning to get under the skin.

SAVORY-SWEET TURKEY LEGS

When it comes to fair food, the turkey leg is king of food-on-a-stick. I've learned that, sadly, almost all fair, festival, and commercial turkey legs come from food purveyors precooked and frozen. The good news is you can find them fresh in smaller quantities at the mega-superstores. Turkey legs are really inexpensive, and nothing beats preparing them low-and-slow on a wood pellet grill smoker. The tough meat and tendons really benefit from the long cook.

Ingredients
1 gallon hot water
1 cup curing salt (such as Morton Tender Quick)
¼ cup packed light brown sugar
1 teaspoon freshly ground black pepper
1 teaspoon ground cloves
1 bay leaf
2 teaspoons liquid smoke
4 turkey legs
Mandarin Glaze, for serving

Preparation time: 15 minutes + overnight brining

Smoking time: 4 to 5 hours
Temperature: 225°F
Portions: 4
Recommended pellets: Apple
Recommended sides: Grill roasted vegetables with pine nut pesto

Instructions
1. In a large container with a lid, stir together the water, curing salt, brown sugar, pepper, cloves, bay leaf, and liquid smoke until the salt and sugar are dissolved; let come to room temperature.
2. Submerge the turkey legs in the seasoned brine, cover, and refrigerate overnight.
3. When ready to smoke, remove the turkey legs from the brine and rinse them; discard the brine.

4. Supply your smoker with wood pellets and follow the manufacturer's specific start-up procedure. Preheat, with the lid closed, to 225°F.
5. Arrange the turkey legs on the grill, close the lid, and smoke for 4 to 5 hours, or until dark brown and a meat thermometer inserted in the thickest part of the meat reads 165°F.
6. Serve with Mandarin Glaze on the side or drizzled over the turkey legs.

Secret tip: Curing salt often used on meats to add texture, flavor, and color (a hot dog wouldn't be that lovely pink color without similar cures). Use it instead of table salt in this brine to give the turkey a succulent, ham-like texture.

JAMAICAN JERK CHICKEN QUARTERS

Jamaican Jerk cuisine has a couple of standard traits. Your recipe needs Scotch bonnet peppers to give it a spice kick, and you have to grill over pimento wood. Unfortunately, both Scotch bonnets and pimento wood are hard to find in the United States. Habanero peppers are close enough (found in the paste) and we sneak in the pimento wood flavor via dried pimento berries, also known as allspice. Add a handful to the mesquite pellets in the bottom of your hopper (or in a smoker tube). The fantastic aroma is a combination of spices like cloves, cinnamon, nutmeg, and ginger, thus its name—allspice.

Ingredients
4 chicken leg quarters, scored
¼ cup canola oil
½ cup Jamaican Jerk Paste
1 tablespoon whole allspice (pimento) berries

Preparation time: 15 minutes
Smoking time: 1 to 2 hours
Temperature: 275°F
Portions: 4
Recommended pellets: Mesquite
Recommended sides: Roasted okra

Instructions
1. Supply your smoker with wood pellets and follow the manufacturer's specific start-up procedure. Preheat, with the lid closed, to 275°F.
2. Brush the chicken with canola oil, then brush 6 tablespoons of the Jerk paste on and under the skin. Reserve the remaining 2 tablespoons of paste for basting.
3. Throw the whole allspice berries in with the wood pellets for added smoke flavor.
4. Arrange the chicken on the grill, close the lid, and smoke for 1 hour to 1 hour 30 minutes, or until a meat thermometer inserted in the thickest part of the thigh reads 165°F.
5. Let the meat rest for 5 minutes and baste with the reserved jerk paste prior to serving.

SMO-FRIED CHICKEN

I use only five herbs and spices to get get fried chicken with a Traeger, but with the addition of smoke, even the Colonel would deem this finger-lickin' good! You'll need your grill's higher temperature to produce the crunchy "fried" skin. The flavor and crunch end up better on the grill, and your kitchen will remain cool and clean in the process.

Ingredients
1 egg, beaten

½ cup milk
1 cup all-purpose flour
2 tablespoons salt
1 tablespoon freshly ground black pepper
2 teaspoons freshly ground white pepper
2 teaspoons cayenne pepper
2 teaspoons garlic powder
2 teaspoons onion powder
1 teaspoon smoked paprika
8 tablespoons (1 stick) unsalted butter, melted
1 whole chicken, cut up into pieces

Preparation time: 30 minutes
Smoking time: 55 minutes
Temperature: 375°F, 325°F
Portions: 4 to 6
Recommended pellets: Pecan, Alder
Recommended sides: Biscuits, cornbread

Instructions
1. Supply your smoker with wood pellets and follow the manufacturer's specific start-up procedure. Preheat, with the lid closed, to 375°F.
2. In a medium bowl, combine the beaten egg with the milk and set aside.
3. In a separate medium bowl, stir together the flour, salt, black pepper, white pepper, cayenne, garlic powder, onion powder, and smoked paprika.
4. Line the bottom and sides of a high-sided metal baking pan with aluminum foil to ease cleanup.
5. Pour the melted butter into the prepared pan.
6. Dip the chicken pieces one at a time in the egg mixture, and then coat well with the seasoned flour. Transfer to the baking pan.
7. Smoke the chicken in the pan of butter ("smo-fry") on the grill, with the lid closed, for 25 minutes, then reduce the heat to 325°F and turn the chicken pieces over.
8. Continue smoking with the lid closed for about 30 minutes, or until a meat thermometer inserted in the thickest part of each chicken piece reads 165°F.
9. Serve immediately.

Secret tip: Whole chickens are often cheaper than individual parts, especially when you're buying organic. Save a few bucks by learning how to quickly break the bird down yourself.

APPLEWOOD-SMOKED WHOLE TURKEY

Turkey has never been easier to cook than on a wood pellet grill. Just remember to rub a bit of the poultry seasoning under the skin and into the muscle. Seasoning will not penetrate thick turkey skin from the outside in.

Ingredients
1 (10- to 12-pound) turkey, giblets removed
Extra-virgin olive oil, for rubbing
¼ cup poultry seasoning
8 tablespoons (1 stick) unsalted butter, melted
½ cup apple juice
2 teaspoons dried sage
2 teaspoons dried thyme

Preparation time: 10 minutes
Smoking time: 5 to 6 hours
Temperature: 250°F
Portions: 6 to 8
Recommended pellets: Apple, Apple mash blend
Recommended sides: Roasted smashed potatoes, green bean casserole

Instructions
1. Supply your smoker with wood pellets and follow the manufacturer's specific start-up procedure. Preheat, with the lid closed, to 250°F.
2. Rub the turkey with oil and season with the poultry seasoning inside and out, getting under the skin.
3. In a bowl, combine the melted butter, apple juice, sage, and thyme to use for basting.

4. Put the turkey in a roasting pan, place on the grill, close the lid, and grill for 5 to 6 hours, basting every hour, until the skin is brown and crispy, or until a meat thermometer inserted in the thickest part of the thigh reads 165°F.
5. Let the bird rest for 15 to 20 minutes before carving.

Secret tip: Salt is a preservative, so the shelf life of salted butter is longer than unsalted; however, I don't recommend using them interchangeably. I use unsalted butter in most recipes to control the amount of salt being added. If you use salted butter, make sure you taste as you go. It does make a difference.

SMOKED AIRLINE CHICKEN

You may not have heard, but the airline chicken is going extinct. No, it's not a breed of bird; it's a now rarely seen cut of chicken. Sometimes called "Statler chicken," "hotel cut," or a "frenched breast," it is a skin-on, boneless chicken breast with the first segment of the wing, or drumette, still attached. It's a relic of the days when many flights offered "fancy" hot meals. You never find this cut in the grocery store, so you'll need to trim your own from a whole bird or have a butcher do it for you. I prefer white meat over dark, so this combines my favorite parts of the chicken. Plus, the pellet smoke adds incredible flavor that the airlines could never achieve.

Ingredients
2 boneless chicken breasts with drumettes attached
½ cup soy sauce
½ cup teriyaki sauce
¼ cup canola oil
¼ cup white vinegar
1 tablespoon minced garlic
¼ cup chopped scallions
2 teaspoons freshly ground black pepper
1 teaspoon ground mustard

Preparation time: 20 minutes + 4 hours to marinate

Smoking time: 1 to 2 hours
Temperature: 250°F
Portions: 4
Recommended pellets: Pecan, Oak
Recommended sides: Potatoes vegetable hash, Brussels Sprout Bites with Cilantro-Balsamic Drizzle

Instructions
1. Place the chicken in a baking dish.
2. In a bowl, whisk together the soy sauce, teriyaki sauce, canola oil, vinegar, garlic, scallions, pepper and ground mustard, then pour this marinade over the chicken, coating both sides.
3. Refrigerate the chicken in marinade for 4 hours, turning over every hour.
4. When ready to smoke the chicken, supply your smoker with wood pellets and follow the manufacturer's specific start-up procedure. Preheat, with the lid closed, to 250°F.
5. Remove the chicken from the marinade but do not rinse. Discard the marinade.
6. Arrange the chicken directly on the grill, close the lid, and smoke for 1 hour 30 minutes to 2 hours, or until a meat thermometer inserted in the thickest part of the meat reads 165°F.
7. Let the meat rest for 3 minutes before serving.

TRADITIONAL BBQ CHICKEN

A simple moist chicken breast with smoke flavor is something wood pellet grills do very well. I recommend taking it low and slow to allow the white meat to absorb as much smoke as possible. However, if you are in a hurry, you can boost the cook temperature to 350°F and cut the cook time down to 30 minutes. Note: I suggest using a sweet wood pellet flavor in this recipe to complement the barbecue sauce.

Ingredients
8 boneless, skinless chicken breasts
2 teaspoons salt
2 teaspoons freshly ground black pepper
2 teaspoons garlic powder
2 cups The Ultimate BBQ Sauce or your preferred barbecue sauce, divided

Preparation time: 10 minutes
Smoking time: 1 to 2 hours
Temperature: 225°F
Portions: 8
Recommended pellets: Maple, Cherry
Recommended sides: Mexican Street Corn with Chipotle Butter

Instructions
1. Supply your smoker with wood pellets and follow the manufacturer's specific start-up procedure. Preheat, with the lid closed, to 250°F.
2. Place the chicken breasts in a large pan and sprinkle both sides with the salt, pepper, and garlic powder, being sure to rub under the skin.
3. Place the roasting pan on the grill, close the lid, and smoke for 1 hour 30 minutes to 2 hours, or until a meat thermometer inserted in the thickest part of each breast reads 165°F. During the last 15 minutes of cooking, cover the chicken with 1 cup of barbecue sauce.
4. Serve the chicken warm with the remaining 1 cup of barbecue sauce.

WILD WEST WINGS

Wood pellet smokers are a secret weapon for preparing wings on the grill. On typical grills, fatty drippings inevitably cause massive flareups and grease fires. Not so with pellet power. The indirect heat and large drip pan protect against flareups. Salt, pepper, and smoke alone are enough to make wings delicious, but if you like to experiment, try this zesty ranch rub instead. For a double dose of ranch, you can serve these wings with ranch dressing as a dipping sauce.

Ingredients
2 pounds chicken wings
2 tablespoons extra-virgin olive oil
2 packages ranch dressing mix (such as Hidden Valley brand)
¼ cup prepared ranch dressing (optional)

Preparation time: 10 minutes
Smoking time: 1 hour
Temperature: 350°F
Portions: 4
Recommended pellets: Oak
Recommended sides: Bacon-Wrapped Jalapeño Poppers

Instructions
1. Supply your smoker with wood pellets and follow the manufacturer's specific start-up procedure. Preheat, with the lid closed, to 350°F.
2. Place the chicken wings in a large bowl and toss with the olive oil and ranch dressing mix.
3. Arrange the wings directly on the grill, or line the grill with aluminum foil for easy cleanup, close the lid, and smoke for 25 minutes.
4. Flip and smoke for 20 to 35 minutes more, or until a meat thermometer inserted in the thickest part of the wings reads 165°F and the wings are crispy. (Note: The wings will likely be done after 45 minutes, but an extra 10 to 15 minutes makes them crispy without drying the meat.)
5. Serve warm with ranch dressing (if using).

BUTTERED THANKSGIVING TURKEY

Injecting turkey with butter instead of the usual tea gives a moistness and flavor to your turkey, something you can't get in an oven.

Ingredients
1 whole turkey (make sure the turkey is not pre-brined)
2 batches Garlic Butter Injectable
3 tablespoons olive oil
1 batch Chicken Rub
2 tablespoons butter

Preparation time: 25 minutes
Smoking time: 5 to 6 hours
Temperature: 180°F and 375°F
Portions: 12 to 14
Recommended pellets: Hickory
Recommended sides: Brussel sprouts and speck gratin

Instructions
1. Supply your smoker with wood pellets and follow the manufacturer's specific start-up procedure. Preheat the grill, with the lid closed, to 180°F.
2. Inject the turkey throughout with the garlic butter injectable. Coat the turkey with olive oil and season it with the rub. Using your hands, work the rub into the meat and skin.
3. Place the turkey directly on the grill grate and smoke for 3 or 4 hours (for an 8- to 12-pound turkey, cook for 3 hours; for a turkey over 12 pounds, cook for 4 hours), basting it with butter every hour.
4. Increase the grill's temperature to 375°F and continue to cook until the turkey's internal temperature reaches 170°F.
5. Remove the turkey from the grill and let it rest for 10 minutes, before carving and serving.

Secret tip: Save these leftovers! Smoked buttered turkey makes the best sandwiches.

SPATCHCOCKED TURKEY

Spatchcocked turkey—turkey split in half and laid flat by removing its backbone—is an easy way to cut your cooking time and get crispier skin.

Ingredients
1 whole turkey
2 tablespoons olive oil
1 batch Chicken Rub

Preparation time: 25 minutes
Smoking time: 2 hours
Temperature: 350°F
Portions: 10 to 14
Recommended pellets: Apple
Recommended sides: Sweet potato and chive damper

Instructions
1. Supply your smoker with wood pellets and follow the manufacturer's specific start-up procedure. Preheat the grill, with the lid closed, to 350°F.
2. To remove the turkey's backbone, place the turkey on a work surface, on its breast. Using kitchen shears, cut along one side of the turkey's backbone and then the other. Pull out the bone.
3. Once the backbone is removed, turn the turkey breast-side up and flatten it.
4. Coat the turkey with olive oil and season it on both sides with the rub. Using your hands, work the rub into the meat and skin.
5. Place the turkey directly on the grill grate, breast-side up, and cook until its internal temperature reaches 170°F.
6. Remove the turkey from the grill and let it rest for 10 minutes, before carving and serving.

Secret tip: For crispier skin, wait until your turkey reaches an internal temperature of 160°F, then turn up your grill's temperature to 450°F and cook until the turkey's internal temperature reaches 170°F.

SMOKED TURKEY BREAST

Turkey breasts are so good for when you want turkey but don't want a full 10-plus-pound bird. As I mentioned earlier, turkey has always been one of my favorite things to grill. To get my turkey fix, I'll often smoke a turkey breast for the family. Typically, one breast is enough for all of us and doesn't make it past night one.

Ingredients
1 (3-pound) turkey breast
Salt
Freshly ground black pepper
1 teaspoon garlic powder

Preparation time: 15 minutes
Smoking time: 1 to 2 hours
Temperature: 180°F and 350°F
Portions: 2 to 4
Recommended pellets: Mesquite Blend
Recommended sides: Roasted vegetables, collard greens, garlic mashed potatoes

Instructions
1. Supply your smoker with wood pellets and follow the manufacturer's specific start-up procedure. Preheat the grill, with the lid closed, to 180°F.

2. Season the turkey breast all over with salt, pepper, and garlic powder.
3. Place the breast directly on the grill grate and smoke for 1 hour.
4. Increase the grill's temperature to 350°F and continue to cook until the turkey's internal temperature reaches 170°F. Remove the breast from the grill and serve immediately.

Secret tip: If you haven't already done so, get yourself a big spatula. The big spatula is my go-to for managing large cuts of poultry, including full birds.

CORNISH GAME HEN

Cornish game hens have become my favorite food for impressing guests. First, the game hen sounds way more exotic than it is (it's really just a chicken). Second, these birds are readily available at most supermarkets. Finally, each plate is a feast for the eyes because everyone gets their own bird! Plus, there's no fighting over drumsticks.

Ingredients
4 Cornish game hens
Extra-virgin olive oil, for rubbing
2 teaspoons salt
1 teaspoon freshly ground black pepper
1 teaspoon celery seeds

Preparation time: 10 minutes
Smoking time: 2 to 3 hours
Temperature: 225°F
Portions: 4
Recommended pellets: Apple, Bourbon Brown Sugar Blend
Recommended sides: Roasted carrots, sweet potatoes, and onions

Instructions
1. Supply your smoker with wood pellets and follow the manufacturer's specific start-up procedure. Preheat, with the lid closed, to 275°F.
2. Rub the game hens over and under the skin with olive oil and season all over with the salt, pepper, and celery seeds.
3. Place the birds directly on the grill grate, close the lid, and smoke for 2 to 3 hours, or until a meat thermometer inserted in each bird reads 170°F.
4. Serve the Cornish game hens hot.

SMOKED TURKEY WINGS

Smoked turkey wings are the flavorful big brother to chicken wings. One of the upsides to turkey wings is that they pack all the turkey flavor of the rest of the bird. Though you could cover turkey wings with sauce, you rarely see it done because they are so naturally flavorful. Smoke turkey wings on your pellet grill or smoker for a great turkey snack, or add your favorite potatoes to make a full meal.

Ingredients
4 turkey wings
1 batch Sweet and Spicy Cinnamon Rub

Preparation time: 15 minutes

Smoking time: 1 hour
Temperature: 180°F and 325°F
Portions: 2
Recommended pellets: Hickory
Recommended sides: Corn casserole

Instructions
1. Supply your smoker with wood pellets and follow the manufacturer's specific start-up procedure. Preheat the grill, with the lid closed, to 180°F.
2. Using your hands, work the rub into the turkey wings, coating them completely.
3. Place the wings directly on the grill grate and cook for 30 minutes.
4. Increase the grill's temperature to 325°F and continue to cook until the turkey's internal temperature reaches 170°F. Remove the wings from the grill and serve immediately.

Secret tip: If you absolutely need a sauce for these wings, serve it on the side. The meat stands on its own, so give it a chance before smothering it in your favorite sweet or spicy sauce.

LAMB AND GAME

There's more to barbecue than just ribs, chicken, burgers, and brisket. Wood pellet grills make low and slow so easy, it's understandable that you may want to stick with what you know. But because your grill can also maintain 425°F just as easily as a steady 180°F, your options are almost endless. If you're a hunter, here is where you can pick up a few ideas for how to infuse smoke into pheasant, venison, and quail. If you're not a hunter but want to purchase wild or farmed game, just check with your nearest wild game processor or taxidermist. They often offer fresh or frozen meats for sale in-store, or they will happily point you to the nearest market. If you want to branch out to other mainstream regional specialties, check out the leg of lamb, kielbasa, and gyro recipes later in this chapter. Read on!

SMOKED PHEASANT

A feast of pheasant has long been considered a delicacy, not only in America but also worldwide. In fact, pheasant hunting is popular in just about every part of the United States, but it is especially popular in the Great Plains. Like me, pheasants are officially omnivores (but they eat a lot more seeds and bugs than I do). Wild pheasants are typically smaller than farm-raised birds. They cook quicker, so adjust the grill time accordingly.

Ingredients
1 gallon hot water
1 cup salt
1 cup packed brown sugar
2 (2- to 3-pound) whole pheasants, cleaned and plucked
¼ cup extra-virgin olive oil
2 tablespoons onion powder
2 tablespoons freshly ground black pepper

2 tablespoons cayenne pepper
1 tablespoon minced garlic
2 teaspoons smoked paprika
1 cup molasses

Preparation time: 25 minutes + overnight brining

Smoking time: 3 to 4 hours
Temperature: 250°F
Portions: 4 to 6
Recommended pellets: Hickory, Apple, Cherry
Recommended sides: Potluck Salad with Smoked Cornbread

Instructions
1. In a large container with a lid, combine the hot water, salt, and brown sugar, stirring to dissolve the salt and sugar. Let cool to room temperature, then submerge the pheasants in the brine, cover, and refrigerate for 8 to 12 hours.
2. Remove the pheasants from the brine, then rinse them and pat dry. Discard the brine.
3. Supply your smoker with wood pellets and follow the manufacturer's specific start-up procedure. Preheat, with the lid closed, to 250°F.
4. In a small bowl, combine the olive oil, black pepper, cayenne pepper, onion powder, garlic, and paprika to form a paste.
5. Rub the pheasants with the paste and place breast-side up on the grill grate. Close the lid and smoke for 1 hour.
6. Open the smoker and baste the pheasants with some of the molasses. Close the lid and continue smoking for 2 to 3 hours, basting with the molasses every 30 minutes, until a meat thermometer inserted into the thigh reads 160°F.
7. Remove the pheasants from the grill and let rest for 20 minutes before serving warm or cold.

SUCCULENT LAMB CHOPS

Lamb chops are underrated by barbecue fans. The fatty, bone-in succulence is perfect for the licking flames of a high-heat grill. It's preferable for lamb to be on the medium-rare side; to achieve that with your pellet smoker, start your grill out low and slow, and wait until the end of your cook to give the chops a high-temperature "reverse" sear. You can use pricier rib lamb chops for this recipe, but I prefer little loin chops. They are a bit meatier, with the same great flavor, and you get extra points because they look like tiny T-bone steaks.

Ingredients
½ cup rice wine vinegar
1 teaspoon liquid smoke
2 tablespoons extra-virgin olive oil
2 tablespoons dried minced onion
1 tablespoon chopped fresh mint
8 (4-ounce) lamb chops
½ cup hot pepper jelly
1 tablespoon Sriracha
1 teaspoon salt
1 teaspoon freshly ground black pepper

Preparation time: 15 minutes + 2 hours to marinate

Smoking time: 10 to 20 minutes
Temperature: 165°F, 450°F
Portions: 4 to 6
Recommended pellets: Cherry

Recommended sides: Roasted smashed potatoes

Instructions
1. In a small bowl, whisk together the rice wine vinegar, liquid smoke, olive oil, minced onion, and mint. Place the lamb chops in an aluminum roasting pan. Pour the marinade over the meat, turning to coat thoroughly. Cover with plastic wrap and marinate in the refrigerator for 2 hours.
2. Supply your smoker with wood pellets and follow the manufacturer's specific start-up procedure. Preheat, with the lid closed, to 165°F, or the "Smoke" setting.
3. On the stove top, in a small saucepan over low heat, combine the hot pepper jelly and Sriracha and keep warm.
4. When ready to cook the chops, remove them from the marinade and pat dry. Discard the marinade.
5. Season the chops with the salt and pepper, then place them directly on the grill grate, close the lid, and smoke for 5 minutes to "breathe" some smoke into them.
6. Remove the chops from the grill. Increase the pellet cooker temperature to 450°F, or the "High" setting. Once the grill is up to temperature, place the chops on the grill and sear, cooking for 2 minutes per side to achieve medium-rare chops. A meat thermometer inserted in the thickest part of the meat should read 145°F. Continue grilling, if necessary, to your desired doneness.
7. Serve the chops with the warm Sriracha pepper jelly on the side.

Secret tip: Shop for grass-fed lamb for the best flavor, and balance the fatty richness by experimenting with acids such as vinegar and lemon juice in your marinade.

SMOKED CHRISTMAS CROWN ROAST OF LAMB

I like to imagine that the crown roast comes from one rack of ribs. In reality, that double-length dachshund lamb would look a little freaky. You'll need to purchase two bone-in racks of lamb and have your butcher trim and french them, then tie them into a crown. Frenching is the process of removing the meat between each bone using a small knife, so that 1½ inch of bone is exposed at the end.

Ingredients
2 racks of lamb, trimmed, frenched, and tied into a crown
1¼ cups extra-virgin olive oil, divided
2 tablespoons chopped fresh basil
2 tablespoons chopped fresh rosemary
2 tablespoons ground sage
2 tablespoons ground thyme
8 garlic cloves, minced
2 teaspoons salt
2 teaspoons freshly ground black pepper

Preparation time: 1 hour
Smoking time: 1 to 2 hours
Temperature: 275°F
Portions: 4
Recommended pellets: Apple, Oak, Cherry
Recommended sides: Roasted vegetables, garlic mashed potatoes

Instructions
1. Set the lamb out on the counter to take the chill off, about an hour.
2. In a small bowl, combine 1 cup of olive oil, the basil, rosemary, sage, thyme, garlic, salt, and pepper.
3. Baste the entire crown with the herbed olive oil and wrap the exposed frenched bones in aluminum foil.
4. Supply your smoker with wood pellets and follow the manufacturer's specific start-up procedure. Preheat, with the lid closed, to 275°F.

5. Put the lamb directly on the grill, close the lid, and smoke for 1 hour 30 minutes to 2 hours, or until a meat thermometer inserted in the thickest part reads 140°F.
6. Remove the lamb from the heat, tent with foil, and let rest for about 15 minutes before serving. The temperature will rise about 5°F during the rest period, for a finished temperature of 145°F.

Secret tip: The "guard of honor" style is another super regal way to present your lamb. Tie the two racks side to side, with the bones arching inward and crossing like the rifles of an honor guard. And yes, people will laugh if you cap the bones with little white paper booties.

SPATCHCOCKED QUAIL WITH SMOKED FRUIT

It's the same technique for quail as it is for turkey and chicken, but you are simply removing the spine of a smaller bird. If you need help with this, you can ask your butcher to do it for you. Smoking the spatchcocked quail under a foil-wrapped brick flattens it and promotes more even cooking.

Ingredients
4 quail, spatchcocked
2 teaspoons salt
2 teaspoons freshly ground black pepper
2 teaspoons garlic powder
4 ripe peaches or pears
4 tablespoons (½ stick) salted butter, softened
1 tablespoon sugar
1 teaspoon ground cinnamon

Preparation time: 20 minutes
Smoking time: 1 hour

Temperature: 225°F
Portions: 4
Recommended pellets: Hickory
Recommended sides: Brussels Sprout Bites with Cilantro-Balsamic Drizzle.

Instructions
1. Supply your smoker with wood pellets and follow the manufacturer's specific start-up procedure. Preheat, with the lid closed, to 225°F.
2. Season the quail all over with the salt, pepper, and garlic powder.
3. Cut the peaches (or pears) in half and remove the pits (or the cores).
4. In a small bowl, combine the butter, sugar, and cinnamon; set aside.
5. Arrange the quail on the grill grate, close the lid, and smoke for about 1 hour, or until a meat thermometer inserted in the thickest part reads 145°F.
6. After the quail has been cooking for about 15 minutes, add the peaches (or pears) to the grill, flesh-side down, and smoke for 30 to 40 minutes.
7. Top the cooked peaches (or pears) with the cinnamon butter and serve alongside the quail.

YUMMY GYRO

Ingredients
1 pound ground lamb

2 teaspoons salt
1 teaspoon freshly ground black pepper
2 tablespoons chopped fresh oregano
1 tablespoon minced garlic
1 tablespoon onion powder
4 to 6 pocketless pitas
Tzatziki sauce, for serving
1 tomato, chopped, for serving
1 small onion, thinly sliced, for serving

Preparation time: 20 minutes + overnight to marinate

Smoking time: 40 minutes
Temperature: 300°F, 450°F

Portions: 4
Recommended pellets: Apple, Cherry
Recommended sides: Sweet potato chips, Greek salad

Instructions
1. In a medium bowl, combine the lamb, salt, pepper, oregano, garlic, and onion powder; mix well. Cover with plastic wrap and refrigerate overnight.
2. Supply your smoker with wood pellets and follow the manufacturer's specific start-up procedure. Preheat, with the lid closed, to 300°F.
3. Remove the meat mixture from the refrigerator and, on a Frogmat or a piece of heavy-duty aluminum foil, roll and shape it into a rectangular loaf about 8 inches long by 5 inches wide.
4. Place the loaf directly on the grill, close the lid, and smoke for 35 minutes, or until a meat thermometer inserted in the center reads 155°F.
5. Remove the loaf from the heat and increase the temperature to 450°F.
6. Cut the loaf into ⅛-inch slices and place on a Frogmat or a piece of heavy-duty foil.
7. Return the meat (still on the Frogmat or foil) to the smoker, close the lid, and continue cooking for 2 to 4 minutes, or until the edges are crispy.
8. Warm the pitas in the smoker for a few minutes and serve with the lamb, tzatziki sauce, chopped tomato, and sliced onion.

VENISON STEAKS

Game meat is almost always leaner than the meat of farm-raised hogs or cows that are usually bred for tenderness and fat marbling. So be aware that overcooking can really toughen venison. Online markets, such as Dartagnan.com, have sprung up with plenty of venison options, and you can likely also find sources from wild game meat processors used by local hunters.

Ingredients
4 (8-ounce) venison steaks
2 tablespoons extra-virgin olive oil
4 garlic cloves, minced
1 tablespoon ground sage
2 teaspoons sea salt
2 teaspoons freshly ground black pepper

Preparation time: 20 minutes
Smoking time: 1 hour 20 minutes

Temperature: 225°F
Portions: 4
Recommended pellets: Hickory, Cherry
Recommended sides: Sweet Potato Chips

Instructions
1. Supply your smoker with wood pellets and follow the manufacturer's specific start-up procedure. Preheat, with the lid closed, to 225°F.
2. Rub the venison steaks well with the olive oil and season with the garlic, sage, salt, and pepper.
3. Arrange the venison steaks directly on the grill grate, close the lid, and smoke for 1 hour and 20 minutes, or until a meat thermometer inserted in the center reads 130°F to 140°F, depending on desired doneness. If you want a better sear, remove the steaks from the grill at an internal temperature of 125°F, crank up the heat to 450°F, or the "High" setting, and cook the steaks on each side for an additional 2 to 3 minutes.

GREEK LEG OF LAMB

Barbecue is regional across the United States. Even Kentucky has its foot in the ring. Leg of mutton is that foot. Long ago, Kentucky was the top lamb producer in the country, and that legacy lives on—mutton is still a traditional barbecue dish there, served with a savory black sauce. Over the years, mutton has lost out in popularity to lamb (which is the same animal, just under one year of age). The recipe here outlines the more traditional leg of lamb cooking method, but if you crave a variation, it can also be slow-smoked Kentucky mutton style (to a fall-apart internal temp of 205°F), like Pulled Pork Shoulder.

Ingredients
2 tablespoons finely chopped fresh rosemary
1 tablespoon ground thyme
5 garlic cloves, minced
2 tablespoons sea salt
1 tablespoon freshly ground black pepper
Butcher's string
1 whole boneless (6- to 8-pound) leg of lamb
¼ cup extra-virgin olive oil
1 cup red wine vinegar
½ cup canola oil

Preparation time: 15 minutes + 4 hours to marinate

Smoking time: 20 to 25 minutes per pound

Temperature: 325°F
Portions: 12 to 16
Recommended pellets: Oak
Recommended sides: Greek salad, Caprese Salad with Cold-Smoked Mozzarella

Instructions
1. In a small bowl, combine the rosemary, thyme, garlic, salt, and pepper; set aside.
2. Using butcher's string, tie the leg of lamb into the shape of a roast. Your butcher should also be happy to truss the leg for you.
3. Rub the lamb generously with the olive oil and season with the spice mixture. Transfer to a plate, cover with plastic wrap, and refrigerate for 4 hours.
4. Remove the lamb from the refrigerator but do not rinse.
5. Supply your smoker with wood pellets and follow the manufacturer's specific start-up procedure. Preheat, with the lid closed, to 325°F.

6. In a small bowl, combine the red wine vinegar and canola oil for basting.
7. Place the lamb directly on the grill, close the lid, and smoke for 20 to 25 minutes per pound (depending on desired doneness), basting with the oil and vinegar mixture every 30 minutes. Lamb is generally served medium-rare to medium, so it will be done when a meat thermometer inserted in the thickest part reads 140°F to 145°F.
8. Let the lamb rest for about 15 minutes before slicing to serve.

ROSEMARY-SMOKED LAMB CHOPS

Lamb chops take on the flavor of the herbs and spices that surround them. I had no idea how true this was until I smoked my lamb chops on a bed of rosemary for the first time, and this has quickly become my favorite way of preparing lamb.

Ingredients
4½ pounds bone-in lamb chops
2 tablespoons olive oil
Salt
Freshly ground black pepper
1 bunch fresh rosemary

Preparation time: 15 minutes
Smoking time: 2 hours, 5 minutes
Temperature: 180°F and 450°F
Portions: 4
Recommended pellets: Mesquite
Recommended sides: Brussels Sprout Bites with Cilantro-Balsamic Drizzle.

Instructions
1. Supply your smoker with wood pellets and follow the manufacturer's specific start-up procedure. Preheat the grill, with the lid closed, to 180°F.
2. Rub the lamb chops all over with olive oil and season on both sides with salt and pepper.
3. Spread the rosemary directly on the grill grate, creating a surface area large enough for all the chops to rest on. Place the chops on the rosemary and smoke until they reach an internal temperature of 135°F.
4. Increase the grill's temperature to 450°F, remove the rosemary, and continue to cook the chops until their internal temperature reaches 145°F.
5. Remove the chops from the grill and let them rest for 5 minutes before serving.

Secret tip: Reverse-sear your lamb chops over a direct flame or in a cast-iron skillet rather than just increasing the grill's temperature. This gives the chops a quicker sear.

SMOKED RACK OF LAMB

If you want to add wood-fired taste to your lamb, there is no way around it—you need to smoke it low and slow. Slowly smoking your rack of lamb packs it full of hardwood smoke flavor and brings out all the flavors of the meat.

Ingredients
1 (2-pound) rack of lamb
1 batch Rosemary-Garlic Lamb Seasoning

Preparation time: 25 minutes
Smoking time: 4 to 6 hours
Temperature: 225°F
Portions: 6
Recommended pellets: Hickory
Recommended sides: Rosemary and garlic roasted potatoes

Instructions
1. Supply your smoker with wood pellets and follow the manufacturer's specific start-up procedure. Preheat the grill, with the lid closed, to 225°F.
2. Using a boning knife, score the bottom fat portion of the rib meat.

3. Using your hands, rub the rack of lamb all over with the seasoning, making sure it penetrates into the scored fat.
4. Place the rack directly on the grill grate, fat-side up, and smoke until its internal temperature reaches 145°F.
5. Remove the rack from the grill and let it rest for 20 to 30 minutes, before slicing it into individual ribs to serve.

Secret tip: Sear your ribs for 1 or 2 minutes over an open flame or in cast iron before pulling them from the grill.

BURGERS

SMOKED BURGERS

If you haven't smoked burgers before, why not try it? Just like everything else, smoking burgers gives them that wood-fired flavor they don't get from other cooking methods. The beauty of smoking the burgers on your pellet grill or smoker is that it won't take any additional effort. Add a bun and your favorite toppings for an easy, flavorful burger that will put the local dive bar to shame.

Ingredients
1 pound ground beef
1 egg
Wood-Fired Burger Seasoning

Preparation time: 15 minutes
Smoking time: 45 minutes
Temperature: 180°F and 400°F
Portions: 4
Recommended pellets: Competition Blend
Recommended sides: Bun, salad, tomatoes, The Ultimate BBQ Sauce, and fries (or Smoke Roasted Potatoes)

Instructions
1. Supply your Traeger with wood pellets and follow the start-up procedure. Preheat the grill, with the lid closed, to 180°F.
2. In a medium bowl, thoroughly mix together the ground beef and egg. Divide the meat into 4 portions and shape each into a patty. Season the patties with the burger shake.
3. Place the burgers directly on the grill grate and smoke for 30 minutes.
4. Increase the grill's temperature to 400°F and continue to cook the burgers until their internal temperature reaches 145°F. Remove the burgers from the grill and serve as you like.

Secret tip: To add even more flavor to your burgers, dice ½ package of pellet-grilled bacon (try Apple-Smoked Bacon) and mix it into the ground beef with the egg.

RANCH BURGERS

Ingredients
1 lb ground beef (preferably 80% lean 20% fat ground chuck)

1/2 yellow onion, chopped
1 package ranch dressing mix (1 oz)
1 cup cheddar cheese, shredded
1 egg, beaten
4 buns, toasted (optional)
3/4 cup bread crumbs
3/4 cup mayonnaise
1/4 cup relish
1/4 cup ketchup
2 tbsp Worcestershire sauce

Preparation time: 10 minutes
Smoking time: 30 minutes
Temperature: 180°F and 400°F
Portions: 4
Recommended pellets: Hickory, Oak, Mesquite
Recommended sides: Fries, beans, salad, potato salad, corn, mashed potatoes, potato chips

Instructions
1. Mix ground beef, cheese, ranch dressing mix, egg, bread crumbs, and onion in a bowl until evenly combined.
2. Form burger mixture into 1/4 pound circular patties.
3. Preheat pellet grill to 350°F.
4. Lightly oil grill grate and place burger patties on the grill.
5. Cook burgers until they reach an internal temperature of 155°F (typically cooks for about 6 minutes per side).
6. Remove burgers once done and let rest at room temperature for 15 minutes.
7. Combine sauce ingredients in a bowl and whisk well.
8. Place burger patties on buns and top with desired toppings, including homemade sauce.

Secret tip: For burgers made with store bought ground beef, you should make sure your meat is cooked to an internal temperature of 160°F. If you don't have a probe thermometer, cook until at least lightly pink in center.

CHILE CHEESEBURGERS

Ingredients
1 lb ground chuck (80% lean, 20% fat)
4 Monterey Jack cheese slices
1/4 cup yellow onion, finely chopped
4 hamburger buns
2 tbsp hatch chiles, peeled and chopped
6 tbsp hatch chile salsa
•1 tsp kosher salt
Mayonnaise, to taste
1 tsp ground black pepper

Preparation time: 15 minutes
Smoking time: 30 minutes
Temperature: 350°F
Portions: 4
Recommended pellets: Hickory, Oak, Mesquite
Recommended sides: Bun, salad, tomatoes, The Ultimate BBQ Sauce, and fries (or Smoke Roasted Potatoes). Sliced onions, guacamole, tomatoes, and mushrooms.

Instructions
1. In a bowl, combine beef, diced onion, chopped hatch chiles, salt, and fresh ground pepper. Once evenly mixed, shape into 4 burger patties
2. Preheat pellet grill to 350°F3. Place burgers on grill, and cook for about 6 minutes per side or until both sides of each burger are slightly crispy
4. After burger is cooked to desired doneness and both sides have light sear, place cheese slices on each burger. Allow to heat for around 45 seconds or until cheese melts
5. Remove from grill and allow to rest for about 10 minutes6. Spread a little bit of mayonnaise on both sides of each bun. Place burger patty on bottom side of the bun, then top with hatch chile salsa on top to taste

Secret tip: Toast buns in the oven beforehand for about 30-45 seconds on high heat, buttering the open ends if desired.

BISON BURGERS

Did you know buffalo and bison are actually two different animals? It's true. Early American explorers mistakenly referred to bison as buffalo because the animals resembled Old World buffalo, but they are really a separate species. Here in the States, what you may have heard called buffalo meat is really the meat of a bison. Bison burgers offer a leaner, healthier alternative to ground beef burgers.

Ingredients
2 pounds ground bison
2 tablespoons steak seasoning
4 tablespoons (½ stick) unsalted butter, cut into pieces
1 large onion, finely minced
6 slices Swiss cheese
6 ciabatta buns, split
Sweet and Spicy Jalapeño Relish, for serving
Lettuce and sliced tomatoes, for serving

Preparation time: 30 minutes
Smoking time: 17 to 19 minutes
Temperature: 425°F
Portions: 6
Recommended pellets: Mesquite

Instructions
1. Supply your smoker with wood pellets and follow the manufacturer's specific start-up procedure. Preheat, with the lid closed, to 425°F.
2. In a large bowl, combine the ground bison and steak seasoning until well blended.
3. Shape the meat mixture into 6 patties and make a thumb indentation in the center of each. Set aside.
4. Place a rimmed baking sheet on the grill and add the butter and onion. Sauté for 5 minutes, or until the onion is translucent. Top with the bison burger patties, indention-side down.
5. Close the lid and smoke for 6 to 7 minutes, then flip the burgers and smother them in the sautéed onion. Close the lid again and continue smoking for 6 to 7 minutes. During the last few minutes of cooking, top each burger with a slice of Swiss cheese. For safe consumption, the internal temperature should reach between 140°F (medium) and 160°F (well-done).
6. Lightly toast the ciabatta buns, split-side down, on one side of the smoker.
7. Serve the onion-smothered cheeseburgers on the toasted buns with jalapeño relish, lettuce, and tomato—or whatever toppings you like.

Secret tip: For a kicked-up game burger, try adding Smoked Goose Bacon on top!

FRENCH ONION BURGERS

French onion soup has a lot of the savory flavors I want in a burger. You could top a shoe with that hot, stringy cheese, and I'd want to pick off every last bit. I know it looks like there is a lot involved in this recipe for a simple burger, but I promise you won't be disappointed.

Ingredients
1 pound lean ground beef
1 tablespoon minced garlic
1 teaspoon Better Than Bouillon Beef Base
1 teaspoon dried chives
1 teaspoon freshly ground black pepper
8 slices Gruyère cheese, divided
½ cup soy sauce
1 tablespoon extra-virgin olive oil
1 teaspoon liquid smoke
3 medium onions, cut into thick slices (do not separate the rings)
1 loaf French bread, cut into 8 slices
4 slices provolone cheese

Preparation time: 35 minutes
Smoking time: 20 to 25 minutes
Temperature: 425°F
Portions: 4
Recommended pellets: Oak
Recommended sides: Bun, salad, tomatoes, and fries (or Smoke Roasted Potatoes)

Instructions
1. In a large bowl, mix together the ground beef, minced garlic, beef base, chives, and pepper until well blended
2. Divide the meat mixture and shape into 8 thin burger patties
3. Top each of 4 patties with one slice of Gruyère, then top with the remaining 4 patties to create 4 stuffed burgers
4. Supply your smoker with wood pellets and follow the manufacturer's specific start-up procedure. Preheat, with the lid closed, to 425°F5. Arrange the burgers directly on one side of the grill, close the lid, and smoke for 10 minutes. Flip and smoke with the lid closed for 10 to 15 minutes more, or until a meat thermometer inserted in the burgers reads 160°F. Add another Gruyère slice to the burgers during the last 5 minutes of smoking to melt.
6. Meanwhile, in a small bowl, combine the soy sauce, olive oil, and liquid smoke
7. Arrange the onion slices on the grill and baste on both sides with the soy sauce mixture. Smoke with the lid closed for 20 minutes, flipping halfway through
8. Lightly toast the French bread slices on the grill. Layer each of 4 slices with a burger patty, a slice of provolone cheese, and some of the smoked onions. Top each with another slice of toasted French bread. Serve immediately

Secret tip: Don't buy more than 80 percent lean ground beef to make hamburgers. An 80/20 lean-to-fat ratio makes for the tastiest burgers.

PORK FENNEL BURGER

For this burger, you need fat. Pork shoulder is almost imperative for the correct balance of lean and fat. You need strong spices; as a starting point, you cannot beat fennel seeds and black pepper. And you need adequate salt, an essential in any good burger.

Ingredients
1 fennel bulb, trimmed and cut into large chunks
3 to 4 garlic cloves
2 ½ pounds boneless pork shoulder, with some of the fat, cut into 1-inch cubes
1 tablespoon fennel seeds
1 teaspoon caraway seeds (optional)
1 teaspoon salt
½ teaspoon pepper, or more to taste
Peeled orange slices to garnish (optional)
Chopped olives to garnish (optional)
Chopped parsley to garnish (optional)
Chopped roasted red pepper to garnish (optional)
Fennel slices, to garnish (optional)

Preparation time: 10 minutes
Smoking time: 30 minutes
Temperature: 180°F and 400°F
Portions: 4
Recommended pellets: Competition Blend
Recommended sides: Bun, salad, tomatoes, The Ultimate BBQ Sauce, and fries (or Smoke Roasted Potatoes)

Instructions
1. Put fennel and garlic into a food processor and pulse until just chopped; remove to a large bowl. Put pork fat in processor and grind until just chopped; add to bowl. Working in batches, process meat with fennel seeds, caraway, if using and salt and pepper, until meat is just chopped (be careful not to over-process). Add to bowl and mix well. Shape mixture into 8 patties.
2. Supply your smoker with wood pellets and follow the manufacturer's specific start-up procedure. Preheat, with the lid closed, to 425°F3. Arrange the burgers directly on one side of the grill, close the lid, and smoke for 10 minutes. Flip and smoke with the lid closed for 10 to 15 minutes more, or until a meat thermometer inserted in the burgers reads 160°F. Add another Gruyère slice to the burgers during the last 5 minutes of smoking to melt.
4. Garnish with peeled orange slices, chopped olives, chopped parsley, chopped roasted red pepper and fennel slices, to taste.

Secret tip: Variations, of course, are not just possible but advisable. Chopped fresh fennel or chopped onion are spectacular additions. When it is cooked over high heat, whether on a grill or in a pan or broiler, until just done, the result is consistently juicy, super flavorful and sublimely tender. And it browns, developing a dark, crisp crust like no beef burger I've ever had.

PORK AND PORTOBELLO BURGERS

This is a new-age version of a veggie burger (as in half and half, not a burger made from vegetables and grain), which you might also think of as a stuffed mushroom. It's terrific, hearty, unusual and really cool: a portobello filled with sausage meat and grilled.

Ingredients
1 pound ground pork
1 tablespoon minced garlic
1 teaspoon minced fresh rosemary, fennel seed or parsley
Salt and ground black pepper
4 large portobello mushroom caps, stems removed
Olive oil
4 burger buns
Any burger fixings you like

Preparation time: 10 minutes
Smoking time: 30 minutes
Temperature: 180°F and 400°F
Portions: 4
Recommended pellets: Competition Blend
Recommended sides: Bun, salad, tomatoes, The Ultimate BBQ Sauce, and fries (or Smoke Roasted Potatoes)

Instructions
1. Combine the ground pork, garlic, rosemary and a sprinkle of salt and pepper. Use a spoon to lightly scrape away the gills of the mushrooms and hollow them slightly. Drizzle the mushrooms (inside and out) with olive oil and sprinkle with salt and pepper. Press 1/4 of the mixture into each of the hollow sides of the mushrooms; you want the meat to spread all the way across the width of the mushrooms. They should look like burgers.
2. Grill the burgers, meat side down, until the pork is well browned, 4 to 6 minutes. Flip and cook until the top side of the mushrooms are browned and the mushrooms are tender, another 6 to 8 minutes. If you like, use an instant-read thermometer to check the interior temperature of the pork, which should be a minimum of 145 degrees.
3. Serve the burgers on buns (toasted, if you like) with any fixings you like.

Secret tip: Try it with ground lamb also.

SAUSAGES

SMOKED BRATS

In the United States, brats have become a football tailgate staple. But bratwurst is actually an old German name. Derived from brät, which is finely chopped meat, and wurst, which means sausage, brats are almost like fine cheese in that there are so many different varieties. The main thing to keep in mind is that the inside of a fresh brat is raw, unlike a hot dog that is always precooked. You'll want to use an instant-read meat thermometer to confirm that you're hitting an internal temperature of 160°F.

Ingredients
4 (12-ounce) cans of beer
2 onions, sliced into rings
2 green bell peppers, sliced into rings
2 tablespoons unsalted butter, plus more for the rolls
2 tablespoons red pepper flakes
10 brats, uncooked
10 hoagie rolls, split
Mustard, for serving

Preparation time: 10 minutes
Smoking time: 1 to 2 hours
Temperature: 225°F
Portions: 12 to 15
Recommended pellets: Oak, Pecan

Instructions
1. On your kitchen stove top, in a large saucepan over high heat, bring the beer, onions, peppers, butter, and red pepper flakes to a boil.
2. Supply your smoker with wood pellets and follow the manufacturer's specific start-up procedure. Preheat, with the lid closed, to 225°F.
3. Place a disposable pan on one side of grill, and pour the warmed beer mixture into it, creating a "brat tub" (see Tip below).
4. Place the brats on the other side of the grill, directly on the grate, and close the lid and smoke for 1 hour, turning 2 or 3 times.
5. Add the brats to the pan with the onions and peppers, cover tightly with aluminum foil, and continue smoking with the lid closed for 30 minutes to 1 hour, or until a meat thermometer inserted in the brats reads 160°F.
6. Butter the cut sides of the hoagie rolls and toast cut-side down on the grill.
7. Using a slotted spoon, remove the brats, onions, and peppers from the cooking liquid and discard the liquid.
8. Serve the brats on the toasted buns, topped with the onions and peppers and mustard (ketchup optional).

Secret tip: When grilling brats for a crowd, have a "brat tub" on the grill to act as a holding tank once your sausages are cooked. This will allow you to keep the pellet grill running without burning your brats, and the sliced onions and green bell peppers can also be used as toppings.

TRAEGER SMOKED SAUSAGE

Pork to fork wood-fired goodness. Ground pork, onion, garlic and ground mustard pair perfectly for this homemade mesquite smoked sausage. You'll never go back to store-bought.

Ingredients
3 Pound ground pork
1/2 Tablespoon ground mustard
1 Tablespoon onion powder
1 Tablespoon garlic powder
1 Teaspoon pink curing salt
1 Tablespoon salt
4 Teaspoon black pepper
1/2 Cup ice water
Hog casings, soaked and rinsed in cold water

Preparation time: 30 minutes
Smoking time: 3 hours
Temperature: 225°F and 155°F
Portions: 4 to 6
Recommended pellets: Apple
Recommended sides: Garlic mashed potatoes, twice smoked potatoes

Instructions
1. In a medium bowl, combine the meat and seasonings, mix well.
2. Add ice water to meat and mix with hands working quickly until everything is incorporated.
3. Place mixture in a sausage stuffer and follow manufacturer's instructions for operating. Use caution not to overstuff or the casing might burst.
4. Once all the meat is stuffed, determine your desired link length and pinch and twist a couple of times or tie it off. Repeat for each link.
5. When ready to cook, set Traeger temperature to 225°F and preheat, lid closed for 15 minutes. For optimal flavor, use Super Smoke if available.
6. Place links directly on the grill grate and cook for 1 to 2 hours or until the internal temperature registers 155°F. Let sausage rest a few minutes before slicing. Enjoy!

SMOKED SAUSAGE & POTATOES

Serve this high-protein dish for breakfast, or dish it out for a side at the next potluck.

Ingredients
2 Pound Hot Sausage Links
2 Pound Potatoes, fingerling
1 Tablespoon fresh thyme
4 Tablespoon butter

Preparation time: 15 minutes
Smoking time: 50 minutes
Temperature: 375°F and 275°F
Portions: 4 to 6
Recommended pellets: Hickory, Apple

Instructions
1. When ready to cook, set the Traeger to 375°F and preheat, lid closed for 15 minutes.

2. Put your sausage links on the grill to get some color. This should take about 3 minutes on each side.
3. While sausage is cooking, cut the potatoes into bite size pieces all about the same size so they cook evenly. Chop the thyme and butter, then combine all the ingredients into a Traeger cast iron skillet.
4. Pull your sausage off the grill, slice into bite size pieces and add to your cast iron.
5. Turn grill down to 275°F and put the cast iron in the grill for 45 minutes to an hour or until the potatoes are fully cooked.
6. After 45 minutes, use a butter knife to test your potatoes by cutting into one to see if its done. To speed up cook time you can cover cast iron will a lid or foil. Serve. Enjoy!

GRILLED BACON DOG

Come hungry for this one. Bacon-wrapped hot dogs are grilled and covered with onions, tomatoes, jalapenos, lettuce, BBQ sauce and doused with a creamy cheese sauce.

Ingredients
16 Hot Dogs
16 Slices Bacon, sliced
2 Onion, sliced
16 hot dog buns
As Needed The Ultimate BBQ Sauce
As Needed Cheese

Preparation time: 20 minutes
Smoking time: 25 minutes
Temperature: 375°F
Portions: 4 to 6
Recommended pellets: Hickory, Oak, Mesquite

Instructions
1. When ready to cook, set the Traeger to 375°F and preheat, lid closed for 15 minutes.
2. Wrap bacon strips around the hot dogs, and grill directly on the grill grate for 10 minutes each side. Grill onions at the same time as the hot dogs, and cook for 10 -15 minutes.
3. Open hot dog buns and spread BBQ sauce, the grilled hot dogs, cheese sauce and grilled onions. Top with vegetables. Serve, enjoy!

SAUSAGE PEPPER SKEWERS

Gather your mates & fire up these Australian skewers to watch the Rio Olympic games.

Ingredients
12 Ounce andouille sausage, cut into 2 inch slices
1/2 Whole red onion, sliced
1 Whole Green Bell Pepper, Sliced
1 Whole Yellow Bell Pepper, sliced
To Taste olive oil
To Taste Cajun Shake
1/2 Cup Minced Tomatoes
1/2 Tablespoon Minced Chipotle in Adobo Sauce
1/4 Teaspoon cracked black pepper
1 Teaspoon honey

1/4 Teaspoon ancho chile powder
1/4 Teaspoon garlic powder
1/4 Teaspoon onion powder
1/4 Teaspoon Kosher Sea Salt

Preparation time: 15 minutes
Smoking time: 10 minutes
Temperature: 350°F
Portions: 6 to 8
Recommended pellets: Hickory

Instructions
1. If using wooden skewers, soak skewers in water for about 30 minutes prior to cooking.
2. Start the Traeger on High heat, lid closed, for 10 to 15 minutes.
3. Cut pepper, onion and sausage into chunks. Thread skewer alternating between meat and vegetables.
4. Drizzle each of the skewers with olive oil and season on all sides with the Traeger Cajun Rub.
5. Put skewers directly on grill grate and cook for about 5 minutes. Flip skewers over and cook for an additional 5 minutes.
6. Spicy Ketchup Dipping: Mix together sauce ingredients and transfer to a small serving bowl.
7. Pull skewers off grill and serve with spicy dipping sauce. Enjoy!

POLISH KIELBASA

Making sausage from scratch can be a lot of fun. If you're making links, as you will be with this kielbasa, you'll need to make a decision about the proper casing. Your choice is between natural or synthetic. I recommend natural casings, which come from the intestines of hogs or other animals and are known to give sausage a telltale snap with every bite. Medium casings are 32 to 35mm (1¼ to 1⅓ inches), and large casings are 35 to 44mm (1⅓ to 1¾ inches). Medium casings are a good choice for this recipe.

Ingredients
4 pounds ground pork
½ cup water
2 garlic cloves, minced
4 teaspoons salt
1 teaspoon freshly ground black pepper
1 teaspoon dried marjoram
½ teaspoon ground allspice
14 feet natural hog casings, medium size

Preparation time: 1 hour + overnight to refrigerate

Smoking time: 1 to 2 hours
Temperature: 225°F
Portions: 8
Recommended pellets: Pecan, Oak, Hickory
Recommended sides: Twice smoked potatoes, smoked cabbage

Instructions
1. In a large bowl, combine the pork, water, garlic, salt, pepper, marjoram, and allspice.
2. Stuff the casings according to the instructions on your sausage stuffing device, or use a funnel (see Tip).
3. Twist the casings according to your desired length and prick each with a pin in several places so the kielbasa won't burst.
4. Transfer the kielbasa to a plate, cover with plastic wrap, and refrigerate for at least 8 hours or overnight.

5. Remove from the refrigerator and allow the links to come to room temperature.
6. Supply your smoker with wood pellets and follow the manufacturer's specific start-up procedure. Preheat, with the lid closed, to 225°F.
7. Place the kielbasa directly on the grill grate, close the lid, and smoke for 1 hour 30 minutes to 2 hours, or until a meat thermometer inserted in each link reads 155°F. (The internal temperature will rise about 5°F when resting, for a finished temp of 160°F.)
8. Serve with buns and condiments of your choosing, or cut up the kielbasa and serve with smoked cabbage

Secret tip: Stuffing sausage casings is made easier by enlisting the help of a mechanical sausage stuffer. KitchenAid even makes a grinding and stuffing attachment for their famous stand mixers. Run water through the casing to rinse and then slip the open end over the tip of the stuffer or funnel. Push the casing up over the tip, leaving only two inches remaining, and tie off the end. Using your stuffing device or your fingers, push the ground sausage slowly into the casing, being careful not to overfill and break the casing.

RUBS, SEASONINGS, INJECTABLES, AND SAUCES

Seasoning and flavoring your meat correctly is one of the most critical steps to becoming a pit master. From selecting the proper shake to knowing how much to use, the seasoning process is important.

Rubs, injectables, marinades, and mops—each has a specific purpose and should be used accordingly. Though all of these have very different flavor characteristics, some have moisture and texture specifics that only work correctly with the proper recipe. Don't worry—we set you up here with a solid repertoire of recipes and the marketplace is ever growing with new products to try.

Never feel that you need to heavily coat your meat with spices and rubs. Remember, all our tastes are different, and sometimes BBQ spices can be a little on the salty side. With any of the following recipes, never feel bound to use the entire rub, especially on a smaller cut. Save it for next time instead.

PORK RUB

A quality pork rub is a dry rub that can be used for just about everything. Pork rubs tend to rely on both herby and salty undertones to create a perfect sidekick for many meats. Pork rubs—and in particular this rub—go great with pork, but also with poultry and even beef.

Ingredients
1/2 cup smoked paprika
1/3 cup dried thyme
1/4 cup salt
1/4 cup garlic powder
2 tablespoons black pepper
2 tablespoons chili powder
2 tablespoons onion powder
2 tablespoons chipotle chili pepper
1 tablespoon oregano
1 tablespoon crushed celery seeds

Time 5 minutes
Portions: 1/4 cup (enough to coat 2 or 3 pounds)

Instructions
1. In a small airtight container or zip-top bag, combine the thyme, paprika, salt, garlic powder, onion powder, chili powder, oregano, black pepper, chipotle pepper, and celery seed.
2. Close the container and shake to mix. Unused rub will keep in an airtight container for months.

Secret tip: Use a handheld electric mixer to ensure your spices are mixed well.

CHICKEN RUB

If you are going to own a pellet grill, you need a good chicken rub. Chicken rub is perfect for all varieties of poultry and pork.

Ingredients
2 tablespoons packed light brown sugar
1½ teaspoons coarse kosher salt
1¼ teaspoons garlic powder

½ teaspoon onion powder
½ teaspoon freshly ground black pepper
½ teaspoon ground chipotle chile pepper
½ teaspoon smoked paprika
¼ teaspoon dried oregano leaves
¼ teaspoon mustard powder
¼ teaspoon cayenne pepper

Time 5 minutes
Portions: 1/4 cup (enough to coat 4 or 5 pounds)

Instructions
1. In a small airtight container or zip-top bag, combine the brown sugar, salt, garlic powder, onion powder, black pepper, chipotle pepper, paprika, oregano, mustard, and cayenne.
2. Close the container and shake to mix. Unused rub will keep in an airtight container for months.

Secret tip: Any of the spice rubs in this chapter can be made in large batches and stored in an airtight container for months. To make up a large batch, simply double, triple, quadruple—or more.

DILL SEAFOOD RUB

Sour and citrusy flavors go extremely well with seafood and fish. With these flavors in mind, dill is a perfect addition to the seafood flavor profile.

Ingredients
2 tablespoons coarse kosher salt
2 tablespoons dried dill weed
1 tablespoon garlic powder
1½ teaspoons lemon pepper

Time 5 minutes
Portions: 5 tablespoons (enough to coat 2 or 3 pounds)

Instructions
1. In a small airtight container or zip-top bag, combine the salt, dill, garlic powder, and lemon pepper.
2. Close the container and shake to mix. Unused rub will keep in an airtight container for months.

Secret tip: Dill seafood rub is not just for seafood. Use it on chicken for an unusual yet satisfying flavor.

CAJUN RUB

Chicken, fish, pork, beef—all of it can be spiced to perfection with a good Cajun rub. In barbecuing throughout the years, I've found Cajun flavor never goes out of style on my spice rack and I am constantly searching for the best Cajun seasonings out there. Though this isn't a Louisiana-born recipe, it's the next best thing and you'll have no trouble rolling it out for next year's Mardi Gras party.

Ingredients
1 teaspoon freshly ground black pepper

1 teaspoon onion powder
1 teaspoon coarse kosher salt
1 teaspoon garlic powder
1 teaspoon sweet paprika
½ teaspoon cayenne pepper
½ teaspoon red pepper flakes
½ teaspoon dried oregano leaves
½ teaspoon dried thyme
½ teaspoon smoked paprika

Time 5 minutes
Portions: 3 tablespoons (enough to coat 4 to 6 pounds)

Instructions
1. In a small airtight container or zip-top bag, combine the black pepper, onion powder, salt, garlic powder, sweet paprika, cayenne, red pepper flakes, oregano, thyme, and smoked paprika.
2. Close the container and shake to mix. Unused rub will keep in an airtight container for months.

Secret tip: Use Cajun rub as a way to spice up everything from popcorn to tomato soup.

ESPRESSO BRISKET RUB

The perfect beef rub is the perfect brisket rub. This rub not only gives you the best flavor, but also the best bark. Adding the ground espresso adds flavor as well as a dark color that you won't get with other rubs.

Ingredients
3 tablespoons coarse kosher salt
2 tablespoons ground espresso coffee
2 tablespoons freshly ground black pepper
1 tablespoon garlic powder
1 tablespoon light brown sugar
1½ teaspoons dried minced onion
1 teaspoon ground cumin

Time 5 minutes
Portions: 1/2 cup (enough to coat 4 to 6 pounds)

Instructions
1. In a small airtight container or zip-top bag, combine the salt, espresso, black pepper, garlic powder, brown sugar, minced onion, and cumin.
2. Close the container and shake to mix. Unused rub will keep in an airtight container for months.

Secret tip: Use brisket rub for all beef cuts. It's great on steaks and roasts, as well.

SWEET BROWN SUGAR RUB

A sweet rub is perfect for your poultry and pork cuts. Sweet rubs work to bring a sweet flavor while highlighting the salty flavor of the meat. Sweet rubs are awesome with ribs, especially pork ribs.

Ingredients

2 tablespoons light brown sugar
1 teaspoon coarse kosher salt
1 teaspoon garlic powder
1 teaspoon onion powder
1 teaspoon sweet paprika
½ teaspoon freshly ground black pepper
½ teaspoon cayenne pepper
½ teaspoon dried oregano leaves
¼ teaspoon smoked paprika

Time 5 minutes
Portions: 1/4 cup (enough to coat 3 to 5 pounds)

Instructions
1. In a small airtight container or zip-top bag, combine the brown sugar, salt, garlic powder, onion powder, sweet paprika, black pepper, cayenne, oregano, and smoked paprika.
2. Close the container and shake to mix. Unused rub will keep in an airtight container for months.

Secret tip: Use this sweet rub on dark-meat chicken. The sweet flavor complements the salty, fatty dark meat well.

ALL-PURPOSE DRY RUB

Here is a rub that provides a fast, flavorful coating for barbecue: beef, pork, chicken, lamb, venison. The recipe is forgiving. You might add granulated onion or garlic powder to it, or omit the coriander if you don't have any. Be careful with the paprika, as there are so many different varieties afoot: if it's smoked, you'll need less, and if it's fiery you may need less cayenne. No cayenne? Use red pepper flakes. Adjust the seasonings to your taste, then apply liberally.

Ingredients
½ cup paprika, or 1/3 cup smoked paprika
¼ cup kosher salt
¼ cup freshly ground black pepper
¼ cup brown sugar
¼ cup chile powder
3 tablespoons ground cumin
2 tablespoons ground coriander
1 tablespoon cayenne pepper, or to taste

Time 5 minutes
Portions: 2 and ½ cups (enough to coat 8 to 10 pounds, depending on the meat)

Instructions
Combine all ingredients in a bowl and mix well with a fork to break up the sugar and combine the spices. Mixture will keep in an airtight container, out of the light, for a few months.

Secret tip: Not only is this rub delicious on steaks, I've also used it as the seasoning for roasted nuts. Melt some unsalted butter, stir in some of your favorite nuts (I use any combination of pecans, almonds, macadamia, and cashews), then add enough of the rub to evenly coat all the nuts. Bake a single layer at about 250 for 30-45 minutes, stirring occasionally. Sprinkle a bit of kosher salt over them when they come out and let cool.

ALL-PURPOSE CALIFORNIA BEEF RUB

A good rub makes grilling or roasting easy. This one combines the best of the salt-pepper-garlic notes of Santa Maria-style barbecue with the depth of coffee and clove. Diners will be hard-pressed to place its complex flavor until you tell them the components.

Ingredients
2 tablespoons finely ground coffee
1 ½ tablespoons kosher salt
1 ½ tablespoons granulated garlic
1 heaping teaspoon black pepper
1 tablespoon brown sugar
¼ teaspoon cayenne pepper
¼ teaspoon ground cloves
¼ teaspoon cinnamon

Time 5 minutes
Portions: 1/3 cup (enough to coat 3 to 4 pounds)

Instructions
Combine all ingredients in a bowl and mix well with a fork to break up the sugar and combine the spices. Mixture will keep in an airtight container, out of the light, for a few months.

Secret tip: Coat your beef cuts in soy sauce prior to applying a rub. It works great with this recipe, first allowing the soy sauce to dry a little so it is nice and sticky. The salty soy seals in the juices, and this delicious rub gave it a great crust. Leave out the salt, should you decide to use the soy sauce.

SWEET AND SPICY CINNAMON RUB

Although a sweet rub is great, spice is about the only thing to make it better. This rub is so sweet and delicious that you can't stop eating it, but it's also so hot that you'll wish you could stop.

Ingredients
2 tablespoons light brown sugar
1 teaspoon coarse kosher salt
1 teaspoon garlic powder
1 teaspoon onion powder
1 teaspoon sweet paprika
½ teaspoon freshly ground black pepper
½ teaspoon cayenne pepper
½ teaspoon dried oregano leaves
½ teaspoon ground ginger
½ teaspoon ground cumin
¼ teaspoon smoked paprika
¼ teaspoon ground cinnamon
¼ teaspoon ground coriander
¼ teaspoon chili powder

Time 5 minutes
Portions: 1/4 cup (enough to coat 3 to 5 pounds)

Instructions

1. In a small airtight container or zip-top bag, combine the brown sugar, salt, garlic powder, onion powder, sweet paprika, black pepper, cayenne, oregano, ginger, cumin, smoked paprika, cinnamon, coriander, and chili powder.
2. Close the container and shake to mix. Unused rub will keep in an airtight container for months.

Secret tip: This sweet and spicy rub is the ticket for your next candied bacon. The flavor is beyond reproach, but the spice is there to put it over the top.

COFFEE-CHILE RUB

This easy-to-make seasoning mixture gives meat a spicy, slightly sweet flavor. Apply a thin coating before grilling beef, pork or lamb. Or use as a condiment to season the meat once you've carved and portioned it.

Ingredients
¼ cup finely ground dark-roast coffee
¼ cup ancho chile powder
¼ cup dark brown sugar, tightly packed
2 tablespoons smoked paprika
2 tablespoons kosher salt
1 tablespoon ground cumin

Time 5 minutes
Portions: 1 cup (enough to coat 4 to 6 steaks)

Instructions
1 In a small bowl, mix all the ingredients thoroughly, massaging the mixture with your fingers to break down the dark brown sugar into fine crystals.
2. Liberally sprinkle a thin layer of the rub onto the steak, then pat it in with your fingers so it adheres.

Secret tip: Consider adding, or substituting, unsweetened Dutch process Cocoa, coarse or fine-ground coriander, grains of paradise. These can all add to a hearty rub.

CUMIN SALT

This easy-to-make cumin-flavored salt is traditionally served with Moroccan roast lamb, but it's good on just about everything, even fried eggs. It tastes best freshly made, but will keep for about a month in a closed container.

Ingredients
1 teaspoon cumin seeds
¼ cup medium-coarse or flaky sea salt
Pinch red pepper flakes (optional)
Pinch cayenne or hot paprika (optional)

Time 5 minutes
Portions: 1/4 cup (enough to coat 3 to 5 pounds)

Instructions
1. Toast cumin seeds in a dry skillet over medium-high heat until fragrant and lightly colored, about 1 minute.
2. Grind very coarsely in a mortar or spice mill.
3. Combine in a bowl with salt and stir together.
4. Add red pepper flakes or cayenne, if using.

WOOD-FIRED BURGER SEASONING

The perfect burger is a delight. The pellet grill and smoker give you the edge when it comes to mastering the perfect burgers. Whether you sear or smoke the burgers, wood-fired flavor kills the competition. To gain that extra bit of flavor, sprinkle a little bit of this seasoning over your next flame-broiled burger.

Ingredients
1 teaspoon coarse kosher salt
1 teaspoon garlic powder
1 teaspoon dried minced onion
1 teaspoon onion powder
1 teaspoon freshly ground black pepper
½ teaspoon sweet paprika
¼ teaspoon mustard powder
¼ teaspoon celery seed

Time 5 minutes
Portions: 2 tablespoons (enough to coat 8 400-pounds burgers)

Instructions
1. In a small airtight container or zip-top bag, combine the salt, garlic powder, minced onion, onion powder, black pepper, sweet paprika, mustard powder, and celery seed.
2. Close the container and shake to mix. Unused burger shake will keep in an airtight container for months.

Secret tip: Use this hamburger seasoning on formed patties, not mixed into the meat. This will prevent the salt from drying out the hamburger meat.

JERK SEASONING

Ingredients
1 tablespoon allspice berries
¼ teaspoon nutmeg pieces (crack a whole nutmeg with a hammer)
1 teaspoon black peppercorns
2 teaspoons dried thyme
1 teaspoon cayenne, or to taste
1 tablespoon paprika
1 tablespoon sugar
1 tablespoon salt
2 teaspoons minced garlic
2 teaspoons minced ginger (or 2 teaspoons ground ginger)

Time 5 minutes
Portions: ¼ cup (enough for 2 to 3 pounds of meat)

Instructions
1 Put allspice, nutmeg, peppercorns and thyme in a spice or coffee grinder and grind to a fine powder.

2. Mix in remaining ingredients and use immediately. To use later, omit garlic and ginger and store in a tightly covered container; add garlic and ginger immediately before using.

Secret tip: Add scotch bonnet peppers for extra heat.

ROSEMARY-GARLIC LAMB SEASONING

Lamb loves an herby garlic flavor profile. I find that rosemary complements lamb well, adding a sweetness you don't get with other herbs. Whether you're cooking loin chops or a full leg of lamb, this seasoning is key for the perfect wood-fired lamb smoke.

Ingredients
2 teaspoons dried rosemary leaves
2 teaspoons coarse kosher salt
1 teaspoon garlic powder
1 teaspoon freshly ground black pepper
½ teaspoon onion powder
½ teaspoon dried minced onion

Time 5 minutes
Portions: 2 tablespoons (enough to coat 3 or 4 pounds)

Instructions
1. In a small airtight container or zip-top bag, combine the rosemary, salt, garlic powder, black pepper, onion powder, and minced onion.
2. Close the container and shake to mix. Unused seasoning will keep in an airtight container for months.

Secret tip: Lamb seasoning also goes great with beef or game. Any red meat takes well to the rosemary flavor.

TEA INJECTABLE

It's easy to inject your meats full of amazing, moist flavor. By using spices you have on hand, you can create a flavorful yet inexpensive injection option.

Ingredients
¼ cup favorite spice rub or shake
2 cups water

Time 30 minutes
Portions: 2 cups (enough to inject 10 to 14 pounds)

Instructions
1. Place the rub in a standard paper coffee filter and tie it up with kitchen string to seal.
2. In a small pot over high heat, bring the water to a boil.
3. Drop the filter into the boiling water and remove the pot from the heat. Let it steep for 30 minutes.
4. Remove and discard the filter. Discard any unused tea after injecting the meat.

Secret tip: To get more flavor from your spices, let the tea bag steep for a couple of hours, gently squeezing it every 10 minutes or so.

GARLIC BUTTER INJECTABLE

Sometimes we just need a little more butter in our lives to make us happy and cooking with butter makes your meats so much moister and tastier.

Ingredients
16 tablespoons (2 sticks) salted butter
2 tablespoons salt
1½ tablespoons garlic powder

Time 5 minutes
Portions: 2 cups (enough to inject up to 20 pounds)

Instructions
1. In a small skillet over medium heat, melt the butter.
2. Stir in the salt and garlic powder until well mixed. Use immediately.

Secret tip: Use this injectable quickly and clean up with hot water. Because butter solidifies so quickly, it can easily clog your injector.

COMPOUND BUTTER

A mixture of butter and other ingredients makes a compound butter, which can be used as a sauce on top of grilled meat, vegetables or fish. A classic variety is maître d'hotel butter, which uses thyme and lemon juice as flavoring agents.
But a cilantro-and-lime-juice compound butter is a marvelous thing to apply to fish, and you could even think of adding a tiny dice of jalapeño pepper to the mix. Lemon-basil is terrific as well — you could add some garlic to that and omit the shallots. Some cooks take maître d'hotel butter and add Roquefort cheese to it as a topping for steak. Compound butter is a theme on which to improvise. The following recipe provides the basic instructions.

Ingredients
8 tablespoons unsalted butter
1 tablespoon herb leaves, minced
1 small shallot, peeled and minced
2 teaspoons freshly squeezed lemon or lime juice
 Splash Champagne or white-wine vinegar

Preparation time 10 minutes + cooling

Portions: 1/2 cup

Instructions
1. Put the butter on a cutting board and, using a fork, cut the other ingredients into it until the butter is creamy and smooth. Scrape the butter together with a chef's knife, and form it into a rough log. If making ahead of time, roll it tightly in a sheet of plastic wrap and refrigerate or freeze until ready to use.

Secret tip: Blanch your fresh green herbs in boiling water for 30 sec, shock in ice-water and then carefully dry them before mincing and grinding them with butter. This step will help preserve the fresh vibrant green color and also set the flavors so your butter or sauces don't become a dull green grey or worse black from the action of enzymes due to browning from air.

LOBSTER BUTTER

This is an American take on the classic French recipe for beurre de homard, which incorporates cooked lobster meat into a compound butter. It is thriftier, using the shells to bring flavor instead of the lobster meat, but is no less delicious for that. The process is akin to making a lobster stock, with butter in place of water. Use the lobster butter as a melted dip for shrimp or yet more lobster.

Ingredients
Shells of cooked lobsters, crushed into small pieces
8 tablespoons (1 stick) unsalted butter per lobster

Preparation time 5 minutes + cooling

Cooking time: 40 minutes

Portions: 1/2 cup

Instructions
1. Heat grill to 300 degrees. Put lobster shells on the largest sheet pan you can fit in the oven, and allow them to dry and roast, about 15 to 20 minutes. Remove and set aside.
2. Meanwhile, melt 1 stick butter per lobster in a large bowl or double boiler set over simmering water, making sure bowl does not touch the surface of water. Add lobster shells to the melted butter and simmer gently, without boiling, for about 20 minutes.
3. Strain the melted butter through a cheesecloth-lined sieve into another bowl, then set that bowl into ice to chill. Cover bowl and refrigerate to set, then skim off the top and discard any liquids. Use within a few days, or freeze for up to a few weeks.

Secret tip: Not ready to make the butter? Put lobster shells (after you eat the lobster) bagged in the freezer until you need them.

QUICK AND EASY TERIYAKI MARINADE

Teriyaki is the key to turning meat into candy. It is the perfect sweet complement to pork and poultry. Use teriyaki as either a marinade or an injectable. As a marinade, it can take effect in as little as 30 minutes, so remember: Some marinade is better than no marinade.

Ingredients
¼ cup water
¼ cup soy sauce
¼ cup packed light brown sugar
¼ cup Worcestershire sauce
2 garlic cloves, sliced
Time 5 minutes
Portions: 1 cup (enough to marinate 4 to 6 pounds)

Instructions
1. In a small bowl, whisk the water, soy sauce, brown sugar, Worcestershire sauce, and garlic until combined. Refrigerate any unused marinade in an airtight container for 2 or 3 days.

Secret tip: Marinate your meats in a zip-top bag, not in a dish. A bag forms around your meat, allowing you to use less marinade.

ITALIAN MARINADE

I have used fresh herbs, though dried ones are more traditional, and have upped the flavor slightly with the use of lemon zest. Once you've got the marinade made, simply cut the meat — chicken or beef, lamb or pork — into 1- or 2-inch cubes, and submerge it in the liquid for a couple of days (10 to 12 hours for chicken), covered, in the refrigerator.

Ingredients
1 cup extra-virgin olive oil
¾ cup red wine vinegar
Zest of 1 lemon
¼ cup freshly squeezed lemon juice (about 2 lemons)
4 cloves garlic, peeled, smashed and roughly chopped
1 bay leaf
1 tablespoon thyme leaves
1 tablespoon oregano leaves
1 tablespoon basil leaves, rolled and chopped into chiffonade
1 teaspoon granulated sugar
1 teaspoon kosher salt
1 teaspoon freshly cracked black pepper
1 teaspoon red pepper flakes, or to taste

Time 5 minutes
Portions: 1 cup (enough to marinate 2 to 3 pounds)

Instructions
1. Whisk together all the ingredients in a large bowl. Refrigerate any unused marinade in an airtight container for 2 or 3 days.

Secret tip: It works extremely well on veggies, too. Use roasted eggplants, roasted pepper, and artichokes to get a whiff of Italy in you barbecue.

SPICY TOFU MARINADE

This is the perfect compliment to a vegetarian grill.

Ingredients
¼ cup soy sauce
1 tablespoon rice vinegar
1 teaspoon brown sugar
2 tablespoons mirin (sweet Japanese rice wine)
1 to 2 garlic cloves, to taste, minced or puréed
1 tablespoon minced or grated fresh ginger
1 teaspoon Asian chili paste or cayenne to taste
2 tablespoons dark sesame oil

Time 5 minutes
Portions: 1/2 cup (enough to marinate 1 pound of tofu)

Instructions
1. Whisk together all of the ingredients in a bowl. Use as a marinade and/or dipping sauce for pan-seared, grilled or plain tofu.

Secret tip: Advance preparation: This will keep for 3 or 4 days in the refrigerator

THANKSGIVING TURKEY BRINE

The perfect turkey is within your reach with the pellet grill. From smoking to roasting, you can do it all. To step up your turkey game, you need to brine the turkey, which just means soaking it in a liquid mixture so it absorbs the flavor.

Ingredients
2 gallons water
2 cups coarse kosher salt
2 cups packed light brown sugar

Time 5 minutes
Portions: 1 brine (enough for 1 16-pound turkey)

Instructions
1. In a clean 5-gallon bucket, stir together the water, salt, and brown sugar until the salt and sugar dissolve completely.

Secret tip: If you can, boil your brine before adding the turkey to ensure the salt and sugar are completely dissolved into the solution. This allows the mixture to actually penetrate the meat. The better dissolved, the more of the mixture will pass through the turkey. Just bring the brine to a boil over high heat, remove, and let cool. Use immediately.

LEMON BUTTER MOP FOR SEAFOOD

Whether you serve it with steamed clams or king crab, this lemon butter mixture will keep you eating seafood for days.

Ingredients
8 tablespoons (1 stick) butter
Juice of 1 small lemon
1 tablespoon fine salt
1½ teaspoons garlic powder
1½ teaspoons dried dill weed

Time 5 minutes
Portions: 1 and 1/2 cups (enough for 4 pounds)

Instructions
1. In a small skillet over medium heat, melt the butter.
2. Stir in the lemon juice, salt, garlic powder, and dill, stirring until well mixed. Use immediately.

Secret tip: This mixture can be used as a mop, for dipping, or even for cooking. It's an ideal mop for shrimp and crab.

WORCESTERSHIRE MOP AND SPRITZ

Mopping and spritzing your meats is essential to keeping them moist throughout a long cook. Cuts like brisket, pork shoulder, and the like don't stand a chance without some added moisture. Keep a good spritz or mop handy for those long smokes.

Ingredients
½ cup water
½ cup Worcestershire sauce
2 garlic cloves, sliced

Time 5 minutes
Portions: 1 cup (enough to spritz 3 to 4 pounds)

Instructions
1. In a small bowl, stir together the water, Worcestershire sauce, and garlic until mixed.
2. Transfer to a spray bottle for spritzing. Refrigerate any unused spritz for up to 3 days and use for all kinds of meats.

Secret tip: This spritz is great for beef, but works just as well for lamb and many game meats. Deer and elk both pair well with the Worcestershire flavor.

THE ULTIMATE BBQ SAUCE

This tangy sauce is the perfect blend of sweet, tart, and smoky, and works well with several of the recipes in this book.

Ingredients
1 small onion, finely chopped
2 garlic cloves, finely minced
2 cups ketchup
1 cup water
½ cup molasses
½ cup apple cider vinegar
5 tablespoons granulated sugar
5 tablespoons light brown sugar
1 tablespoon Worcestershire sauce
1 tablespoon freshly squeezed lemon juice
2 teaspoons liquid smoke
1½ teaspoons freshly ground black pepper
1 tablespoon yellow mustard

Preparation time: 5 minutes
Cooking time: 30 minutes
Portions: 3 cups

Instructions
1. On the stovetop, in a saucepan over medium heat, combine the onion, garlic, ketchup, water, molasses, apple cider vinegar, granulated sugar, brown sugar, Worcestershire sauce, lemon juice, liquid smoke, black pepper, and mustard. Bring to a boil, then reduce the heat to low and simmer for 30 minutes, straining out any bigger chunks, if desired.
2. Let the sauce cool completely, then transfer to an airtight container and refrigerate for up to 2 weeks, or use a canning process to store for longer.

EASTERN NORTH-CAROLINA BBQ SAUCE

Chris Schlesinger is the chef and an owner of the East Coast Grill in Cambridge, Mass., which he opened in 1985. He is also the author, with John Willoughby, of six cookbooks that relate somehow to the pleasures of fire. This is an adaptation of his recipe for barbecue sauce meant to be served with pulled pork.

Ingredients
½ cup white vinegar
½ cup cider vinegar
½ tablespoon sugar
½ tablespoon crushed red pepper flakes
½ tablespoon Tabasco sauce
Salt and freshly cracked black pepper to taste

Preparation time: 5 minutes
Portions: 1 cup

Instructions
1. Whisk ingredients together in a bowl. Drizzle on barbecued meat. Covered, sauce will keep about 2 months.

Secret tip: Great on chicken and collard greens.

WHITE BBQ SAUCE

White barbecue sauce is indigenous to northern Alabama. It melts into beautiful lacquer over the grill, bringing a tangy slickness to all that it touches. It's also quite good on bluefish.

Ingredients
1 ½ cups mayonnaise
⅓ cup plus 2 tablespoons apple-cider vinegar
2 tablespoons lemon juice
2 tablespoons prepared horseradish
1 teaspoon mustard powder
Kosher salt and freshly ground black pepper, to taste
cayenne pepper, to taste

Preparation time: 10 minutes
Portions: 3 cups

Instructions
1. Combine the mayonnaise, vinegar, lemon juice, horseradish and mustard powder in a medium nonreactive bowl, and whisk until smooth.
2. Add salt, pepper and cayenne to taste. Brush on grilled or roasted chicken during the end of the cooking process, and pass remaining sauce at the table.

Secret tip: It's good on anything grilled or smoked. Chicken, pork, burgers and on and on....

HOT SAUCE WITH CILANTRO

Ingredients:
½ tsp coriander
½ tsp cumin seeds
¼ tsp black pepper
2 green cardamom pods
2 garlic cloves
1 tsp salt
1 oz. parsley
2 tablespoons olive oil

Preparation time: 10 minutes
Portions: 4 serves

Instructions:
1. In a blender place all ingredients and blend until smooth
2. Pour sauce in a bowl and serve

BASIL PESTO SAUCE

Ingredients:
2 cloves garlic
2 oz. basil leaves
1 tablespoon pine nuts
1 oz. parmesan cheese
½ cup olive oil

Preparation time: 10 minutes
Portions: 4 serves

Instructions:
1. In a blender place all ingredients and blend until smooth
2. Pour sauce in a bowl and serve

VEGAN PESTO

This works perfectly on grilled veggies and every vegan guest will thank you.

Ingredients:
1 cup cilantro leaves
1 cup basil leaves
1 cup parsley leaves
½ cup mint leaves
½ cup walnuts
1 tsp miso
1 tsp lemon juice
¼ cup olive oil

Preparation time: 10 minutes
Portions: 4 serves

Instructions:
1. In a blender place all ingredients and blend until smooth
2. Pour sauce in a bowl and serve

FENNEL AND ALMONDS SAUCE

Ingredients:
1 cup fennel bulb
1 cup olive oil
1 cup almonds
1 cup fennel fronds

Preparation time: 10 minutes
Portions: 4 serves

Instructions:
1. In a blender place all ingredients and blend until smooth
2. Pour sauce in a bowl and serve

HONEY DIPPING SAUCE

Ingredients:
5 tablespoons unsalted butter
8 tablespoons kimchi paste
2 tablespoons honey
1 tsp sesame seeds

Preparation time: 10 minutes
Portions: 4 serves

Instructions:
1. In a blender place all ingredients and blend until smooth
2. Pour sauce in a bowl and serve

GINGER DIPPING SAUCE

Ingredients:
6 tablespoons ponzu sauce
2 tablespoons scallions
2 tsp ginger
2 tsp mirin
1 tsp sesame oil
¼ tsp salt

Preparation time: 10 minutes
Portions: 4 serves

Instructions:
1. In a blender place all ingredients and blend until smooth

2. Pour sauce in a bowl and serve

THAI DIPPING SAUCE

Ingredients:
6 tsp garlic sauce
2 tablespoons fish sauce
2 tablespoons lime juice
1 tablespoon brown sugar
1 tsp chili flakes

Preparation time: 10 minutes
Portions: 4 serves

Instructions:
1. In a blender place all ingredients and blend until smooth
2. Pour sauce in a bowl and serve

COCONUT DIPPING SAUCE

Ingredients:
4 tablespoons coconut milk
1 tablespoon curry paste
2 tablespoons lime juice
2 tsp soy sauce
1 oz. parsley
2 tablespoons olive oil

Preparation time: 10 minutes
Portions: 4 serves

Instructions:
1. In a blender place all ingredients and blend until smooth
2. Pour sauce in a bowl and serve

BLACK BEAN DIPPING SAUCE

Ingredients:
2 tablespoons black bean paste
2 tablespoons peanut butter
1 tablespoon maple syrup
2 tablespoons olive oil

Preparation time: 10 minutes
Portions: 4 serves

Instructions:
1. In a blender place all ingredients and blend until smooth
2. Pour sauce in a bowl and serve

MAPLE SYRUP DIPPING SAUCE

Ingredients:
2 tablespoons peanut butter
2 tablespoons maple syrup
2 tsp olive oil
2 tablespoon Korean black bean paste

Preparation time: 10 minutes
Portions: 4 serves

Instructions:
1. In a blender place all ingredients and blend until smooth
2. Pour sauce in a bowl and serve

SOY DIPPING SAUCE

Ingredients:
¼ cup soy sauce
¼ cup sugar
¼ cup rice vinegar
½ cup scallions
½ cup cilantro

Preparation time: 10 minutes
Portions: 4 serves

Instructions:
1. In a blender place all ingredients and blend until smooth
2. Pour sauce in a bowl and serve

AVOCADO SALSA

Ingredients:
2 avocados
1 onion
1 jalapeno
2 garlic cloves
¼ cup red wine vinegar

1 tablespoon lime juice
¼ cup parsley leaves

Preparation time: 10 minutes
Portions: 4 serves

Instructions:
1. In a blender place all ingredients and blend until smooth
2. Pour sauce in a bowl and serve

ALDER-SMOKED SALT

Smoking salt will change the way you look at food. No longer are your smoke-filled masterpieces bound by the restraint of being outdoors. Smoked salt can now be used in place of any other salt in your kitchen, seasoning everything from meats to desserts with its hint of smoke.

Ingredients
1 pound coarse sea salt

Preparation time: 5 minutes
Smoking time: 4 hours
Temperature: 120°F
Portions: 1 pound
Recommended pellets: Alder

Instructions
1. Supply your smoker with wood pellets and follow the manufacturer's specific start-up procedure. Preheat the grill, with the lid closed, to 120°F.
2. Pour the salt onto a rimmed baking sheet and smoke for 4 hours, stirring every hour.
3. Remove the salt from the smoker, let it cool, and store in an airtight container.

Secret tip: Substitute whatever salt you like in this recipe, as long as it is sea salt.

FISH AND SEAFOOD

Salmon is by far the most popular fish to smoke. These days, we're even seeing it at the market alongside traditional beef jerky. Its oily flesh makes it the perfect canvas for absorbing smoke flavor. But there's an endless variety of seafood that can also take on smoke incredibly well. The rule of thumb is the fattier the fish, the smokier flavor you'll taste. Salmon and trout have high fat content and are ideal for wood pellet smokers. That's because the smokers allow you to easily maintain the lower, sub-200°F temperatures that let the fish slowly absorb the subtle wood flavors—without fear of overcooking the delicate flesh. As with smoked meats, the process of smoking fish started as a way of not only cooking, but also of preserving the food. The bold flavors and superior health benefits continue to stand the test of time.

The lightness of seafood is a perfect match for wood pellet smokers. The light flesh picks up subtle flavors nicely, and because most seafood is quick to cook, the lower temperature settings of pellet grills can help prevent overcooking.

The best seafood for your smoker depends on where you live. Shopping local means you can get the freshest product possible. Shrimp is my local favorite, and there are plenty of ways to prepare it (just ask Bubba Gump for his list). Lobster is an uncommon but elegant treat on the smoker that is much easier to prepare than you may think.
Smoked fish is another staple of the pellet smoker.
Salmon to tuna, the oilier the fish, the better for absorbing smoke flavor.
Oysters and hardwood smoke are also a great combination—you can host a real oyster roast instead of serving the more typical steamed oysters. Here, we roast them on the half shell topped with a seasoned butter.
One other consideration with fish and seafood is what's in season where you live. But don't let locale or seasonality deter you too much from what you crave. Good markets, modern seafood farming, and modern distribution make most seafood accessible year-round.

At the Fish Market
Shopping for fish can seem complicated. More than just type, you have to decide on whole or cleaned, farm-raised or local, fresh or frozen.
When shopping for fresh fish, look with your nose first. Fresh fish should smell clean and briny, not "off" or overly fishy. The eyes should appear shiny and full, not cloudy or sunken. Skin and scales should look shiny and metallic. With fillets, flesh should be firm and bright (not dull)—and never slimy.

TECHNIQUES
Smoking fish with the skin on can help the flesh retain moisture, but you don't want to eat all kinds of fish skin. Many people love the taste of salmon skin when fried crisp. Pellet smoking will not crisp the skin to many people's liking, but you'll still want to leave it on one side of the fillet to allow for easier maneuverability on the grill.

RULES TO GRILL BY
Fish over wood fire is one of the greatest combinations in culinary history. But there are a few things to keep in mind for seafood success:

1. Use kosher salt in these recipes, not table salt. The latter may contain iodide and anti-caking agents that can give fish an off flavor.

2. Blotting and drying the surface of the pre-smoked fish fillet allows for the formation of a pellicle, a sticky, thin, lacquer-like film on the surface of the fish that helps smoke adhere to the meat.
Choose skin-off fillets or thin-skinned fish for the best absorption of smoke flavors.

3. While cleaning (and before seasoning), use your fingers to inspect fish fillets like salmon and trout for pin bones and remove them.

4. Fish is notorious for messy cleanup. Use aluminum foil (pierced with vent holes) or Frogmats to minimize hassle.

5. Enlist the help of a grill basket to protect the flesh of the fish, or place pieces skin-side down on the grate.

6. Light-flavored foods call for more delicate and aromatic wood flavors. Fruit and alder wood pellets are fish favorites

7. A fish spatula is slotted, thin, and flexible, making it the perfect tool for lifting and moving delicate pieces of fish.

8. Use tongs and a cloth or paper towel dipped in vegetable oil to brush oil on the grill grate to prevent sticking.

PACIFIC NORTHWEST SALMON

There are all sorts of ways to add wood flavor to your salmon, but nothing works better than good old-fashioned wood smoke. Before grilling your salmon, give it a short alder wood smoke for that smoky flavor native to the birthplace of the pellet grill. Alder trees are scattered throughout Oregon and the Pacific Northwest, and alder is a primary base wood on the West Coast.

Ingredients
1 (2-pound) half salmon fillet
1 batch Dill Seafood Rub
2 tablespoons butter, cut into 3 or 4 slices

Preparation time: 15 minutes
Smoking time: 1 hour, 15 minutes
Temperature: 180°F and 300°F
Portions: 4
Recommended pellets: Alder
Recommended sides: Rosemary and garlic roasted potatoes

Instructions
1. Supply your smoker with wood pellets and follow the manufacturer's specific start-up procedure. Preheat the grill, with the lid closed, to 180°F.
2. Season the salmon all over with the rub. Using your hands, work the rub into the flesh.
3. Place the salmon directly on the grill grate, skin-side down, and smoke for 1 hour.
4. Place the butter slices on the salmon, equally spaced. Increase the grill's temperature to 300°F and continue to cook until the salmon's internal temperature reaches 145°F. Remove the salmon from the grill and serve immediately.

Secret tip: Serve the salmon with lemon. This might sound like a no-brainer, but it goes perfectly with the dill, creating a sour tang that intensifies the salmon's overall flavor.

GRILLED SALMON

Grilled salmon is great. Made on a pellet grill, it's even better, but the one thing that can ruin it is overcooking it and drying it out. To combat your chances of this happening, rub it with a little mayonnaise before cooking. Only a thin layer is needed and, I swear, you won't notice the mayo flavor. This will keep your salmon moist, even if you leave it on the grill a little longer than intended.

Ingredients
1 (2-pound) half salmon fillet
3 tablespoons mayonnaise
1 batch Dill Seafood Rub

Preparation time: 25 minutes
Smoking time: 25 minutes
Temperature: 325°F
Portions: 4
Recommended pellets: Alder
Recommended sides: Rosemary and garlic roasted potatoes

Instructions
1. Supply your smoker with wood pellets and follow the manufacturer's specific start-up procedure. Preheat the grill, with the lid closed, to 325°F.
2. Using your hands, rub the salmon fillet all over with the mayonnaise and sprinkle it with the rub.
3. Place the salmon directly on the grill grate, skin-side down, and grill until its internal temperature reaches 145°F. Remove the salmon from the grill and serve immediately.

Secret tip: When cooking fish, rub your grill grates with oil to prevent the scales from sticking. Even though most pellet grill grates are coated with porcelain, fish has a tendency to stick to the grates, making a stinky mess to clean up.

HOT-SMOKED SALMON

The hours spent smoking salmon are always worth it, as smoked salmon is perfect for snacking or topping a salad. There's really no end to what you can do with wood pellet–smoked salmon.

Ingredients
1 (2-pound) half salmon fillet
1 batch Dill Seafood Rub

Preparation time: 15 minutes
Smoking time: 4 to 6 hours
Temperature: 180°F
Portions: 4
Recommended pellets: Hickory
Recommended sides: Rosemary and garlic roasted potatoes

Instructions
1. Supply your smoker with wood pellets and follow the manufacturer's specific start-up procedure. Preheat the grill, with the lid closed, to 180°F.
2. Season the salmon all over with the rub. Using your hands, work the rub into the flesh.
3. Place the salmon directly on the grill grate, skin-side down, and smoke until its internal temperature reaches 145°F. Remove the salmon from the grill and serve immediately.

Secret tip: Focus on temperature, not time. Like many grillers learning the craft, I used to set my timer, leave the salmon, and when I returned, I'd wonder why it was dry. Always cook to temperature. Salmon's ideal temperature is 145°F. Pull it off then and you will never fail.

WOOD-FIRED HALIBUT

Another common seafood is halibut. This fish has a flesh texture and flavor that's very different from salmon, with pale white flesh and a much milder fishy flavor. Halibut is an extremely popular fish to grill and can be imbued with wood-fired flavor on a pellet grill.

Ingredients
1 pound halibut fillet
1 batch Dill Seafood Rub

Preparation time: 5 minutes
Smoking time: 20 minutes
Temperature: 325°F
Portions: 4
Recommended pellets: Hickory
Recommended sides: Green salad

Instructions
1. Supply your smoker with wood pellets and follow the manufacturer's specific start-up procedure. Preheat the grill, with the lid closed, to 325°F.
2. Sprinkle the halibut fillet on all sides with the rub. Using your hands, work the rub into the meat.
3. Place the halibut directly on the grill grate and grill until its internal temperature reaches 145°F. Remove the halibut from the grill and serve immediately.

Secret tip: I like halibut paired with citrus, including citrus-flavored rubs. One of my favorite rubs to use on halibut is Louisiana Grills' Caribbean Key Lime.

SEARED TUNA STEAKS

Only sear your tuna steaks a few minutes per side, leaving the center an untouched pink.

Ingredients
2 (1½- to 2-inch-thick) tuna steaks
2 tablespoons olive oil
Salt
Freshly ground black pepper

Preparation time: 10 minutes
Smoking time: 10 minutes
Temperature: 500 °F
Portions: 2
Recommended pellets: Oak
Recommended sides: Greek salad

Instructions
1. Supply your smoker with wood pellets and follow the manufacturer's specific start-up procedure. Preheat the grill, with the lid closed, to 500°F.
2. Rub the tuna steaks all over with olive oil and season both sides with salt and pepper.
3. Place the tuna steaks directly on the grill grate and grill for 3 to 5 minutes per side, leaving a pink center. Remove the tuna steaks from the grill and serve immediately.

Secret tip: Ask your fishmonger to cut your tuna steaks to order. There is no reason to eat a small frozen steak when you can eat one freshly cut to your desired thickness. I aim for at least 1½- to 2-inch steaks.

BARBECUED SHRIMP

Ingredients
1 pound peeled and deveined shrimp, with tails on
2 tablespoons olive oil
1 batch Dill Seafood Rub

Preparation time: 15 to 30 minutes
Smoking time: 10 minutes
Temperature: 375°F
Portions: 4
Recommended pellets: Mesquite
Recommended sides: Rosemary and garlic roasted potatoes

Instructions
1. Soak wooden skewers in water for 30 minutes.
2. Supply your smoker with wood pellets and follow the manufacturer's specific start-up procedure. Preheat the grill, with the lid closed, to 375°F.
3. Thread 4 or 5 shrimp per skewer.
4. Coat the shrimp all over with olive oil and season each side of the skewers with the rub.

5. Place the skewers directly on the grill grate and grill the shrimp for 5 minutes per side. Remove the skewers from the grill and serve immediately.

Secret tip: Save yourself time and use a grill basket. Although those skewers are cute and look fun when you serve them, grilling shrimp in a grill basket is so much easier. From the prep to the cooking to even the serving, it is so much easier to throw the shrimp in a basket and go

CAJUN-BLACKENED SHRIMP

Ingredients
1 pound peeled and deveined shrimp, with tails on
1 batch Cajun Rub
8 tablespoons (1 stick) butter
¼ cup Worcestershire sauce

Preparation time: 10 minutes
Smoking time: 20 minutes
Temperature: 450°F
Portions: 4
Recommended pellets: Alder
Recommended sides: Fresh Broccoli Salad

Instructions
1. Supply your smoker with wood pellets and follow the manufacturer's specific start-up procedure. Preheat the grill, with the lid closed, to 450°F and place a cast-iron skillet on the grill grate. Wait about 10 minutes after your grill has reached temperature, allowing the skillet to get hot.
2. Meanwhile, season the shrimp all over with the rub.
3. When the skillet is hot, place the butter in it to melt. Once the butter melts, stir in the Worcestershire sauce.
4. Add the shrimp and gently stir to coat. Smoke-braise the shrimp for about 10 minutes per side, until opaque and cooked through. Remove the shrimp from the grill and serve immediately.

OYSTERS IN THE SHELL

Ingredients
8 medium oysters, unopened, in the shell, rinsed and scrubbed
1 batch Lemon Butter Mop for Seafood

Preparation time: 5 minutes
Smoking time: 20 minutes
Temperature: 375°F
Portions: 4
Recommended pellets: Oak
Recommended sides: Roasted fingerlingpotatoes

Instructions
1. Supply your smoker with wood pellets and follow the manufacturer's specific start-up procedure. Preheat the grill, with the lid closed, to 375°F.
2. Place the unopened oysters directly on the grill grate and grill for about 20 minutes, or until the oysters are done and their shells open.

3. Discard any oysters that do not open. Shuck the remaining oysters, transfer them to a bowl, and add the mop. Serve immediately.

Secret tip: I use barbecue gloves and a butter knife when shucking oysters, but if you find the right tools, it can make your life so much easier. Leather gloves are perfect. And pick up an oyster knife, unless you like your significant other harassing you over improperly using kitchen utensils.

CAJUN CATFISH

Cajun flavors are perfect for seafood and nowhere is that more apparent than on catfish.

Ingredients
2½ pounds catfish fillets
2 tablespoons olive oil
1 batch Cajun Rub

Preparation time: 15 minutes
Smoking time: 15 minutes
Temperature: 300°FPortions: 6
Recommended pellets: Mesquite
Recommended sides: Crispy Baked Asparagus Fries

Instructions
1. Supply your smoker with wood pellets and follow the manufacturer's specific start-up procedure. Preheat the grill, with the lid closed, to 300°F.
2. Coat the catfish fillets all over with olive oil and season with the rub. Using your hands, work the rub into the flesh.
3. Place the fillets directly on the grill grate and smoke until their internal temperature reaches 145°F. Remove the catfish from the grill and serve immediately

Secret tip: If your grill has an open flame option, once your catfish reaches 140°F, reverse-sear it over the flame for 1 minute. Cooking over the open flame for that short time will give your catfish a little bit of char and flavor.

GRILLED KING CRAB LEGS

King crab legs are not the cheapest endeavor, but when you have a chance to cook them on your pellet grill, you won't regret it.

Ingredients

Preparation time: 5 minutes
Smoking time: 10 minutes
Temperature: 325 °F
Portions: 4
Recommended pellets: Alder
Recommended sides: Green salad

Instructions
1. Supply your smoker with wood pellets and follow the manufacturer's specific start-up procedure. Preheat the grill, with the lid closed, to 325°F.

2. Place the crab legs directly on the grill grate and grill for 10 minutes, flipping once after 5 minutes. Serve the crab with the mop on the side for dipping.

Secret tip: Use a pair of kitchen shears to cut through the shells.

LOBSTER TAIL

The taste of lobster mixed with the wood-fired smoke is a killer combination. By cooking your lobster on a wood pellet grill or smoker, you assure it will be enhanced by hardwood smoke.

Ingredients
2 lobster tails
Salt
Freshly ground black pepper
1 batch Lemon Butter Mop for Seafood

Preparation time: 25 minutes
Smoking time: 25 minutes
Temperature: 375°F
Portions: 2
Recommended pellets: Hickory
Recommended sides: Corn on the cob

Instructions
1. Supply your smoker with wood pellets and follow the manufacturer's specific start-up procedure. Preheat the grill, with the lid closed, to 375°F.
2. Using kitchen shears, slit the top of the lobster shells, through the center, nearly to the tail. Once cut, expose as much meat as you can through the cut shell.
3. Season the lobster tails all over with salt and pepper.
4. Place the tails directly on the grill grate and grill until their internal temperature reaches 145°F. Remove the lobster from the grill and serve with the mop on the side for dipping.

BARBECUED SCALLOPS

Scallops taste amazing, and they are even better cooked on a pellet grill. Adding the wood fire smoke to the tender, sweet scallop meat will keep you coming back for more.

Ingredients
1 pound large scallops
2 tablespoons olive oil
1 batch Dill Seafood Rub

Preparation time: 10 minutes
Smoking time: 10 minutes
Temperature: 375 °F
Portions: 4
Recommended pellets: Mesquite
Recommended sides: Green salad

Instructions

1. Supply your smoker with wood pellets and follow the manufacturer's specific start-up procedure. Preheat the grill, with the lid closed, to 375°F.
2. Coat the scallops all over with olive oil and season all sides with the rub.
3. Place the scallops directly on the grill grate and grill for 5 minutes per side. Remove the scallops from the grill and serve immediately.

Secret tip:
Be extremely careful when turning and pulling your scallops on the grill because, once cooked, they love to fall apart. Try tongs to pull and flip the scallops, but use caution. Oiling your grill grates before cooking can help reduce the chances of the scallops sticking.

CHARLESTON CRAB CAKES WITH REMOULADE

If you've ever handpicked a blue crab, you know what a luxury food a crab cake is. It's an extra-nice treat when someone else has done the hard handpicking work. Remoulade may seem a bit fancy for beach food, but top as you like. A remoulade is a French condiment that is aioli- or mayonnaise-based, and I like to think of it as a distant cousin of tartar sauce.

Ingredients
1¼ cups mayonnaise
¼ cup yellow mustard
2 tablespoons sweet pickle relish, with its juices
1 tablespoon smoked paprika
2 teaspoons Cajun seasoning
2 teaspoons prepared horseradish
1 teaspoon hot sauce
1 garlic clove, finely minced
2 pounds fresh lump crabmeat, picked clean
20 butter crackers (such as Ritz brand), crushed
2 tablespoons Dijon mustard
1 cup mayonnaise
2 tablespoons freshly squeezed lemon juice
1 tablespoon salted butter, melted
1 tablespoon Worcestershire sauce
1 tablespoon Old Bay seasoning
2 teaspoons chopped fresh parsley
1 teaspoon ground mustard
2 eggs, beaten
¼ cup extra-virgin olive oil, divided

Preparation time: 30 minutes
Smoking time: 45 minutes
Temperature: 375°F
Portions: 4
Recommended pellets: Apple
Recommended sides: Potato fries

Instructions
For the remoulade:
1.In a small bowl, combine the mayonnaise, mustard, pickle relish, paprika, Cajun seasoning, horseradish, hot sauce, and garlic.
2.Refrigerate until ready to serve.
For the crab cakes:

1. Supply your smoker with wood pellets and follow the manufacturer's specific start-up procedure. Preheat, with the lid closed, to 375°F.
2. Spread the crabmeat on a foil-lined baking sheet and place over indirect heat on the grill, with the lid closed, for 30 minutes.
3. Remove from the heat and let cool for 15 minutes.
4. While the crab cools, combine the crushed crackers, Dijon mustard, mayonnaise, lemon juice, melted butter, Worcestershire sauce, Old Bay, parsley, ground mustard, and eggs until well incorporated.
5. Fold in the smoked crabmeat, then shape the mixture into 8 (1-inch-thick) crab cakes.
6. In a large skillet or cast-iron pan on the grill, heat 2 tablespoons of olive oil. Add half of the crab cakes, close the lid, and smoke for 4 to 5 minutes on each side, or until crispy and golden brown.
7. Remove the crab cakes from the pan and transfer to a wire rack to drain. Pat them to remove any excess oil.
8. Repeat steps 6 and 7 with the remaining oil and crab cakes.
9. Serve the crab cakes with the remoulade.

Secret tip: If you're shopping for crab and instead find "krab," steer clear. Imitation crab is widely available in all shapes and sizes, but it doesn't hold a candle to the real deal.

CITRUS-SMOKED TROUT

Have you heard that goldfish can be overfed and die because they don't know when to stop eating? Similarly, trout spend about 80 percent of their day foraging for food and eating. No wonder I can relate to them. Trout are generally plentiful and, as members of the salmon family, they grow fairly large. The biggest rainbow trout on record was caught in Canada in 2009, weighing in at 48 pounds!

Ingredients
6 to 8 skin-on rainbow trout, cleaned and scaled
1 gallon orange juice
½ cup packed light brown sugar
¼ cup salt
1 tablespoon freshly ground black pepper
Nonstick spray, oil, or butter, for greasing
1 tablespoon chopped fresh parsley
1 lemon, sliced

Preparation time: 10 minutes + brining

Smoking time: 1 to 2 hours
Temperature: 225°F
Portions: 6
Recommended pellets: Alder, Oak
Recommended sides: Rosemary and garlic roasted potatoes

Instructions
1. Fillet the fish and pat dry with paper towels.
2. Pour the orange juice into a large container with a lid and stir in the brown sugar, salt, and pepper.
3. Place the trout in the brine, cover, and refrigerate for 1 hour.
4. Cover the grill grate with heavy-duty aluminum foil. Poke holes in the foil and spray with cooking spray (see Tip).
5. Supply your smoker with wood pellets and follow the manufacturer's specific start-up procedure. Preheat, with the lid closed, to 225°F.
6. Remove the trout from the brine and pat dry. Arrange the fish on the foil-covered grill grate, close the lid, and smoke for 1 hour 30 minutes to 2 hours, or until flaky.
7. Remove the fish from the heat. Serve garnished with the fresh parsley and lemon slices.

Secret tip: Fish has a tendency to stick to the grill, so to aid in cleanup, cover the grate with heavy-duty aluminum foil. Poke holes in the foil so the smoke can get through, and spray with nonstick spray to further prevent sticking. You could also use a greased Frogmat.

DIJON-SMOKED HALIBUT

For this recipe, we opt for a premium Dijon mustard over the more common everyday yellow mustard. I usually use the cheap yellow variety, because its purpose is more as a spice adherent and it only imparts a light layer of flavor in the final dish. But in this case, the mustard flavor shares the stage with the fish. Think of it as an opportunity to explore the vast world of gourmet mustards that are so trendy right now.

Ingredients
4 (6-ounce) halibut steaks
¼ cup extra-virgin olive oil
2 teaspoons kosher salt
1 teaspoon freshly ground black pepper
½ cup mayonnaise
½ cup sweet pickle relish
¼ cup finely chopped sweet onion
¼ cup chopped roasted red pepper
¼ cup finely chopped tomato
¼ cup finely chopped cucumber
2 tablespoons Dijon mustard
1 teaspoon minced garlic

Preparation time: 25 minutes + 4 hours to marinate

Smoking time: 2 hours
Temperature: 200°F
Portions: 6
Recommended pellets: Alder, Oak
Recommended sides: Roasted fingerling potatoes

Instructions
1. Rub the halibut steaks with the olive oil and season on both sides with the salt and pepper. Transfer to a plate, cover with plastic wrap, and refrigerate for 4 hours.
2. Supply your smoker with wood pellets and follow the manufacturer's specific start-up procedure. Preheat, with the lid closed, to 200°F.
3. Remove the halibut from the refrigerator and rub with the mayonnaise.
4. Put the fish directly on the grill grate, close the lid, and smoke for 2 hours, or until opaque and an instant-read thermometer inserted in the fish reads 140°F.
5. While the fish is smoking, combine the pickle relish, onion, roasted red pepper, tomato, cucumber, Dijon mustard, and garlic in a medium bowl. Refrigerate the mustard relish until ready to serve.
6. Serve the halibut steaks hot with the mustard relish.

Secret tip: This recipe also works great with swordfish or tuna.

CURED COLD-SMOKED LOX

People pay $30 to $50 a pound for lox, the cured and smoked belly of the salmon, but it's really easy to make at home—and at a third of the cost, why not? You'll need to have the ability to cold-smoke at temperatures lower than many wood pellet grill smokers can sustain without an attachment or accessory like a smoker tube (see Accessories). Be sure to use sashimi-grade salmon, which is safe to eat raw. The dry-curing and cold-smoking process may not kill all bacteria that can occur in salmon, so if you're not using sashimi-grade, you'll need to freeze the salmon for 24 hours before starting to cold-smoke to kill any bacteria.

Ingredients
¼ cup salt
¼ cup sugar
1 tablespoon freshly ground black pepper
1 bunch dill, chopped
1 pound sashimi-grade salmon, skin removed
1 avocado, sliced
8 bagels
4 ounces cream cheese
1 bunch alfalfa sprouts
1 (3.5-ounce) jar capers

Preparation time: 24 hours to cure + 24 hours to refrigerate + 20 minutes
Smoking time: 6 hours
Temperature: 80°F
Portions: 6
Recommended pellets: Alder

Instructions
1. In a small bowl, combine the salt, sugar, pepper, and fresh dill to make the curing mixture. Set aside.
2. On a smooth surface, lay out a large piece of plastic wrap and spread half of the curing salt mixture in the middle, spreading it out to about the size of the salmon.
3. Place the salmon on top of the curing salt.
4. Top the fish with the remaining curing salt, covering it completely. Wrap the salmon, leaving the ends open to drain.
5. Place the wrapped fish in a rimmed baking pan or dish lined with paper towels to soak up liquid.
6. Place a weight on the salmon evenly, such as a pan with a couple of heavy jars of pickles on top.
7. Put the salmon pan with weights in the refrigerator. Place something (a dishtowel, for example) under the back of the pan in order to slightly tip it down so the liquid drains away from the fish.
8. Leave the salmon to cure in the refrigerator for 24 hours.
9. Place the wood pellets in the smoker, but do not follow the start-up procedure and do not preheat.
10. Remove the salmon from the refrigerator, unwrap it, rinse it off, and pat dry.
11. Put the salmon in the smoker while still cold from the refrigerator to slow down the cooking process. You'll need to use a cold-smoker attachment or enlist the help of a smoker tube to hold the temperature at 80°F and maintain that for 6 hours to absorb smoke and complete the cold-smoking process.
12. Remove the salmon from the smoker, place it in a sealed plastic bag, and refrigerate for 24 hours. The salmon will be translucent all the way through.
13. Thinly slice the lox and serve with sliced avocado, bagels, cream cheese, alfalfa sprouts, and capers.

Secret tip: There are lots of varieties of smoked salmon, including cured cold-smoked and cooked hot-smoked. But to many people's surprise, real lox is not necessarily smoked. It's just salt-brined.

SUMMER PAELLA

Paella is the ultimate one-pan dish for the backyard barbecue. Thanks to the steady temperature of your wood pellet grill, the process has never been easier to tackle at home. If you don't own a thin carbon-steel paella pan, feel free to use a large stainless-steel or aluminum skillet. Cast iron and nonstick pans are discouraged for paella.

Ingredients

6 tablespoons extra-virgin olive oil, divided, plus more for drizzling
2 green or red bell peppers, cored, seeded, and diced
2 medium onions, diced
2 garlic cloves, slivered
1 (29-ounce) can tomato purée
1½ pounds chicken thighs
Kosher salt
1½ pounds tail-on shrimp, peeled and deveined
1 cup dried thinly sliced chorizo sausage
1 tablespoon smoked paprika
1½ teaspoons saffron threads
2 quarts chicken broth
3½ cups white rice
2 (7½-ounce) cans chipotle chiles in adobo sauce
1½ pounds fresh clams, soaked in cold water for 15 to 20 minutes2 tablespoons chopped fresh parsley
2 lemons, cut into wedges, for serving

Preparation time: 1 hour
Smoking time: 45 minutes
Temperature: 450°F
Portions: 6
Recommended pellets: Alder
Recommended sides: Rosemary and garlic roasted potatoes

Instructions

1. Make the sofrito: On the stove top, in a saucepan over medium-low heat, combine ¼ cup of olive oil, the bell peppers, onions, and garlic, and cook for 5 minutes, or until the onions are translucent.
2. Stir in the tomato purée, reduce the heat to low, and simmer, stirring frequently, until most of the liquid has evaporated, about 30 minutes. Set aside. (Note: The sofrito can be made in advance and refrigerated.)
3. Supply your smoker with wood pellets and follow the manufacturer's specific start-up procedure. Preheat, with the lid closed, to 450°F.
4. Heat a large paella pan on the smoker and add the remaining 2 tablespoons of olive oil.
5. Add the chicken thighs, season lightly with salt, and brown for 6 to 10 minutes, then push to the outer edge of the pan.
6. Add the shrimp, season with salt, close the lid, and smoke for 3 minutes.
7. Add the sofrito, chorizo, paprika, and saffron, and stir together.
8. In a separate bowl, combine the chicken broth, uncooked rice, and 1 tablespoon of salt, stirring until well combined.
9. Add the broth-rice mixture to the paella pan, spreading it evenly over the other ingredients.
10. Close the lid and smoke for 5 minutes, then add the chipotle chiles and clams on top of the rice.
11. Close the lid and continue to smoke the paella for about 30 minutes, or until all of the liquid is absorbed.
12. Remove the pan from the grill, cover tightly with aluminum foil, and let rest off the heat for 5 minutes.
13. Drizzle with olive oil, sprinkle with the fresh parsley, and serve with the lemon wedges.

Secret tip: Sofrito is a Spanish tomato sauce, usually made with olive oil, onions, peppers, and garlic. It's used as a base for many dishes. Variations of the original have spread throughout Latin America, Europe, and the world.

VEGETABLES

Man (and woman) cannot live on meat alone. Traeger owners can enjoy cooking and smoking high- or low-temperature veggies and tasty sides with ease. Because most vegetables have shorter cook times than the meats you smoke, you can prep your veggie sides during the downtime and throw them on the grill in the last minutes of cooking—it's all conveniently coordinated! The wood pellet grill's high-temperature settings allow for effortless baking and browning. Grilled vegetables offer you a far greater variety of flavors to discover than just meat, and the colors can be a dazzling feast for the eyes—especially in the summer months, when the farmers' market is bursting with fresh, locally grown fruit and vegetables. Finally, grilling outside is also the best way to keep your home cool in the hot summer months.

When adding vegetables to your smoker, keep the following in mind for the yummiest results:

1. The water pan is your best friend. This will keep the moisture circulating in the smoking chamber.

2. Wash all of your produce thoroughly. Refer to the "Dirty Dozen" list (www.ewg.org) and consider buying organic. Such smoker favorites as peaches, peppers, and potatoes are on the list of most contaminated vegetables.

3. Marinades help add flavors to vegetables as much as they do to meat—and often more so. Eggplant and zucchini are like sponges for absorbing liquid marinades.

4. If you're cooking vegetables along with your main meat dish, consider their cook times and share the smoker space accordingly.

5. Most veggies don't require anything but a little salt, pepper, and smoke to taste great. But you'll also want to add a light brushing of olive oil to keep them from sticking to the grate, or use Frogmats.

6. Roasted veggies take on an a dense, almost magical texture on your wood pellet grill. 425°F is the sweet spot for roasting when you start with a fully preheated grill.

TWICE-SMOKED POTATOES

With twice the smoke and twice the flavor, these potatoes are the ideal side for steak or any smoked beef. They're so hearty they can almost hold their own as a main course. Shop for starchy baking potatoes with a thick skin, such as the traditional Russet or Idaho, and skip wrapping them in foil.

Ingredients
8 Idaho, Russet, or Yukon Gold potatoes
1 (12-ounce) can evaporated milk, heated
1 cup (2 sticks) butter, melted
½ cup sour cream, at room temperature
1 cup grated Parmesan cheese

½ pound bacon, cooked and crumbled
¼ cup chopped scallions
Salt
Freshly ground black pepper
1 cup shredded Cheddar cheese

Preparation time: 20 minutes
Smoking time: 1 hour 35 minutes
Temperature: 400°F, 375°F
Portions: 16
Recommended pellets: Maple, Pecan

Instructions
1. Supply your smoker with wood pellets and follow the manufacturer's specific start-up procedure. Preheat, with the lid closed, to 400°F.
2. Poke the potatoes all over with a fork. Arrange them directly on the grill grate, close the lid, and smoke for 1 hour and 15 minutes, or until cooked through and they have some give when pinched.
3. Let the potatoes cool for 10 minutes, then cut in half lengthwise.
4. Into a medium bowl, scoop out the potato flesh, leaving ¼ inch in the shells; place the shells on a baking sheet.
5. Using an electric mixer on medium speed, beat the potatoes, milk, butter, and sour cream until smooth.
6. Stir in the Parmesan cheese, bacon, and scallions, and season with salt and pepper.
7. Generously stuff each shell with the potato mixture and top with Cheddar cheese.
8. Place the baking sheet on the grill grate, close the lid, and smoke for 20 minutes, or until the cheese is melted.

Secret tip: One extra step can give your potato a salty crust. Before baking, cover the raw potato with your choice of oil, bacon grease, or butter, then coat the spud with sea salt.

BROCCOLI-CAULIFLOWER SALAD

Ingredients
1½ cups mayonnaise
½ cup sour cream
¼ cup sugar
1 bunch broccoli, cut into small pieces
1 head cauliflower, cut into small pieces
1 small red onion, chopped
6 slices bacon, cooked and crumbled (precooked bacon works well)
1 cup shredded Cheddar cheese

Preparation time: 25 minutes
Portions: 4

Instructions
1. In a small bowl, whisk together the mayonnaise, sour cream, and sugar to make a dressing.
2. In a large bowl, combine the broccoli, cauliflower, onion, bacon, and Cheddar cheese.
3. Pour the dressing over the vegetable mixture and toss well to coat.
4. Serve the salad chilled.

Secret tip: Use your own smoked bacon for an extra smoky kick.

CAROLINA BAKED BEANS

Everyone touts Boston as the baked bean capital. Back in the day, the city was a big locale for distilling rum, and thus had an abundance of molasses. Bostonians added that surplus molasses to their bean recipes, and it was so good, the city earned the nickname "Beantown." In fact, baked beans and brown bread have been a traditional weekend meal in Massachusetts for generations. This recipe adds sweet barbecue sauce, mustard, bacon, onions, and bell pepper rings for a zesty Carolina twist.

Ingredients
3 (28-ounce) cans baked beans (I like Bush's brand)
1 large onion, finely chopped
1 cup The Ultimate BBQ Sauce
½ cup light brown sugar
¼ cup Worcestershire sauce
3 tablespoons yellow mustard
Nonstick cooking spray or butter, for greasing
1 large bell pepper, cut into thin rings
½ pound thick-cut bacon, partially cooked and cut into quarters

Preparation time: 15 minutes
Smoking time: 2 to 3 hours
Temperature: 300°F
Portions: 12 to 15 minutesRecommended pellets: Mesquite

Instructions
1. Supply your smoker with wood pellets and follow the manufacturer's specific start-up procedure. Preheat, with the lid closed, to 300°F.
2. In a large mixing bowl, stir together the beans, onion, barbecue sauce, brown sugar, Worcestershire sauce, and mustard until well combined
3. Coat a 9-by-13-inch aluminum pan with cooking spray or butter.
4. Pour the beans into the pan and top with the bell pepper rings and bacon pieces, pressing them down slightly into the sauce.
5. Place a layer of heavy-duty foil on the grill grate to catch drips, and place the pan on top of the foil. Close the lid and cook for 2 hours 30 minutes to 3 hours, or until the beans are hot, thick, and bubbly.
6. Let the beans rest for 5 minutes before serving.

Secret tip: You should usually avoid covering your grill grate with foil, but with these beans I recommend it, to protect from sticky spillover. A sheet or two under the shallow pan will do. Just keep the pan uncovered, to allow smoke to penetrate the surface of the beans.

BLT PASTA SALAD

If you don't like a classic BLT sandwich, stop right here! This cool summer pasta salad elevates the great flavors of the sandwich favorite. Hold the toast. Add pasta.

Ingredients
1 pound thick-cut bacon
16 ounces bowtie pasta, cooked according to package directions and drained
2 tomatoes, chopped
½ cup chopped scallions
½ cup Italian dressing
½ cup ranch dressing
1 tablespoon chopped fresh basil

1 teaspoon salt
1 teaspoon freshly ground black pepper
1 teaspoon garlic powder
1 head lettuce, cored and torn

Preparation time: 10 minutes
Smoking time: 35 to 45 minutes
Temperature: 225°F
Portions: 6
Recommended pellets: Hickory

Instructions
1. Supply your smoker with wood pellets and follow the manufacturer's specific start-up procedure. Preheat, with the lid closed, to 225°F.
2. Arrange the bacon slices on the grill grate, close the lid, and cook for 30 to 45 minutes, flipping after 20 minutes, until crisp.
3. Remove the bacon from the grill and chop.
4. In a large bowl, combine the chopped bacon with the cooked pasta, tomatoes, scallions, Italian dressing, ranch dressing, basil, salt, pepper, and garlic powder. Refrigerate until ready to serve.
5. Toss in the lettuce just before serving to keep it from wilting.

Secret tip: If you prefer a quicker method or a crispier outcome, smoke the bacon at 350°F for 6 to 7 minutes per side. Thick-cut bacon is easier to handle on the grill.

POTLUCK SALAD WITH SMOKED CORNBREAD

Sure, you can make the cornbread for this recipe in your kitchen oven, but I suggest breaking out a cast iron skillet and taking advantage of the baking capabilities of your wood pellet grill. If ya got it, why not flaunt it? But even if you decide to bake a box of Jiffy cornbread mix, I urge you to try it just once on the smoker.

Ingredients
1 cup all-purpose flour
1 cup yellow cornmeal
1 tablespoon sugar
2 teaspoons baking powder
1 teaspoon salt
1 cup milk
1 egg, beaten, at room temperature
4 tablespoons (½ stick) unsalted butter, melted and cooled
Nonstick cooking spray or butter, for greasing
½ cup milk
½ cup sour cream
2 tablespoons dry ranch dressing mix
1 pound bacon, cooked and crumbled
3 tomatoes, chopped
1 bell pepper, chopped
1 cucumber, seeded and chopped
2 stalks celery, chopped (about 1 cup)
½ cup chopped scallions

Preparation time: 25 minutes
Smoking time: 35 to 45 minutes

Temperature: 375°F
Portions: 6
Recommended pellets: Oak, Apple, Pecan
Instructions

For the cornbread:
1. In a medium bowl, combine the flour, cornmeal, sugar, baking powder, and salt.
2. In a small bowl, whisk together the milk and egg. Pour in the butter, then slowly fold this mixture into the dry ingredients.
3. Supply your smoker with wood pellets and follow the manufacturer's specific start-up procedure. Preheat, with the lid closed, to 375°F.
4. Coat a cast iron skillet with cooking spray or butter.
5. Pour the batter into the skillet, place on the grill grate, close the lid, and smoke for 35 to 45 minutes, or until the cornbread is browned and pulls away from the side of the skillet.
6. Remove the cornbread from the grill and let cool, then coarsely crumble.

For the salad:
1. In a small bowl, whisk together the milk, sour cream, and ranch dressing mix.
2. In a medium bowl, combine the crumbled bacon, tomatoes, bell pepper, cucumber, celery, and scallions.
3. In a large serving bowl, layer half of the crumbled cornbread, half of the bacon-veggie mixture, and half of the dressing. Toss lightly.
4. Repeat the layering with the remaining cornbread, bacon-veggie mixture, and dressing. Toss again.
5. Refrigerate the salad for at least 1 hour. Serve cold.

Secret tip: As shown throughout this book, cast iron skillet can be a great partner for your wood pellet grill. It can be used to brown steaks as easily as it can be used as a baking pan. Plus, cast iron retains heat well after you take it to the table for serving.

VEGETARIAN RECIPES

SMOKED EGGS

Cold-smoked hardboiled eggs are next-level cooking. Allowing a little wood fire smoke to penetrate your eggs changes the taste entirely. I'm telling you, this is a game changer. Pair a couple of smoked hardboiled eggs with some fruit for a spectacular lunch that won't become a bland routine.

Ingredients
12 hardboiled eggs, peeled and rinsed

Preparation time: 10 minutes
Smoking time: 30 minutes
Temperature: 120°F
Portions: 12
Recommended pellets: Hickory
Recommended sides: Rosemary and garlic roasted potatoes

Instructions
1. Supply your smoker with wood pellets and follow the manufacturer's specific start-up procedure. Preheat the grill, with the lid closed, to 120°F.
2. Place the eggs directly on the grill grate and smoke for 30 minutes. They will begin to take on a slight brown sheen.
3. Remove the eggs and refrigerate for at least 30 minutes before serving. Refrigerate any leftovers in an airtight container for 1 or 2 weeks.

Secret tip: Serve smoked hardboiled eggs to cause a buzz at the next holiday party. You can follow this recipe exactly to smoke eggs, or halve them, placing the yolks and whites in separate pans to smoke separately.

MEXICAN STREET CORN WITH CHIPOTLE BUTTER

Corn on the cob has always made great barbecue food. You can cook it in the husk or out of the husk wrapped in foil, and it's nearly impossible to burn. Plus, it's handheld! The only trick has been getting the salt and butter to stick. We fix that by pouring on a spicy butter topping and wrapping the corn in foil to cook. It's finished with a topping of salty fresh Parmesan cheese, so every bite is coated with flavor and there's no fumbling around trying to butter your cob.

Ingredients
4 ears corn
½ cup sour cream
½ cup mayonnaise
¼ cup chopped fresh cilantro, plus more for garnish
Chipotle Butter, for topping
1 cup grated Parmesan cheese

Preparation time: 10 minutes
Smoking time: 12 to 14 minutes
Temperature: 450°F
Portions: 4
Recommended pellets: Hickory, Mesquite

Instructions
1. Supply your smoker with wood pellets and follow the manufacturer's specific start-up procedure. Preheat, with the lid closed, to 450°F.
2. Shuck the corn, removing the silks and cutting off the cores.
3. Tear four squares of aluminum foil large enough to completely cover an ear of corn.
4. In a medium bowl, combine the sour cream, mayonnaise, and cilantro. Slather the mixture all over the ears of corn.
5. Wrap each ear of corn in a piece of foil, sealing tightly. Place on the grill, close the lid, and smoke for 12 to 14 minutes.
6. Remove the corn from the foil and place in a shallow baking dish. Top with chipotle butter, the Parmesan cheese, and more chopped cilantro.
7. Serve immediately.

Secret tip: After the initial 12- to 14-minute cook time, move the corn to indirect heat to keep warm as you cook the rest of your meal. It's very difficult to burn corn on the cob.

ROASTED OKRA

As with many of the higher-temperature recipes in this book, this one can be prepared on the grill or in the oven if you need to conserve grill space. You may think of okra as a product of the American South, but its geographical origins trace back to South Asia, Ethiopia, and West Africa. From there it made its way to North and South America via the slave trade.

Ingredients
Nonstick cooking spray or butter, for greasing
1 pound whole okra

2 tablespoons extra-virgin olive oil
2 teaspoons seasoned salt
2 teaspoons freshly ground black pepper

Preparation time: 10 minutes
Smoking time: 30 minutes
Temperature: 400°F
Portions: 4
Recommended pellets: Hickory, Mesquite

Instructions
1. Supply your smoker with wood pellets and follow the manufacturer's specific start-up procedure. Preheat, with the lid closed, to 400°F. Alternatively, preheat your oven to 400°F.
2. Line a shallow rimmed baking pan with aluminum foil and coat with cooking spray.
3. Arrange the okra on the pan in a single layer. Drizzle with the olive oil, turning to coat. Season on all sides with the salt and pepper.
4. Place the baking pan on the grill grate, close the lid, and smoke for 30 minutes, or until crisp and slightly charred. Alternatively, roast in the oven for 30 minutes.
5. Serve hot.

Secret tip: Whether you make this okra in the oven or in your wood pellet grill, be sure to fully preheat the oven or cook chamber for the best results.

SWEET POTATO CHIPS

All yams are sweet potatoes, but a yam is only one of many varieties of sweet potatoes. But all sweet potatoes enjoy the title of superfood. They are loaded with beta carotene, which is an antioxidant and provides vitamin A in abundance. Sweet potatoes are naturally sweet, but their natural sugars are slowly released into the bloodstream, ensuring a balanced source of energy without causing the blood sugar spikes that are linked to fatigue and weight gain. Sweet and healthy? Win-win!

Ingredients
2 sweet potatoes
1 quart warm water
1 tablespoon cornstarch, plus 2 teaspoons
¼ cup extra-virgin olive oil
1 tablespoon salt
1 tablespoon packed brown sugar
1 teaspoon ground cinnamon
1 teaspoon freshly ground black pepper
½ teaspoon cayenne pepper

Preparation time: 40 minutes
Smoking time: 35 to 45 minutes
Temperature: 375°F
Portions: 3
Recommended pellets: Maple

Instructions
1. Using a mandolin, thinly slice the sweet potatoes.
2. Pour the warm water into a large bowl and add 1 tablespoon of cornstarch and the potato slices. Let soak for 15 to 20 minutes.

3. Supply your smoker with wood pellets and follow the manufacturer's specific start-up procedure. Preheat, with the lid closed, to 375°F.
4. Drain the potato slices, then arrange in a single layer on a perforated pizza pan or a baking sheet lined with aluminum foil. Brush the potato slices on both sides with the olive oil.
5. In a small bowl, whisk together the salt, brown sugar, cinnamon, black pepper, cayenne pepper, and the remaining 2 teaspoons of cornstarch. Sprinkle this seasoning blend on both sides of the potatoes.
6. Place the pan or baking sheet on the grill grate, close the lid, and smoke for 35 to 45 minutes, flipping after 20 minutes, until the chips curl up and become crispy.
7. Store in an airtight container.

Secret tip: Avoid storing your sweet potatoes in the refrigerator's produce bin, which tends to give them a hard center and an unpleasant flavor. What, you don't have a root cellar? Just keep them in a cool, dry area of your kitchen.

BUNNY DOGS WITH SWEET AND SPICY JALAPEÑO RELISH

Roast the carrots until they are golden brown, and be sure to enjoy with your favorite toppings.

Ingredients
8 hot dog-size carrots, peeled
¼ cup honey
¼ cup yellow mustard
Nonstick cooking spray or butter, for greasing
Salt
Freshly ground black pepper
8 hot dog buns
Sweet and Spicy Jalapeño Relish

Preparation time: 20 minutes
Smoking time: 35 to 40 minutes
Temperature: 375°F
Portions: 8
Recommended pellets: Cherry

Instructions
1. Prepare the carrots by removing the stems and slicing in half lengthwise.
2. In a small bowl, whisk together the honey and mustard.
3. Supply your smoker with wood pellets and follow the manufacturer's specific start-up procedure. Preheat, with the lid closed, to 375°F.
4. Line a baking sheet with aluminum foil and coat with cooking spray.
5. Brush the carrots on both sides with the honey mustard and season with salt and pepper; put on the baking sheet.
6. Place the baking sheet on the grill grate, close the lid, and smoke for 35 to 40 minutes, or until tender and starting to brown.
7. To serve, lightly toast the hot dog buns on the grill and top each with two slices of carrot and some relish.

Secret tip: Be sure to fully preheat your smoker to the temperature called for before placing carrots (or any roasting vegetables) on the grill.

MEXICAN STREET CORN WITH CHIPOTLE BUTTER

Brussels sprouts have become a popular appetizer and side dish in fine restaurants, but they're nothing new. In fact, they have been popular for ages in Brussels, Belgium, and I presume that's the origin of the name. There are myriad cooking options, from sautéing to pickling, but fire-roasting brings out some of the best flavors.

Ingredients
16 to 20 long toothpicks
1 pound Brussels sprouts, trimmed and wilted, leaves removed
½ pound bacon, cut in half
1 tablespoon packed brown sugar
1 tablespoon Cajun seasoning
¼ cup balsamic vinegar
¼ cup extra-virgin olive oil
¼ cup chopped fresh cilantro
2 teaspoons minced garlic

Preparation time: 15 minutes
Smoking time: 45 minutes
Temperature: 300°F
Portions: 6
Recommended pellets: Maple

Instructions

1. Soak the toothpicks in water for 15 minutes.
2. Supply your smoker with wood pellets and follow the manufacturer's specific start-up procedure. Preheat, with the lid closed, to 300°F.
3. Wrap each Brussels sprout in a half slice of bacon and secure with a toothpick.
4. In a small bowl, combine the brown sugar and Cajun seasoning. Dip each wrapped Brussels sprout in this sweet rub and roll around to coat.
5. Place the sprouts on a Frogmat or parchment paper–lined baking sheet on the grill grate, close the lid, and smoke for 45 minutes to 1 hour, turning as needed, until cooked evenly and the bacon is crisp.
6. In a small bowl, whisk together the balsamic vinegar, olive oil, cilantro, and garlic.
7. Remove the toothpicks from the Brussels sprouts, transfer to a plate and serve drizzled with the cilantro-balsamic sauce.

Secret tip: When fully cooked, Brussels sprouts often emit a sulfur-like smell—just another great reason to cook outdoors!

SOUTHERN SLAW

Ingredients
1 head cabbage, shredded
¼ cup white vinegar
¼ cup sugar
1 teaspoon paprika
½ teaspoon salt
½ teaspoon freshly ground black pepper
1 cup heavy (whipping) cream

Preparation time: 1 hour and 10 minutes

Portions: 10

Instructions
1. Place the shredded cabbage in a large bowl.
2. In a small bowl, combine the vinegar, sugar, paprika, salt, and pepper.
3. Pour the vinegar mixture over the cabbage and mix well.
4. Fold in the heavy cream and refrigerate for at least 1 hour before serving.

Secret tip: Serve this slaw with Pulled Pork Shoulder, or with hot dogs and hamburgers, or with an hour of Netflix…

GEORGIA SWEET ONION BAKE

This recipe relies on the perfect sweetness of a Vidalia onion. Vidalia is a city in Toombs County, Georgia, that was able to take full advantage of the low amount of sulfur in the soil there. The name Vidalia has been trademarked, and it's no surprise the Vidalia onion is Georgia's official state vegetable. Feel free to replace with other types of sweet onion, but if you can find Vidalia onions, get 'em!

Ingredients
Nonstick cooking spray or butter, for greasing
4 large Vidalia or other sweet onions
8 tablespoons (1 stick) unsalted butter, melted
4 chicken bouillon cubes
1 cup grated Parmesan cheese

Preparation time: 25 minutes
Smoking time: 1 hour
Temperature: 350°F
Portions: 6
Recommended pellets: Mesquite

Instructions
1. Supply your smoker with wood pellets and follow the manufacturer's specific start-up procedure. Preheat, with the lid closed, to 350°F.
2. Coat a high-sided baking pan with cooking spray or butter.
3. Peel the onions and cut into quarters, separating into individual petals.
4. Spread the onions out in the prepared pan and pour the melted butter over them.
5. Crush the bouillon cubes and sprinkle over the buttery onion pieces, then top with the cheese.
6. Transfer the pan to the grill, close the lid, and smoke for 30 minutes.
7. Remove the pan from the grill, cover tightly with aluminum foil, and poke several holes all over to vent.
8. Place the pan back on the grill, close the lid, and smoke for an additional 30 to 45 minutes.
9. Uncover the onions, stir, and serve hot.

Secret tip: We use unsalted butter in many of the recipes in this book, mainly as a way to control the salt content of each dish.

SCAMPI SPAGHETTI SQUASH

The stringy texture from which it gets its name allows you to replace noodles with a delicious low-carb substitute. The long cook time also allows the squash to absorb some nice smoky flavor. Feel free to use the squash as a blank canvas for your favorite pasta sauce.

Ingredients
1 spaghetti squash
2 tablespoons extra-virgin olive oil
1 teaspoon salt
1 teaspoon freshly ground black pepper
2 teaspoons garlic powder
4 tablespoons (½ stick) unsalted butter
½ cup white wine
1 tablespoon minced garlic
2 teaspoons chopped fresh parsley
1 teaspoon red pepper flakes
½ teaspoon salt
½ teaspoon freshly ground black pepper

Preparation time: 20 minutes
Smoking time: 40 minutes
Temperature: 375°F
Portions: 4
Recommended pellets: Hickory

Instructions
For the squash:
1. Supply your smoker with wood pellets and follow the manufacturer's specific start-up procedure. Preheat, with the lid closed, to 375°F.
2. Cut off both ends of the squash, then cut it in half lengthwise. Scoop out and discard the seeds.
3. Rub the squash flesh well with the olive oil and sprinkle on the salt, pepper, and garlic powder.
4. Place the squash cut-side up on the grill grate, close the lid, and smoke for 40 minutes, or until tender

For the sauce:
1. On the stove top, in a medium saucepan over medium heat, combine the butter, white wine, minced garlic, parsley, red pepper flakes, salt, and pepper, and cook for about 5 minutes, or until heated through. Reduce the heat to low and keep the sauce warm.
2. Remove the squash from the grill and let cool slightly before shredding the flesh with a fork; discard the skin.
3. Stir the shredded squash into the garlic-wine butter sauce and serve immediately.

Secret tip: Firm squash can be very tough to split without a razor-sharp knife. You can microwave the whole squash for 3 minutes to soften it just enough to make it easier to cut through.

VEGAN RECIPES

GRILLED RATATOUILLE SALAD
This brightly colored grilled vegetable salad is loaded with flavor and tastes delicious.

Ingredients
1 Whole sweet potatoes
1 Whole red onion, diced
1 Whole zucchini

1 Whole Squash
1 Large Tomato, diced
As Needed vegetable oil
As Needed salt and pepper

Preparation time: 15 minutes
Smoking time: 25 minutes
Temperature: 225°F
Portions: 6
Recommended pellets: Hickory

Instructions
1. Preheat grill to high setting with the lid closed for 10-15 minutes.
2. Slice all vegetables to a ¼ inch thickness.
3. Lightly brush each vegetable with oil and season with Traeger's Veggie Shake or salt and pepper.
4. Place sweet potato, onion, zucchini, and squash on grill grate and grill for 20 minutes or until tender, turn halfway through.
5. Add tomato slices to the grill during the last 5 minutes of cooking time.
6. For presentation, alternate vegetables while layering them vertically. Enjoy!

GRILLED BABY CARROTS AND FENNEL WITH ROMESCO

Smoked romesco sauce on top of this roasted trio of baby carrots, fingerling potatoes and fennel bulbs will make you sing Hallelujah thanks to it intensely fresh and tangy wood-fired flavor.

Ingredients
1 Pound Slender Rainbow Carrots
2 Whole Fennel, bulb
2 Tablespoon extra-virgin olive oil
1 Teaspoon salt
2 Tablespoon extra-virgin olive oil
To Taste salt
1 Tablespoon fresh thyme

Preparation time: 10 minutes
Smoking time: 45 minutes
Temperature: 225°F
Portions: 8 to 12
Recommended pellets: Hickory

Instructions
1. When ready to cook, set temperature to High and preheat, lid closed for 15 minutes. For optimal results, set to 500°F if available.
2. Trim the carrot tops to 1". Peel the carrots and halve any larger ones so they are all about 1/2" thick. Cut the fennel bulbs lengthwise into 1/2" thick slices.
3. Place the fennel and potato slices in a large mixing bowl. Drizzle with 2 Tbsp of the olive oil and a teaspoon of salt.
4. Toss to coat the vegetables evenly with the oil.
5. Place the carrots on a sheet pan. Drizzle with the additional 2 Tbsp of olive oil and a generous pinch of salt. Brush the olive oil over the carrots to distribute evenly.
6. Add the potatoes and fennel slices to the sheet pan. Nestle a few sprigs of herbs into the vegetables as well.
7. Place the pan directly on the grill grate and cook, stirring occasionally until the vegetables are browned and softened, about 35-45 minutes.

8. Allow to cool and serve with the Smoked Romesco Sauce. Enjoy!

APPETIZERS AND SNACKS

SMOKED CASHEWS

Ingredients
1 pound roasted, salted cashews

Preparation time: 5 minutes
Smoking time: 1 hour
Temperature: 120°F
Portions: 6
Recommended pellets: Hickory
Recommended sides: Rosemary and garlic roasted potatoes

Instructions
1. Supply your smoker with wood pellets and follow the manufacturer's specific start-up procedure. Preheat the grill, with the lid closed, to 120°F.
2. Pour the cashews onto a rimmed baking sheet and smoke for 1 hour, stirring once about halfway through the smoking time.
3. Remove the cashews from the grill, let cool, and store in an airtight container for as long as you can resist.

Secret tip: Substitute any variety of nuts you like in this recipe. The wood-fired flavor works perfectly with any type. If using raw nuts, the time will need to be increased to about 4 hours because raw nuts must be cooked for this recipe to work. I tend to stick with roasted, salted nuts, as they take less time and typically have the right amount of salt.

SMOKED CHEESE

Cold-smoking cheese with your cold smoker or using a smoke tube will turn heads at your next party. Typically reserved for the high-priced deli counter, smoked cheeses are a perfect snack or companion to your favorite wine. Although a medium-sharp Cheddar is usually inexpensive and readily available, any of your favorite cheeses can be smoked with this method. Use smoked cheese as a smoky substitute when a recipe calls for cheese.

Ingredients
1 (2-pound) block medium Cheddar cheese, or your favorite cheese, quartered lengthwise

Preparation time: 5 minutes
Smoking time: 2 hours, 30 minutes, plus overnight chilling

Temperature: 90°F
Portions: 4
Recommended pellets: Hickory
Recommended sides: Rosemary and garlic roasted potatoes

Instructions
1. Supply your smoker with wood pellets and follow the manufacturer's specific start-up procedure. Preheat the grill, with the lid closed, to 90°F.

2. Place the cheese directly on the grill grate and smoke for 2 hours, 30 minutes, checking frequently to be sure it's not melting. If the cheese begins to melt, try flipping it. If that doesn't help, remove it from the grill and refrigerate for about 1 hour and then return it to the cold smoker.
3. Remove the cheese, place it in a zip-top bag, and refrigerate overnight.
4. Slice the cheese and serve with crackers, or grate it and use for making a smoked mac and cheese.

Secret tip: The cold smoker needs to be at its absolute coldest for cheese. The grill should be at its lowest setting and all vents open on the cold smoker. Cheese melts, so place a pan filled with ice under the cheese while it smokes. The ice helps cool the air directly below the cheese, decreasing the chances of your cheese melting into the grill.

BACON-WRAPPED JALAPEÑO POPPERS

These poppers differ from Scotch Eggs and armadillo eggs because the peppers are stuffed and wrapped in bacon instead of sausage. This recipe also works with the "pepper rack" vertical pepper holder you may have seen marketed for grilling. Just stuff them from the top down.

Ingredients
8 ounces cream cheese, softened
½ cup shredded Cheddar cheese
¼ cup chopped scallions
1 teaspoon chipotle chile powder or regular chili powder
1 teaspoon garlic powder
1 teaspoon salt
18 large jalapeño peppers, stemmed, seeded, and halved lengthwise
1 pound bacon (precooked works well)

Preparation time: 20 minutes
Smoking time: 30 minutes
Temperature: 350°F
Portions: 12
Recommended pellets: Hickory, Maple

Instructions
1. Supply your smoker with wood pellets and follow the manufacturer's specific start-up procedure. Preheat, with the lid closed, to 350°F. Line a baking sheet with aluminum foil.
2. In a small bowl, combine the cream cheese, Cheddar cheese, scallions, chipotle powder, garlic powder, and salt.
3. Stuff the jalapeño halves with the cheese mixture.
4. Cut the bacon into pieces big enough to wrap around the stuffed pepper halves.
5. Wrap the bacon around the peppers and place on the prepared baking sheet.
6. Put the baking sheet on the grill grate, close the lid, and smoke the peppers for 30 minutes, or until the cheese is melted and the bacon is cooked through and crisp.
7. Let the jalapeño poppers cool for 3 to 5 minutes. Serve warm.

Secret tip: Grilling bacon is made easier with the indirect heat of a wood pellet grill, but I still like to use precooked bacon to wrap these poppers. The peppers will fully cook as the bacon gets crisp and fully rendered.

PULLED PORK LOADED NACHOS

If you smoke a lot of Boston butts, chances are you will have leftover pulled pork from time to time. I like to utilize the extra pork to top everything from loaded baked potatoes to pizza and more. However, my family's favorite quick fix is this nacho dish. Everything is already cooked, so all you need to do is heat it up and melt the cheese.

Ingredients
2 cups leftover smoked pulled pork
1 small sweet onion, diced
1 medium tomato, diced
1 jalapeño pepper, seeded and diced
1 garlic clove, minced
1 teaspoon salt
1 teaspoon freshly ground black pepper
1 bag tortilla chips
1 cup shredded Cheddar cheese
½ cup The Ultimate BBQ Sauce, divided
½ cup shredded jalapeño Monterey Jack cheese
Juice of ½ lime
1 avocado, halved, pitted, and sliced
2 tablespoons sour cream
1 tablespoon chopped fresh cilantro

Preparation time: 15 minutes
Smoking time: 10 minutes
Temperature: 375°F
Portions: 4
Recommended pellets: Hickory, Mesquite

Instructions
1. Supply your smoker with wood pellets and follow the manufacturer's specific start-up procedure. Preheat, with the lid closed, to 375°F.
2. Heat the pulled pork in the microwave.
3. In a medium bowl, combine the onion, tomato, jalapeño, garlic, salt, and pepper, and set aside.
4. Arrange half of the tortilla chips in a large cast iron skillet. Spread half of the warmed pork on top and cover with the Cheddar cheese. Top with half of the onion-jalapeño mixture, then drizzle with ¼ cup of barbecue sauce.
5. Layer on the remaining tortilla chips, then the remaining pork and the Monterey Jack cheese. Top with the remaining onion-jalapeño mixture and drizzle with the remaining ¼ cup of barbecue sauce.
6. Place the skillet on the grill, close the lid, and smoke for about 10 minutes, or until the cheese is melted and bubbly. (Watch to make sure your chips don't burn!)
7. Squeeze the lime juice over the nachos, top with the avocado slices and sour cream, and garnish with the cilantro before serving hot.

Secret tip: A large cast iron skillet is not only a great cooking vessel for the grill, but it is also an impressive, heat-retaining serving platter. Just invest in a handle hot pad to keep from burning yourself.

PIG POPS (SWEET-HOT BACON ON A STICK)

You'll never forget your first bite of candied bacon. It almost always results in a response like, "Where has this been all my life?" In fact, bacon is notoriously hard to cook on a normal grill because the slices can fall through the grate and there are flareups. Using your wood pellet grill and skewers, a baking sheet, or a Frogmat will make it much easier. Note: For crispier bacon, smoke at 350°F for 25 to 30 minutes.

Ingredients
Nonstick cooking spray, oil, or butter, for greasing
2 pounds thick-cut bacon (24 slices)
24 metal skewers
1 cup packed light brown sugar
2 to 3 teaspoons cayenne pepper
½ cup maple syrup, divided

Preparation time: 15 minutes
Smoking time: 25 to 30 minutes
Temperature: 350°F
Portions: 24
Recommended pellets: Hickory, Maple

Instructions
1. Supply your smoker with wood pellets and follow the manufacturer's specific start-up procedure. Preheat, with the lid closed, to 350°F.
2. Coat a disposable aluminum foil baking sheet with cooking spray, oil, or butter.
3. Thread each bacon slice onto a metal skewer and place on the prepared baking sheet.
4. In a medium bowl, stir together the brown sugar and cayenne.
5. Baste the top sides of the bacon with ¼ cup of maple syrup.
6. Sprinkle half of the brown sugar mixture over the bacon.
7. Place the baking sheet on the grill, close the lid, and smoke for 15 to 30 minutes.
8. Using tongs, flip the bacon skewers. Baste with the remaining ¼ cup of maple syrup and top with the remaining brown sugar mixture.
9. Continue smoking with the lid closed for 10 to 15 minutes, or until crispy. You can eyeball the bacon and smoke to your desired doneness, but the actual ideal internal temperature for bacon is 155°F (if you want to try to get a thermometer into it—ha!).
10. Using tongs, carefully remove the bacon skewers from the grill. Let cool completely before handling.

Secret tip: If you'd prefer to use wooden skewers, soak them in water for 30 minutes before threading on the bacon.

CHORIZO QUESO FUNDIDO

Mexican chorizo is a raw hot sausage that is typically used for Mexican-American dishes like dips, eggs, and tacos. It's different from Spanish chorizo, which is a cured sausage that's more likely to be found with dried sausage and salami. We use the fresh Mexican chorizo in this recipe, and we add it in at the end for a pop of color and signature flavor. Queso fundido is akin to fondue: It's an ooey-gooey, cheesy dip to enjoy with nacho chips.

Ingredients
1 poblano chile
1 cup chopped queso quesadilla or queso Oaxaca
1 cup shredded Monterey Jack cheese
¼ cup milk
1 tablespoon all-purpose flour
2 (4-ounce) links Mexican chorizo sausage, casings removed
⅓ cup beer
1 tablespoon unsalted butter
1 small red onion, chopped
½ cup whole kernel corn
2 serrano chiles or jalapeño peppers, stemmed, seeded, and coarsely chopped
1 tablespoon minced garlic
1 tablespoon freshly squeezed lime juice
1 teaspoon ground cumin
1 teaspoon salt
1 teaspoon freshly ground black pepper
1 tablespoon chopped fresh cilantro
1 tablespoon chopped scallions
Tortilla chips, for serving

Preparation time: 40 minutes
Smoking time: 20 minutes
Temperature: 350°F
Portions: 4 to 6
Recommended pellets: Apple

Instructions
1. Supply your smoker with wood pellets and follow the manufacturer's specific start-up procedure. Preheat, with the lid closed, to 350°F.
2. On the smoker or over medium-high heat on the stove top, place the poblano directly on the grate (or burner) to char for 1 to 2 minutes, turning as needed. Remove from heat and place in a closed-up lunch-size paper bag for 2 minutes to sweat and further loosen the skin.
3. Remove the skin and coarsely chop the poblano, removing the seeds; set aside.
4. In a bowl, combine the queso quesadilla, Monterey Jack, milk, and flour; set aside.
5. On the stove top, in a cast iron skillet over medium heat, cook and crumble the chorizo for about 2 minutes.
6. Transfer the cooked chorizo to a small, grill-safe pan and place over indirect heat on the smoker.
7. Place the cast iron skillet on the preheated grill grate. Pour in the beer and simmer for a few minutes, loosening and stirring in any remaining sausage bits from the pan.
8. Add the butter to the pan, then add the cheese mixture a little at a time, stirring constantly.
9. When the cheese is smooth, stir in the onion, corn, serrano chiles, garlic, lime juice, cuvmin, salt, and pepper. Stir in the reserved chopped charred poblano.
10. Close the lid and smoke for 15 to 20 minutes to infuse the queso with smoke flavor and further cook the vegetables.
11. When the cheese is bubbly, top with the chorizo mixture and garnish with the cilantro and scallions.
12. Serve the chorizo queso fundido hot with tortilla chips.

Secret tip: Try using leftover grilled corn cut from the cob for better texture and added smoke flavor.

SIMPLE CREAM CHEESE SAUSAGE BALLS

Though they can be hard to find, mini filo dough shells are very versatile appetizer bases. So when you do find them, stock up. They freeze well, and the possibilities are endless for time-saving hors d'oeuvres. Plus, because your pellet smoker can maintain baking temperatures, they are now welcome at the grill. Canned biscuits divided in half or wonton wrappers also work in a pinch.

Ingredients
1 pound ground hot sausage, uncooked
8 ounces cream cheese, softened
1 package mini filo dough shells
Preparation time: 15 minutes
Smoking time: 30 minutes
Temperature: 350°F
Portions: 4 to 5
Recommended pellets: Hickory

Instructions
1. Supply your smoker with wood pellets and follow the manufacturer's specific start-up procedure. Preheat, with the lid closed, to 350°F.
2. In a large bowl, using your hands, thoroughly mix together the sausage and cream cheese until well blended.
3. Place the filo dough shells on a rimmed perforated pizza pan or into a mini muffin tin.
4. Roll the sausage and cheese mixture into 1-inch balls and place into the filo shells.
5. Place the pizza pan or mini muffin tin on the grill, close the lid, and smoke the sausage balls for 30 minutes, or until cooked through and the sausage is no longer pink.
6. Plate and serve warm.

Secret tip: Serve these along with Not Yo' Typical Nachos and you've got game day covered!

PIGS IN A BLANKET

When you need a quick and easy appetizer, start the grill and roll these lil' smokies into their dough uniform.

Ingredients
2 Tablespoon Poppy Seeds
1 Tablespoon Dried Minced Onion
2 Teaspoon garlic, minced
2 Tablespoon Sesame Seeds
1 Teaspoon salt
8 Ounce Original Crescent Dough
1/4 Cup Dijon mustard
1 Large egg, beaten

Preparation time: 20 minutes
Smoking time: 15 minutes
Temperature: 350 °F
Portions: 4 to 6
Recommended pellets: Apple

Instructions
1. When ready to cook, start your Traeger at 350 degrees F, and preheat with lid closed, 10 to 15 minutes.
2. Mix together poppy seeds, dried minced onion, dried minced garlic, salt and sesame seeds. Set aside.
3. Cut each triangle of crescent roll dough into thirds lengthwise, making 3 small strips from each roll.
4. Brush the dough strips lightly with Dijon mustard. Put the mini hot dogs on 1 end of the dough and roll up.
5. Arrange them, seam side down, on a greased baking pan. Brush with egg wash and sprinkle with seasoning mixture.
6. Bake in Traeger until golden brown, about 12 to 15 minutes.
7. Serve with mustard or dipping sauce of your choice. Enjoy!

BACON PORK PINWHEELS (KANSAS LOLLIPOPS)

Make everyday Pork Appreciation Day with these savory pork loin bacon roll-ups.

Ingredients
1 Whole Pork Loin, boneless
To Taste salt and pepper
To Taste Greek Seasoning
4 Slices bacon
To Taste The Ultimate BBQ Sauce

Preparation time: 10 minutes
Smoking time: 20 minutes
Temperature: 500°F
Portions: 4 to 6
Recommended pellets: Apple

Instructions
1. When ready to cook, start the Traeger and set temperature to 500F. Preheat, lid closed, for 10 to 15 minutes.
2. Trim pork loin of any unwanted silver skin or fat. Using a sharp knife, cut pork loin length wise, into 4 long strips.
3. Lay pork flat, then season with salt, pepper and Cavender's Greek Seasoning.
4. Flip the pork strips over and layer bacon on unseasoned side. Begin tightly rolling the pork strips, with bacon being rolled up on the inside.
5. Secure a skewer all the way through each pork roll to secure it in place. Set the pork rolls down on grill and cook for 15 minutes.
6. Brush BBQ Sauce over the pork. Turn each skewer over, then coat the other side. Let pork cook for another 5-10 minutes, depending on thickness of your pork. Enjoy!

DELICIOUS DEVILED CRAB APPETIZER

The origin story of deviled crab is tied to smoke—cigar smoke, actually. The discovery of deviled crab has been traced back to a cigar workers' strike in Ybor City, Florida, in the 1920s. I remember having deviled crab as a kid, and it was served in a crab-shaped tin. We prepare it below using a mini muffin pan, but you could just as easily use a real hollowed-out crab shell, find manufactured crab shell tins online, or prepare as small cakes, with no shell, on a baking sheet.

Ingredients
Nonstick cooking spray, oil, or butter, for greasing
1 cup panko breadcrumbs, divided

1 cup canned corn, drained
½ cup chopped scallions, divided
½ red bell pepper, finely chopped
16 ounces jumbo lump crabmeat
¾ cup mayonnaise, divided
1 egg, beaten
1 teaspoon salt
1 teaspoon freshly ground black pepper
2 teaspoons cayenne pepper, divided
Juice of 1 lemon

Preparation time: 25 minutes
Smoking time: 10 minutes
Temperature: 425°F
Portions: 30 mini crab cakes
Recommended pellets: Pecan

Instructions
1. Supply your smoker with wood pellets and follow the manufacturer's specific start-up procedure. Preheat, with the lid closed, to 425°F.
2. Spray three 12-cup mini muffin pans with cooking spray and divide ½ cup of the panko between 30 of the muffin cups, pressing into the bottoms and up the sides. (Work in batches, if necessary, depending on the number of pans you have.)
3. In a medium bowl, combine the corn, ¼ cup of scallions, the bell pepper, crabmeat, half of the mayonnaise, the egg, salt, pepper, and 1 teaspoon of cayenne pepper.
4. Gently fold in the remaining ½ cup of breadcrumbs and divide the mixture between the prepared mini muffin cups.
5. Place the pans on the grill grate, close the lid, and smoke for 10 minutes, or until golden brown.
6. In a small bowl, combine the lemon juice and the remaining mayonnaise, scallions, and cayenne pepper to make a sauce.
7. Brush the tops of the mini crab cakes with the sauce and serve hot.

SMOKED TURKEY SANDWICH

Who hasn't spent the Friday after Thanksgiving in front of the TV watching college football and cramming their face full of sandwiches made from leftover Thanksgiving turkey?

Ingredients
2 slices sourdough bread
2 tablespoons butter, at room temperature
2 (1-ounce) slices Swiss cheese
4 ounces leftover Smoked Turkey
1 teaspoon garlic salt

Preparation time: 15 minutes
Smoking time: 15 minutes
Temperature: 375 °F
Portions: 1
Recommended pellets: Hickory

Instructions

1. Supply your smoker with wood pellets and follow the manufacturer's specific start-up procedure. Preheat the grill, with the lid closed, to 375°F.
2. Coat one side of each bread slice with 1 tablespoon of butter and sprinkle the buttered sides with garlic salt.
3. Place 1 slice of cheese on each unbuttered side of the bread, and then put the turkey on the cheese.
4. Close the sandwich, buttered sides out, and place it directly on the grill grate. Cook for 5 minutes. Flip the sandwich and cook for 5 minutes more. Remove the sandwich from the grill, cut it in half, and serve.

Secret tip: Making this sandwich with turkey that was pre-smoked, or cooked previously on a wood-fired grill, really enhances the smoky flavor.

BAKED GOODS

PRETZEL ROLLS

You don't have to wait for Oktoberfest for melt in your mouth pretzel rolls, this hearty homemade bread Traeger's up moist and delicious & they're perfect for wrapping around a fire-grilled brat any time of year.

Ingredients
2 3/4 Cup Bread Flour
1 Quick-Rising Yeast, envelope
1 Teaspoon salt
1 Teaspoon sugar
1/2 Teaspoon celery seed
1/2 Teaspoon Caraway Seeds
1 Cup hot water
As Needed Cornmeal
8 Cup water
1/4 Cup baking soda
2 Tablespoon sugar
1 Whole Egg White
Coarse salt

Preparation time: 1 hour
Smoking time: 20 minutes
Portions: 6

Instructions
1. Combine bread flour, 1 envelope yeast, salt, 1 teaspoon sugar, caraway seeds and celery seeds in food processor or standing mixer with dough hook and blend.
2. With machine running, gradually pour hot water, adding enough water to form smooth elastic dough. Process 1 minute to knead. (You could also knead it by hand for a few minutes.)
3. Grease medium bowl. Add dough to bowl, turning to coat. Cover bowl with plastic wrap, then towel; let dough rise in warm draft-free area until doubled in volume, about 35 minutes.
4. Flour a large baking sheet. Punch dough down and knead on lightly floured surface until smooth. Divide into 8 pieces. Form each dough piece into a ball.
5. Place dough balls on prepared sheet, flattening each slightly. Using serrated knife, cut X in top center of each dough ball. Cover with towel and let dough balls rise until almost doubled in volume, about 20 minutes.
6. When ready to cook, start the Traeger on Smoke with the lid open until a fire is established (4-5 minutes). Turn temperature to 375 F (190 C) and preheat, lid closed, for 10 to 15 minutes.

7. Grease another baking sheet and sprinkle with cornmeal. Bring water to boil in large saucepan. Add baking soda and sugar (water will foam up). Add 3 rolls (or however many will fit comfortably in the pot) and cook 30 seconds per side.

8. Using slotted spoon, transfer rolls to prepared sheet, arranging X side up. Repeat with remaining rolls. Brush rolls with egg white glaze. Sprinkle rolls generously with coarse salt.

9. Bake rolls until brown, about 20 to 25 minutes. Transfer to racks and cool 10 minutes. Serve rolls warm or at room temperature. Enjoy!

FOCACCIA

Herb-infused flat bread is just the beginning; grab two slabs, pack them with shredded pork or beef, and slather with BBQ sauce for a carnivorous, flavor-packed meal.

Ingredients
1 Cup warm water (110°F to 115°F)
1/2 Ounce Yeast, active
1 Teaspoon sugar
2 1/2 Cup flour
1 Teaspoon salt
1/4 Cup extra-virgin olive oil
1 1/2 Teaspoon Italian herbs, dried
1/8 Teaspoon red pepper flakes
As Needed coarse sea salt

Preparation time: 25 minutes
Smoking time: 40 minutes
Portions: 6

Instructions
1. Measure the water in a glass-measuring cup. Stir in the yeast and sugar. Let rest for in a warm place. After 5 to 10 minutes, the mixture should be foamy, indicating the yeast is "alive." If it does not foam, discard it and start again.
2. Pour the water/yeast mixture in the bowl of a food processor. Add 1 cup of the flour as well as the salt and 1/4 cup of olive oil. Pulse several times to blend. Add the remaining flour, Italian herbs, and hot pepper flakes.
3. Process the dough until it's smooth and elastic and pulls away from the sides of the bowl, adding small amounts of flour or water through the feed tube if the dough is respectively too wet or too dry.
4. Let the dough rise in the covered food processor bowl in a warm place until doubled in bulk, about 1 hour5. Remove the dough from the food processor (it will deflate) and turn onto a lightly floured surface.
6. Oil two 8- to 9-inch round cake pans generously with olive oil. (Just pour a couple of glugs in and tilt the pan to spread the oil.) Divide the dough into two equal pieces, shape into disks, and put one in each prepared cake pan.
7. Oil the top of each disk with olive oil and dimple the dough with your fingertips. Sprinkle lightly with coarse salt, and if desired, additional dried Italian herbs.
8. Cover the focaccia dough with plastic wrap and let the dough rise in a warm place, about 45 minutes to an hour.
9. When ready to cook, start the Traeger grill and set the temperature to 400F and preheat, lid closed, for 10 to 15 minutes.
10. Put the pans with the focaccia dough directly on the grill grate. Bake until the focaccia breads are light golden in color and baked through, 35 to 40 minutes, rotating the pans halfway through the baking time.
11. Let cool slightly before removing from the pans. Cut into wedges for serving.

TRAEGER WHEAT BREAD

Ingredients
As Needed extra-virgin olive oil
2 Cup all-purpose flour
1 Cup whole wheat flour
1 1/4 Ounce Packet, Active Dry Yeast
1 1/4 Teaspoon salt
1 1/2 Cup water
As Needed Cornmeal

Preparation time: 30 minutes
Smoking time: 1 hour
Portions: 6

Instructions
1. Oil a large mixing bowl and set aside. In a second mixing bowl, combine the flours, yeast, and salt.
2. Push your sleeve up to your elbow and form your fingers into a claw. Mix the dry ingredients until well-combined.
3. Add the water and mix until blended. The dough will be wet, shaggy, and somewhat stringy.
4. Tip the dough into the oiled mixing bowl and cover with plastic wrap.
5. Allow the dough to rise at room temperature-- about 70 degrees-- for 2 hours, or until the surface is bubbled.
6. Turn the dough out onto a lightly floured work surface and lightly flour the top. With floured hands, fold the dough over on itself twice. Cover loosely with plastic wrap and allow the dough to rest for 15 minutes.
7. Dust a clean lint-free cotton towel with cornmeal, wheat bran, or flour. With floured hands, gently form the dough into a ball and place it, seam side down, on the towel.
8. Dust the top of the ball with cornmeal, wheat bran, or flour, and cover the dough with a second towel. Let the dough rise until doubled in size; the dough will not spring back when poked with a finger.
9. In the meantime, start the Traeger grill and set temperature to 450 F. Preheat, lid closed, for 10-15 minutes.
10. Put a lidded 6- to 8-quart cast iron Dutch oven - preferably one coated with enamel, on the grill grate.
11. When the dough has risen, remove the top towel, slide your hand under the bottom towel to support the dough, then carefully tip the dough, seam side up, into the preheated pot.
12. Remove the towel. Shake the pot a couple of times if the dough looks lopsided: It will straighten out as it bakes.
13. Cover the pot with the lid and bake the bread for 30 minutes. Remove the lid and continue to bake the bread for 15 to 30 minutes more, or until it is nicely browned and sounds hollow when rapped with your knuckles.
14. Turn onto a wire rack to cool. Slice with a serrated knife. Enjoy!

PIZZA BITES

Cheesy, saucy, and totally shareable. These epic bites are stuffed with mozzarella, pepperoni, and sauce, wrapped in homemade dough, then baked over mesquite hardwood for max flavor.

Ingredients
4 1/2 Cup Bread Flour
1 1/2 Tablespoon sugar
2 Teaspoon Instant Yeast
2 Teaspoon kosher salt
3 Tablespoon extra-virgin olive oil
15 Fluid Ounce Water, Lukewarm
8 Ounce Pepperoni, sliced
1 Cup pizza sauce
1 Cup mozzarella cheese
1 Whole egg, for egg wash
1 As Needed salt

Preparation time: 1 day

Smoking time: 20 minutes
Portions: 6

Instructions
1. For the Pizza Dough: Combine flour, sugar, salt, and yeast in food processor. Pulse 3 to 4 times until incorporated evenly. Add olive oil and water. Run food processor until mixture forms ball that rides around the bowl above the blade, about 15 seconds. Continue processing 15 seconds longer.
2. Transfer dough ball to lightly floured surface and knead once or twice by hand until smooth ball is formed. Divide dough into three even parts and place each into a 1 gallon zip top bag. Place in refrigerator and allow to rise at least one day.
3. At least two hours before baking, remove dough from refrigerator and shape into balls by gathering dough towards bottom and pinching shut. Flour well and place each one in a separate medium mixing bowl. Cover tightly with plastic wrap and allow to rise at warm room temperature until roughly doubled in volume.
4. When ready to cook, set the grill temperature to 350°F and preheat, lid closed for 15 minutes.
5. After the first rise remove the dough from the fridge and let come to room temperature. Roll dough on a flat surface. Cut dough into long strips 3" wide by 18" long.
6. Slice pepperoni into strips.
7. In a medium bowl combine the pizza sauce, mozzarella and pepperoni.
8. Spoon 1 TBSP of the pizza filling onto the pizza dough every two inches, about halfway down the length of the dough. Dip a pastry brush into the egg wash and brush around pizza filling. Fold the half side of the dough (without the pizza filling) over the other the half that contains the pizza filling.
9. Press down between each pizza bite slightly with your fingers. With a ravioli or pizza cutter, cut around each filling- creating a rectangle shape and sealing the crust in.
10. Transfer each pizza bite onto a parchment lined cookie sheet. Cover with a kitchen towel and let them rise for 30 minutes.
11. When ready to cook, preheat the grill to 350°F with the lid closed for 10-15 minutes.
12. Brush the bites with remaining egg wash, sprinkle with salt and place directly on the sheet tray. Bake 10-15 minutes until the exterior is golden brown.
13. Remove from grill and transfer to a serving dish. Serve with extra pizza sauce for dipping and enjoy!

IRISH SODA BREAD

Irish Soda Bread relies on baking soda to rise, not yeast. It bakes up thick and rich with flavor and is wonderful sopped in egg yolks, meat drippings or sauce. Hailing from Northern Ireland, this bread is hearty enough to feed yer herd of blokes.

Ingredients
As Needed Cornmeal
3 1/2 Cup all-purpose flour
1 1/2 Teaspoon sugar
1 1/4 Teaspoon baking soda
1 Teaspoon salt
1 Cup buttermilk
To Taste butter

Preparation time: 15 minutes
Smoking time: 45 minutes
Portions: 8 to 12

Instructions
1. When ready to cook, set the temperature to 400F (205 C) and preheat, lid closed, for 10 to 15 minutes.
2. Lightly dust the bottom of an 8-inch (20-cm) round cake pan with cornmeal and set aside.
3. Tear off a large sheet of wax paper and lay it on your work surface.
4. Combine the flour, sugar, soda, and salt in a large sifter and sift onto the wax paper. Carefully lift up the sides of the wax paper and tip the flour mixture back into the sifter. Re-sift into a large mixing bowl.
5. Lightly flour your work surface. Make a well in the middle of the flour mixture in the bowl and pour in 1 cup (240 mL) of buttermilk. Stir with a wooden spoon. Work quickly and gently as the carbon dioxide bubbles formed when the buttermilk hits the dry ingredients will deflate, the dough will look somewhat shaggy. If the dough seems dryish, add a little more buttermilk.
6. Turn out onto the floured surface, and with floured hands, knead gently for 10 to 20 seconds - just long enough to bring the dough bits together. (It will look more like biscuit dough than bread dough.)
7. Form into a flattish round and transfer to the prepared pan. Flour a sharp knife, and deeply cut a cross in the top of the loaf all the way to the edge of the bread. Quickly get it in to bake, if it sits too long, it will deflate.
8. Bake the bread for 45 to 50 minutes, or until it is browned and the bottom of the loaf sounds hollow when rapped with your knuckles.
9. Remove the bread from the baking pan and cool on a cooling rack. Just be-fore serving, cut the loaf in half and then slice each half into thin slices.
10. Serve with butter. Wrap leftovers tightly in plastic wrap or foil. This bread makes great toast. Enjoy!

QUICK BAKED DINNER ROLLS
Serve these simple homemade rolls alongside a burly brisket or ribs, to sop up excess BBQ sauce, or just enjoy them smothered in butter

Ingredients
1 Cup Water, Lukewarm
2 Tablespoon Yeast, quick rise
1 Teaspoon salt
1/4 Cup sugar
3 33/100 Cup flour
1/4 Cup Unsalted Butter, softened
1 egg
As Needed cooking spray
1 egg, for egg wash

Preparation time: 1 hour
Smoking time: 30 minutes

Portions: 8 to 12

Instructions
1. Combine yeast and warm water in a small bowl to activate the yeast. Let sit until foamy, about 5-10 minutes.
2. Combine salt, sugar, and flour in the bowl of a stand mixer fitted with the dough hook. Pour water and yeast into the dry ingredients with the machine running on low.
3. Add butter and egg and mix for 10 minutes gradually increasing the speed from low to high.
4. Form the dough into a ball and place in a buttered bowl. Cover with a cloth and let the dough rise for approximately 40 minutes.
5. Transfer the risen dough to a lightly floured surface and divide into 8 pieces forming a ball with each.
6. Lightly spray a cast iron pan with cooking spray and arrange balls in the pan. Cover with a cloth and let rise 20 minutes.
7. When ready to cook, set the Traeger to 375°F and preheat, lid closed for 15 minutes.
8. Brush rolls with egg wash and then bake for 30 minutes until lightly browned. Serve hot. Enjoy!

BAKED WOOD-FIRED PIZZA

Get that unbeatable Italian wood-fired pizza taste right on your Traeger. Drop the take-out menu and take your pizza flavors back to Italy.

Ingredients
2/3 Cup warm water (110°F to 115°F)
2 1/2 Teaspoon active dry yeast
1/2 Teaspoon granulated sugar
1 Teaspoon kosher salt
1 Tablespoon oil
2 Cup all-purpose flour
1/4 Cup fine cornmeal
1 Large grilled portobello mushroom, sliced
1 Jar pickled artichoke hearts, drained and chopped
1 Cup shredded fontina cheese
1/2 Cup shaved Parmigiano-Reggiano cheese, divided
To Taste Roasted Garlic, minced
1/4 Cup extra-virgin olive oil
To Taste banana peppers

Preparation time: 20 minutes
Smoking time: 12 minutes
Portions: 6

Instructions
1. In a glass bowl, stir together the warm water, yeast and sugar. Let stand until the mixture starts to foam, about 10 minutes. In a mixer, combine 1-3/4 cup flour, sugar and salt. Stir oil into the yeast mixture. Slowly add the liquid to the dry ingredients while slowly increasing the mixers speed until fully combined. The dough should be smooth and not sticky.
2. Knead the dough on a floured surface, gradually adding the remaining flour as needed to prevent the dough from sticking, until smooth, about 5 to 10 minutes.
3. Form the dough into a ball. Apply a thin layer of olive oil to a large bowl. Place the dough into the bowl and coat the dough ball with a small amount of olive oil. Cover and let rise in a warm place for about 1 hour or until doubled in size.
4. When ready to cook, set Traeger temperature to 450°F and preheat, lid closed for 15 minutes.
5. Place a pizza stone in the grill while it preheats.
6. Punch the dough down and roll it out into a 12-inch circle on a floured surface.

7. Spread the cornmeal evenly on the pizza peel. Place the dough on the pizza peel and assemble the toppings evenly in the following order: olive oil, roasted garlic, fontina, portobello, artichoke hearts, Parmigiano-Reggiano and banana peppers.

8. Carefully slide the assembled pizza from the pizza peel to the preheated pizza stone and bake until the crust is golden brown, about 10 to 12 minutes. Enjoy!

PUMPKIN BREAD

A fall favorite, pumpkin bread brings memories of hot apple cider, pumpkin patches, and crisp leaves gently falling. Enjoy this bread any season of the year.

Ingredients
1 Cup Pumpkin, canned
2 eggs
2/3 Cup vegetable oil
1/2 Cup sour cream
1 Teaspoon vanilla extract
2 1/2 Cup flour
1 1/2 Teaspoon baking soda
1 Teaspoon salt
1/2 Teaspoon ground cinnamon
1/4 Teaspoon ground nutmeg
1/4 Teaspoon ground cloves
1/4 Teaspoon ground ginger
As Needed butter

Preparation time: 15 minutes
Smoking time: 1 hour
Portions: 6

Instructions
1. In a large mixing bowl, combine the pumpkin, eggs, vegetable oil, sour cream, and vanilla and whisk to blend.
2. In a separate bowl, combine the flour, baking soda, salt, cinnamon, nutmeg, cloves, and ginger. Add the dry ingredients to the wet ingredients and stir to combine. Do not overmix.
3. If desired, stir in one or more of the optional ingredients (walnuts, dried cranberries, raisins, or chocolate chips). Butter the interiors of two loaf pans.
4. Sprinkle with flour to coat the buttered surfaces, and tap out any excess. Divide the batter evenly between the two pans.
5. When ready to cook, set the Traeger to 350°F and preheat, lid closed for 15 minutes.
6. Arrange the loaf pans directly on the grill grate. Bake for 45 to 50 minutes, or until a skewer or toothpick inserted in the center comes out clean. Also, the top of the loaf should spring back when pressed gently with a finger.
7. Transfer the loaf pans to a cooling rack and let cool for 10 minutes before carefully turning out the pumpkin bread. Let the loaves cool thoroughly before slicing. Wrap in aluminum foil or plastic wrap if not eating right away. Serve and enjoy!

BEER BREAD

Homemade bread isn't that difficult with beer involved. Grab a light beer and Traeger bake this hearty loaf of Irish beer bread. It's heavy, flavorful, and perfect for sopping in meat juices or slathered in butter.

Ingredients
400 g all-purpose flour
2 Tablespoon sugar
1 Tablespoon baking powder
1 Teaspoon salt
12 Ounce beer
2 Tablespoon honey
6 Tablespoon butter, melted

Preparation time: 20 minutes
Smoking time: 1 hour

Portions: 6

Instructions
1. Start the Traeger grill on set the temperature to 350F (180 C) and preheat, lid closed, for 10 to 15 minutes.
2. Spray a loaf pan (9x5x3 inches) (55x12x20 cm) with nonstick cooking spray and set aside.
3. Put the flour, sugar, baking powder, and salt in a large mixing bowl. Whisk with a wire whisk to combine and aerate. Add the beer and honey and stir with a wooden spoon until the batter is just mixed. (Do not overmix.) If desired, gently stir in one or more of the optional add-ins.
4. Pour half of the melted butter in the prepared loaf pan and spoon in the batter. Pour the remainder of the butter over the top of the loaf.
5. Put the loaf pan directly on the grill grate and bake until a wooden skewer or toothpick inserted in the center of the loaf comes out clean, 50 to 60 minutes, and the bread is golden-brown. (Note: If using a glass loaf pan, the baking time might be shorter.)
6. Let the loaf cool slightly in the pan before removing from the pan. Leftovers make great toast.
7. Optional Add-ins: Bacon, cooked and crumbled, 1 cup (100 g) Grated Cheese, Red Bell Pepper and Onion, diced and sauted in Butter (1/4 cup each), Green Onions, minced, Dried Herbs such as Dill, Rosemary, Mixed Italian Herbs, etc,.Cracked Black Pepper, Your favorite Barbecue Rub, such as Traeger's Pork and Poultry Shake, Ground Cinnamon, Dry Ranch Dressing Mix, Coarse-grained Mustard.

ZUCCHINI BREAD

Baking Zucchini Bread on the Traeger brings out fall flavors. The wood-fired smoke encircles and infuses a flavorful addition that creates an amazingly delicious breakfast treat.

Ingredients
1 Cup Walnuts, Chopped
2 Large zucchini
1 Teaspoon salt
1 Teaspoon ground cinnamon
1/4 Teaspoon ground cloves
1/4 Teaspoon baking powder
3 Cup all-purpose flour
1 eggs
2 Cup sugar
1/2 Cup vegetable oil
1/2 Cup Yogurt

1 1/2 Teaspoon vanilla extract

Preparation time: 10 minutes
Smoking time: 50 minutes
Portions: 6

Instructions
1. Grease and flour two 9- by 5-inch bread pans, preferably nonstick.
2. When ready to cook, set the temperature to 350°F and preheat, lid closed for 15 minutes.
3. Spread the walnuts on a pie plate and toast for 10 minutes, stirring once. Let cool, then coarsely chop. Set aside.
4. Trim the ends off the zucchini, then coarsely grate into a colander set over the sink on a box grater (or use the shredding disk on a food processor). You'll need 2 cups.
5. Sprinkle with the salt and let drain for 30 minutes. Press on the zucchini with paper towels to expel excess water.
6. Sift the flour, baking powder, cinnamon, and cloves in a mixing bowl or on a large sheet of parchment or wax paper.
7. Combine the eggs, sugar, oil, yogurt, and vanilla in a large mixing bowl and mix on medium speed. (You can mix the batter by hand, if desired.) Add half the dry ingredients and mix on low speed; add the remaining dry ingredients and mix until just combined.
8. Stir in the walnuts and zucchini by hand.
9. Divide the batter between the prepared baking pans.
10. Arrange the pans directly on the grill grate and bake for 50 minutes, or until a bamboo skewer inserted in the center of the breads comes out clean.
11. Transfer to a wire rack and let cool for 10 minutes, then remove the breads from the pans. For best results, let the breads cool completely before slicing.

SWEET CHEESE MUFFINS

These muffins are a crowd-pleaser. But it's hard to stop at eating just one, so be careful when you serve them before the main course. Because your wood pellet grill can hold a steady baking temperature, you can use it to prepare these on the grill, but they are just as easy to make in your kitchen oven. They fall somewhere between a sweet muffin and savory cornbread. The secret ingredient is the cake mix. You won't have any of these muffins left over, I guarantee.

Ingredients
1 package butter cake mix
1 package Jiffy Corn Muffin Mix
1 cup self-rising or cake flour
12 tablespoons (1½ sticks) unsalted butter, softened, plus 8 tablespoons (1 stick) melted
3½ cups shredded Cheddar cheese
2 eggs, beaten, at room temperature
2¼ cups buttermilk
Nonstick cooking spray or butter, for greasing
¼ cup packed brown sugar

Preparation time: 15 minutes
Smoking time: 12 to 15 minutes
Temperature: 375°F
Portions: 3 dozens mini muffins
Recommended pellets: Maple, Cherry

Instructions
1. Supply your smoker with wood pellets and follow the manufacturer's specific start-up procedure. Preheat, with the lid closed, to 375°F.

2. In a large mixing bowl, combine the cake mix, corn muffin mix, and flour.
3. Slice the 1½ sticks of softened butter into pieces and cut into the dry ingredients. Add the cheese and mix thoroughly.
4. In a medium bowl, combine the eggs and buttermilk, then add to the dry ingredients, stirring until well blended.
5. Coat three 12-cup mini muffin pans with cooking spray and spoon ¼ cup of batter into each cup.
6. Transfer the pans to the grill, close the lid, and smoke, monitoring closely, for 12 to 15 minutes, or until the muffins are lightly browned.
7. While the muffins are cooking, make the topping: In a small bowl, stir together the remaining 1 stick of melted butter and the brown sugar until well combined.
8. Remove the muffins from the grill. Brush the tops with the sweet butter and serve warm.

DESSERTS

BACON CHOCOLATE CHIP COOKIES

Bacon salt, bacon lip balm, bacon whiskey . . . I've always said bacon is the duct tape of food, but lately it's become an obsession. So much so that there is an annual Baconfest in Lathrop, California. The event features pig races, cooking competitions, and the dreaded bacon eating contest. Sounds gut-wrenching! These cookies bake just fine in the oven, but the lick of smoke they get from hardwood fire makes them unique. With or without the smoke, though, it seems everything's better with bacon.

Ingredients
2¾ cups all-purpose flour
1½ teaspoons baking soda
½ teaspoon salt
12 tablespoons (1½ sticks) unsalted butter, softened
1 cup light brown sugar
1 cup granulated sugar
2 eggs, at room temperature
2½ teaspoons apple cider vinegar
1 teaspoon vanilla extract
2 cups semisweet chocolate chips
8 slices bacon, cooked and crumbled

Preparation time: 20 minutes
Smoking time: 10 to 12 minutes
Temperature: 375°F
Portions: 2 dozen cookies
Recommended pellets: Maple

Instructions
1. In a large bowl, combine the flour, baking soda, and salt, and mix well.
2. In a separate large bowl, using an electric mixer on medium speed, cream the butter and sugars. Reduce the speed to low and mix in the eggs, vinegar, and vanilla.
3. With the mixer speed still on low, slowly incorporate the dry ingredients, chocolate chips, and bacon pieces.
4. Supply your smoker with wood pellets and follow the manufacturer's specific start-up procedure. Preheat, with the lid closed, to 375°F.
5. Line a large baking sheet with parchment paper.
6. Drop rounded teaspoonfuls of cookie batter onto the prepared baking sheet and place on the grill grate. Close the lid and smoke for 10 to 12 minutes, or until the cookies are browned around the edges.

Secret tip: Try to match your pellet hardwood to your bacon. If you are using hickory-smoked bacon, use hickory pellets.

S'MORES DIP SKILLET

It's always great to reflect on childhood memories when grilling. No recipe does that better than the Scout's classic, s'mores. This dip will leave everyone wanting s'more.

Ingredients
2 tablespoons salted butter, melted
¼ cup milk
12 ounces semisweet chocolate chips
16 ounces Jet-Puffed marshmallows
Graham crackers and apple wedges, for serving

Preparation time: 5 minutes
Smoking time: 6 to 8 minutes
Temperature: 450°F
Portions: 4 to 6
Recommended pellets: Apple, Cherry

Instructions
1. Supply your smoker with wood pellets and follow the manufacturer's specific start-up procedure. Preheat, with the lid closed, to 450°F.
2. Place a cast iron skillet on the preheated grill grate and pour in the melted butter and milk, stirring for about 1 minute.
3. Once the mixture starts to heat, top with the chocolate chips in an even layer and arrange the marshmallows standing up to cover all of the chocolate.
4. Close the lid and smoke for 5 to 7 minutes, or until the marshmallows are lightly toasted.
5. Remove from the heat and serve immediately with graham crackers and apple wedges for dipping.

Secret tip: Your pellet grill will toast marshmallows easier than a raging campfire, but beware! Like bread, marshmallows will burn quickly on the grill, so keep a very close eye on them. And remember: no double dipping!

SMOKED BLACKBERRY PIE

If you've ever picked wild blackberries, you may remember that they are actually red before they ripen. You may have heard the old expression, "Blackberries are red when they're green." In this recipe, the dark, plump blackberries are a feast for the eyes, and they're healthy, thanks to their high levels of dietary fiber, vitamin C, and vitamin K.

Ingredients
Nonstick cooking spray or butter, for greasing
1 box (2 sheets) refrigerated piecrusts
8 tablespoons (1 stick) unsalted butter, melted, plus 8 tablespoons (1 stick) cut into pieces
½ cup all-purpose flour
2 cups sugar, divided
2 pints blackberries
½ cup milk
Vanilla ice cream, for serving

Preparation time: 15 minutes
Smoking time: 20 to 25 minutes
Temperature: 375°F
Portions: 4 to 6
Recommended pellets: Apple, Cherry

Instructions
1. Supply your smoker with wood pellets and follow the manufacturer's specific start-up procedure. Preheat, with the lid closed, to 375°F.
2. Coat a cast iron skillet with cooking spray.
3. Unroll 1 refrigerated piecrust and place in the bottom and up the side of the skillet. Using a fork, poke holes in the crust in several places.
4. Set the skillet on the grill grate, close the lid, and smoke for 5 minutes, or until lightly browned. Remove from the grill and set aside.
5. In a large bowl, combine the stick of melted butter with the flour and 1½ cups of sugar.
6. Add the blackberries to the flour-sugar mixture and toss until well coated.
7. Spread the berry mixture evenly in the skillet and sprinkle the milk on top. Scatter half of the cut pieces of butter randomly over the mixture.
8. Unroll the remaining piecrust and place it over the top of skillet or slice the dough into even strips and weave it into a lattice. Scatter the remaining pieces of butter along the top of the crust.
9. Sprinkle the remaining ½ cup of sugar on top of the crust and return the skillet to the smoker.
10. Close the lid and smoke for 15 to 20 minutes, or until bubbly and brown on top. It may be necessary to use some aluminum foil around the edges near the end of the cooking time to prevent the crust from burning.
11. Serve the pie hot with vanilla ice cream.

Secret tip: If you opt to use different kinds of berries, remember that raspberries are delicate. Avoid washing them under hard running water; instead, place in a colander and immerse in a water bath.

CARROT CAKE

No one really knows who came up with the idea of putting carrots in a cake, but it does have attributes that trace back to medieval times, when people would often make a carrot pudding. I guess the carrots add moisture and were something sweet when you couldn't find corn syrup. In fact, this carrot cake is the only vegetable cake I know of (I'm not counting zucchini bread as cake).

Ingredients
8 carrots, peeled and grated
4 eggs, at room temperature
1 cup vegetable oil
½ cup milk
1 teaspoon vanilla extract
2 cups sugar
2 cups self-rising or cake flour
2 teaspoons baking soda
1 teaspoon salt
1 cup finely chopped pecans
Nonstick cooking spray or butter, for greasing
8 ounces cream cheese
1 cup confectioners' sugar
8 tablespoons (1 stick) unsalted butter, at room temperature
1 teaspoon vanilla extract

½ teaspoon salt
2 tablespoons to ¼ cup milk

Preparation time: 20 minutes
Smoking time: 1 hour
Temperature: 350°F
Portions: 4 to 6
Recommended pellets: Apple, Cherry

Instructions

For the cake:
1. Supply your smoker with wood pellets and follow the manufacturer's specific start-up procedure. Preheat, with the lid closed, to 350°F.
2. In a food processor or blender, combine the grated carrots, eggs, oil, milk, and vanilla, and process until the carrots are finely minced.
3. In a large mixing bowl, combine the sugar, flour, baking soda, and salt.
4. Add the carrot mixture to the flour mixture and stir until well incorporated. Fold in the chopped pecans.
5. Coat a 9-by-13-inch baking pan with cooking spray.
6. Pour the batter into prepared pan and place on the grill grate. Close the lid and smoke for about 1 hour, or until a toothpick inserted in the center comes out clean.
7. Remove the cake from the grill and let cool completely.

For the frosting:
1. Using an electric mixer on low speed, beat the cream cheese, confectioners' sugar, butter, vanilla, and salt, adding 2 tablespoons to ¼ cup of milk to thin the frosting as needed.
2. Frost the cooled cake and slice to serve.

Secret tip: The carrot is the special ingredient here, and you want to avoid any large chunks. Use a handheld grater and be sure to protect your fingers by grasping the carrot with a kitchen towel.

SMOKIN' LEMON BARS

These bars are smokin'. Our homemade lemon bars are made with fresh squeezed lemon juice, sugar, zest and baked over applewood for some serious dessert perfection.

Ingredients
3/4 Cup lemon juice
1 1/2 Cup sugar
2 eggs
3 Egg Yolk
1 1/2 Teaspoon cornstarch
Pinch sea salt
4 Tablespoon unsalted butter
1/4 Cup olive oil
1/2 Tablespoon lemon zest
1 1/4 Cup flour
1/4 Cup granulated sugar
3 Tablespoon Confectioner's Sugar
1 Teaspoon lemon zest
1/4 Teaspoon Sea Salt, Fine
10 Tablespoon Unsalted Butter, Cut Into Cubes

Preparation time: 30 minutes
Smoking time: 1 hour
Temperature: 350°F
Portions: 8 to 12
Recommended pellets: Maple, Cherry

Instructions
1. When ready to cook, set grill temperature to 180°F and preheat, lid closed for 15 minutes.
2. In a small mixing bowl, whisk together lemon juice, sugar, eggs and yolks, cornstarch and fine sea salt. Pour into a sheet tray or cake pan and place on grill. Smoke for 30 minutes whisking mixture halfway through smoking. Remove from grill and set aside.
3. Pour mixture into a small saucepan. Place on stove top set to medium heat until boiling. Once boiling, boil for 60 seconds. Remove from heat and strain through a mesh strainer into a bowl. Whisk in cold butter, olive oil, and lemon zest.
4. To make a crust, pulse together the flour, granulated sugar, confectioners' sugar, lemon zest and salt in a food processor. Add butter and pulse until just mixed into a crumbly dough. Press dough into a prepared 9" by 9" baking dish lined with parchment paper that is long enough to hang over 2 of the sides.
5. When ready to cook, set the Traeger to 350°F and preheat, lid closed for 15 minutes.
6. Bake until crust is very lightly golden brown, about 30 to 35 minutes.
7. Remove from grill and pour the lemon filling over the crust. Return to grill and continue to bake until filling is just set about 15 to 20 minutes.
8. Allow to cool at room temperature, then refrigerate until chilled before slicing into bars. Sprinkle with confectioners' sugar and flaky sea salt right before serving. Enjoy!

DOUBLE CHOCOLATE CHIP BROWNIE PIE

These Traeger-baked brownies will satisfy the family's Sunday night chocolate sweet-tooth craving.

Ingredients
1/2 Cup Semisweet Chocolate Chips
1 Cup butter
1 Cup brown sugar
1 Cup sugar
4 Whole eggs
2 Teaspoon vanilla extract
2 Cup all-purpose flour
333/500 Cup Cocoa Powder, Unsweetened
1 Teaspoon baking soda
1 Teaspoon salt
1 Cup Semisweet Chocolate Chips
3/4 Cup White Chocolate Chips
3/4 Cup Nuts (optional)
1 Whole Hot Fudge Sauce, 8oz
2 Tablespoon Guinness Beer
Preparation time: 20 minutes
Smoking time: 45 minutes
Temperature: 350°F
Portions: 8 to 12
Recommended pellets: Maple, Cherry

Instructions

1. Coat the inside of a 10-inch (25 cm) pie plate with non-stick cooking spray.
2. When ready to cook, set the grill temperature to 350°F (180 C) and preheat, lid closed for 15 minutes.
3. Melt 1/2 cup (100 g) of the semi sweet chocolate chips in the microwave. Cream together butter, brown sugar and granulated sugar. Beat in the eggs, adding one at a time and mixing after each egg, and the vanilla. Add in the melted chocolate chips.
4. On a large piece of wax paper, sift together the cocoa powder, flour, baking soda and salt. Lift up the corners of the paper and pour slowly into the butter mixture.
5. Beat until the dry ingredients are just incorporated. Stir in the remaining semi sweet chocolate chips, white chocolate chips, and the nuts. Press the dough into the prepared pie pan.
6. Place the brownie pie on the grill and bake for 45-50 minutes or until the pie is set in the middle. Rotate the pan halfway through cooking. If the top or edges begin to brown, cover the top with a piece of aluminum foil.
7. In a microwave-safe measuring cup, heat the fudge sauce in the microwave. Stir in the Guinness.
8. Once the brownie pie is done, allow to sit for 20 minutes. Slice into wedges and top with the fudge sauce. Enjoy.

BAKED BOURBON MAPLE PUMPKIN PIE

Give your classic pumpkin pie a wood-fired overhaul with a bourbon infusion and chocolate crust twist.

Ingredients
1/4 Cup Cocoa Powder, Unsweetened
1 Tablespoon Cocoa Powder, Unsweetened
3 1/2 Tablespoon sugar
1 Teaspoon salt
1 1/4 Cup all-purpose flour
1 Tablespoon all-purpose flour
6 Tablespoon butter
2 Tablespoon vegetable oil
1 Large Egg Yolk
1/2 Teaspoon apple cider vinegar
1/4 Cup ice water
1 Large egg, beaten
15 Ounce Pumpkin, canned
1/4 Cup sour cream
2 Tablespoon bourbon
1 Teaspoon ground cinnamon
1/2 Teaspoon salt
1/4 Teaspoon ground ginger
1/4 Teaspoon ground nutmeg
1/8 Teaspoon Allspice, ground
1/8 Teaspoon Mace, ground
3 Large eggs
3/4 Cup maple syrup
2 Tablespoon sugar
1/2 Vanilla Bean, halved
1 Cup heavy cream

Preparation time: 30 minutes
Smoking time: 1 hour
Temperature: 375°F
Portions: 6 to 8
Recommended pellets: Maple, Cherry

Instructions

1. For the Chocolate Pie Dough: Pulse cocoa powder, granulated sugar, salt, and 1-1/4 cups plus 1 Tbsp flour in a food processor to combine. Add butter and shortening and pulse until mixture resembles coarse meal with a few pea-sized pieces of butter remaining. Transfer to a large bowl.
2. Whisk together the egg yolk, vinegar, and 1/4 cup ice water in a small bowl. Drizzle half of the egg mixture over flour mixture and, using a fork, mix gently just until combined. Add remaining egg mixture and mix until the dough just comes together (you will have some unincorporated pieces).
3. Turn out dough onto a lightly floured surface, flatten slightly, and cut into quarters. Stack pieces on top of one another. Placing unincorporated dry pieces of dough between layers, and press down to combine. Repeat process twice more (all pieces of dough should be incorporated at this point). Form dough into a 1" thick disk. Wrap in plastic; chill at least 1 hour.
4. Roll out a disk of dough on a lightly floured surface into a 14" round. Transfer to a 9" pie dish. Lift up the edge and allow the dough to slump down into the dish. Trim. Leaving about 1" overhang. Fold overhang under and crimp edge. Chill in freezer 15 minutes.
5. When ready to cook, set the Traeger to 350°F and preheat, lid closed for 15 minutes.
6. Line pie with parchment paper or heavy-duty foil, leaving a 1-1/2" overhang. Fill with pie weights or dried beans. Bake until crust is dry around the edge, about 20 minutes.
7. Remove paper and weights and bake until surface of the crust looks dry, 5-10 minutes.
8. Brush bottom and sides of crust with 1 beaten egg. Return to grill and bake until dry and set, about 3 minutes longer.
9. For the Pumpkin Maple Filling: Whisk together pumpkin puree, sour cream, bourbon, cinnamon, salt, ginger, nutmeg, allspice, mace (optional) and remaining 3 eggs in a large bowl; set aside.
10. Pour maple syrup and 2 tbsp sugar in a small saucepan. Scrape in the seeds from vanilla bean (reserve pod for another use) or add vanilla extract and bring syrup to a boil. Reduce heat to medium-high and simmer, stirring occasionally, until mixture is thickened and small puffs of steam start to release about 3 minutes.
11. Remove from heat and add cream in 3 additions, stirring with a wooden spoon after each addition until smooth. Gradually whisk hot maple cream into pumpkin mixture.
12. Place pie dish on a rimmed baking sheet and pour in pumpkin filling. Bake pie, rotating halfway through, until set around edge but center barely jiggles 50-60 minutes.
13. Transfer pie dish to a wire rack and let the pie cool. Slice and serve. Enjoy!

CONCLUSION

I hope you have enjoyed this book and the recipe within it as much as I've enjoyed writing it and trying them out. Now that you have a deeper understanding of the amazing potential of your Traeger grills, cook, bake, grill, and obviously smoke to your heart's desire! And if you can find some time between cookouts and backyard's breakfast, please leave a review on Amazon to let us know what you liked about this book, your own experiences, and how we can improve it for the next readers!

Made in the USA
Middletown, DE
17 September 2020